FREEDOM FROM THE PRESS
Journalism and State Power in Singapore

Cherian George

NUS PRESS
SINGAPORE

© Cherian George

Published by:

NUS Press
National University of Singapore
AS3-01-02, 3 Arts Link
Singapore 117569

Fax: (65) 6774-0652
E-mail: nusbooks@nus.edu.sg
Website: http://nuspress.nus.edu.sg

ISBN 978-9971-69-594-1 (Paper)

First Edition 2012
Reprint 2015
Reprint 2018

All rights reserved. This book, or parts thereof, may not be reproduced in any form or by any means, electronic or mechanical, including photocopying, recording or any information storage and retrieval system now known or to be invented, without written permission from the Publisher.

National Library Board, Singapore Cataloguing-in-Publication Data

George, Cherian.
  Freedom from the press: journalism and state power in Singapore / Cherian George. – Singapore: NUS Press, c2012.
  p. cm.
  Includes bibliographical references and index.
  ISBN: 978-9971-69-594-1 (pbk.)

  1. Journalism – Political aspects – Singapore. 2. Press and politics – Singapore. 3. Freedom of the press – Singapore. 4. Government and the press – Singapore. I. Title.

PN4751
079.5957 — dc22   OCN760269057

Printed by: Markono Print Media Pte Ltd

For
Alisha, Nicole, Kiran & Cameron

Contents

Acknowledgments ix

Singapore Politics and Media: A Primer xi

1. Introduction: Beyond the Singapore Paradox 1
2. Journalism Tamed: The Mechanics of Media Control 23
3. Inside the Press: Routines, Values and "OB" Markers 46
4. Government Unlimited: The Ideology of State Primacy 71
5. Calibrated Coercion: The State Strategy of Self-Restraint 93
6. The Harmony Myth: Asian Media's Radical Past 117
7. Freedom of the Press: A Cause Without Rebels 137
8. Alternative Online Media: Challenging the Gatekeepers 158
9. Rise of the Unruly: Media Activism and Civil Disobedience 183
10. Networked Hegemony: Consolidating the Political System 200

Notes 226

Bibliography 256

Index 268

Acknowledgments

Many of the arguments and concepts in this book were developed from ideas piloted at various workshops, conferences and other collaborative projects. I thank the fellow scholars whose invitations provided such opportunities. My interest in Asian journalism's radical past was seeded by my involvement in an inter-disciplinary project on Singapore's post-war history led by Michael Barr and Carl Trocki, which led to their edited volume, *Paths Not Taken* (NUS Press, 2008). My concept of networked hegemony was rehearsed in a research project spearheaded by Mely Anthony, which led to the edited book, *Political Change, Democratic Transitions and Security in Southeast Asia* (Routledge, 2009). Nissim Otmazgin's and Eyal Ben-Ari's conference at the Hebrew University of Jerusalem got me thinking about comparing journalism with popular culture. Ideas from my chapter in their book, *Popular Culture and the State in East and Southeast Asia* (Routledge, 2012), have been further developed in the following pages.

The late Kevin Boyle helped me cross disciplinary boundaries and dip my toes in international law on freedom of expression, in the course of our collaborations in Asia-Europe Foundation programmes. My understanding of comparative media law was enriched by my participation in conferences organised by Andrew Kenyon and Amanda Whiting at the Melbourne Law School. A symposium organised by Theodore Glasser and Isabel Awad at Stanford University provided a chance to test ideas about normative diversity within the profession. My colleague Hao Xiaoming led the way for our survey of Singapore journalists, results from which are included in this book. The study was initiated by David Weaver and Lars Willnat as part of their book project on *The Global Journalist* (Routledge, 2012). Arun Mahizhnan and Tan Tarn How at Singapore's Institute of Policy Studies convened several forums for us to grapple with the fast-changing new media landscape, contributing to my thoughts on the subject.

This book was written in the course of my work at Nanyang Technological University's Wee Kim Wee School of Communication and Information, which I must thank for keeping its promise to provide faculty with time for research and writing. Various university research grants and schemes supported my research assistants Mykel Yee, Lin Junjie, Low Wei Xiang — and Justin Zhuang, whose diligence was particularly valuable. Eleanor Wong, Michael Hor, Douglas Wong and Reginald Chua were kind enough to read my first draft and offer comments and suggestions. Tay Kay Chin advised on the cover design and more than 30 Facebook friends chipped in with their views. Prudencio "Dengcoy" Miel lent his creative genius to the cover art.

Most of the work on this book was carried out during a professionally challenging period. For a student of soft-authoritarian domination, the first-hand experience has been both ironic and illuminating, providing a worm's eye view of dynamics that the following pages analyse at higher levels of abstraction. That I could respond philosophically to the situation is thanks in part to the loyalty of several friends. Above all, I thank Zuraidah, whose smile lightens every load and whose strength didn't fail when I needed it.

Singapore Politics and Media: A Primer

*Names and other terms feature prominently in this book are highlighted in **bold**.*

The Republic of Singapore is a city-state of 5 million people, 3.2 million of whom are citizens.[1] It is located at the Southeastern tip of the Asian landmass, on the main maritime route between the Indian and Pacific Oceans. Its closest neighbours are Malaysia and Indonesia. Controlled by the British Empire from 1918, it was occupied from 1942–5 by the Empire of Japan. It was granted internal self-government by the British in 1959 and chose to join the Federation of Malaysia in 1963. The merger failed: Singapore separated from Malaysia to become an independent republic in 1965.[2] In most respects, it is a First World city; it has one of the world's busiest ports and financial markets.

Singapore has been governed by the **People's Action Party** (PAP) continuously since 1959.[3] General Elections decide seats in Singapore's unicameral Parliament, which has a maximum term of five years.[4] The Westminster-style first-past-the-post system means that the margin of victory in each constituency has no bearing on the allocation of seats. As a result, although the PAP's share of the popular vote ranged from 60 to 75 per cent in GEs since the 1990s, its share of seats has always exceeded 90 per cent, giving it virtually unchecked law-making power. In the 2011 general election, the PAP won 81 out of 87 seats. **Lee Hsien Loong** has been prime minister since 2004. He was preceded by **Goh Chok Tong** and, before that, **Lee Kuan Yew**, who was prime minister from 1959 to 1990. Lee Kuan Yew, the father of the current prime minister, dominated Singapore politics and shaped media policy for half a century, only retiring from Cabinet in 2011.

Singapore is a culturally diverse immigrant society. The majority is Chinese (74 per cent) and the main minority groups are Malays (13 per cent) and Indians (9 per cent).[5] There is no dominant religious group. Most Chinese are Buddhists and Taoists; almost all Malays and some Indians are Muslims. There is a growing population of Christians. Singapore has four official languages: English (the main working language and the medium of instruction in schools); Malay (designated as the "national language"); Chinese (with official promotion of Mandarin over dialects); and Tamil (the language of the majority of Indian Singaporeans). The media market is similarly divided on linguistic lines.

Singapore's news industry is dominated by **Singapore Press Holdings** (SPH), a corporation created in 1984 by the merger of two newspaper groups. While not government-owned, it is closely supervised by the political leadership. Its flagship title and *de facto* national paper is the English-language ***Straits Times***, founded in 1845. In 2010, it had an average daily circulation of around 350,000 copies. Its Sunday edition is the *Sunday Times*. SPH's other English-language dailies are *The New Paper*, a downmarket tabloid, and the *Business Times*. The largest Chinese-language daily is SPH's *Lianhe Zaobao*, which had a weekday circulation of around 160,000 in 2010. It has two downmarket sister papers, *Shin Min Daily News* and *Lianhe Wanbao*. SPH's Chinese papers are descended from **Nanyang Siang Pau** and *Sin Chew Jit Poh*. SPH publishes the country's only dailies in Malay (*Berita Harian*, which has a weekday circulation of around 60,000) and Tamil (*Tamil Murasu*, around 15,000).[6] SPH also publishes a bilingual free-sheet, *My Paper*, in English and Chinese. As in other mature markets, newspaper circulations in Singapore are in decline. However, the industry remains financially robust.

Broadcasting is dominated by **MediaCorp**, the sole provider of free-to-air television channels, including Channel NewsAsia, and the main radio station operator. Descended from the government's propaganda department and corporatised in stages, MediaCorp is government-owned but also highly commercial in orientation. Much of its factual programming depends on government grants and subsidies. MediaCorp publishes the only non-SPH Singaporean daily newspaper, ***Today***. The free-sheet claims an average distribution of 300,000 copies on weekdays, 200,000 on Saturdays and 100,000 on Sundays.[7] In return for retreating from its short-lived foray into television, SPH was given a 20 per cent stake in MediaCorp's television business and a 40 per cent stake in its newspaper business. Operationally, however, the two companies remain bitter rivals. Subscription television is provided by Starhub, a public-listed company in which the government-linked Singapore Technologies is the largest shareholder. The second provider of subscription television is government-linked Singapore Telecom's mioTV service. While Starhub and mioTV carry international news channels such as BBC and CNN, neither has a domestic news programme competing with Mediacorp's news output. Due mainly to Singapore's status as a major business and financial hub, several international news organisations have significant operations in the country. For example, Singapore is the Asia base of Thomson Reuters and the headquarters of CNBC Asia.

Commercial news organisations are major providers of online news. In addition, there have been numerous independent sociopolitical websites, notably **The Online Citizen** and **Temasek Review**. All are volunteer-run. Newspapers, and to a lesser extent broadcast stations, remain the main employers of full-time professional journalists and therefore the main producers of news and commentary on current affairs. Journalists tend to be university graduates from a range of academic disciplines, with an increasing number coming from communication schools in Singapore and overseas.

The PAP believes that Singapore needs a strong government with the ability to act decisively against threats and to seize opportunities. To that end, freedom of the press must be "subordinate to the primacy of purpose of an elected government", in the words of Lee Kuan Yew. The main piece of press legislation is the **Newspaper and Printing Presses Act** (NPPA) of 1974. Under the NPPA, newspapers need annual permits. Newspaper companies must also issue management shares to government nominees, opening the door to government intervention over editorial direction and senior editorial appointments. The NPPA also allows the government to restrict the circulation of foreign publications, although in recent years, **libel suits** and prosecutions for **contempt of court** have been more commonly used against foreign media. The **Broadcasting Act** imposes a licensing requirement on radio and television, protecting the state-owned MediaCorp from unwanted competition. Internet regulations under the Act require internet service providers to block any content on the regulator's instruction. In practice, however, no political websites have been blocked. The main regulator is the **Media Development Authority** under the Ministry of Information, Communication and the Arts.

November 2011

For updated information, visit <http://www.freedomfromthepress.info>.

"In such a situation, freedom of the press, freedom of the news media, must be subordinated to the overriding needs of the integrity of Singapore, and to the primacy of purpose of an elected government."

– Lee Kuan Yew, Address to the General Assembly of the International Press Institute, Helsinki, 9 June 1971

CHAPTER 1

Introduction: Beyond the Singapore Paradox

The Newseum in the heart of Washington, D.C. is an inspiring tribute to journalism. Situated on historic Pennsylvania Avenue, close to Capitol Hill, the museum celebrates the role of a free press in building democracy. Its exhibits include a graffiti-strewn section of the Berlin Wall, that 20th-century symbol of the state's instinct to control its people as well as of the people's irrepressible desire for freedom. On a higher floor is a corner reminding visitors of liberty's unfinished business: a "Press Freedom Map" covers a wall, with the nations of the world colour-coded according to how much freedom of expression they enjoy. North America, Europe, Oceania, Japan, Taiwan and South Korea are all coloured a healthy green, illustrating the nexus between political freedom and economic development. There is, however, one small exception. First-World Singapore is coloured the same as most of Africa and the poorer half of Asia: red, for unfree.

The Newseum's Press Freedom Map is based on the annual surveys of Freedom House, a watchdog organisation based in the American capital.[1] Another tabulation that has received much publicity is the Paris-based Reporters Sans Frontieres' Press Freedom Index. Its assessment of Singapore is similar. In 2010, RSF ranked Singapore among the bottom 25 per cent of nations.[2] RSF's methodology is dubious, resulting in the Republic being grouped with regimes where journalists lose not just their liberty but even their lives.[3] Such doubts notwithstanding, nobody denies that Singapore lacks the kind of media freedom found in liberal societies. Indeed, one way in which the government has tried to defend the Republic's honour is to suggest that, if

Singapore ranks so low in such rankings, it only goes to show that press freedom cannot be as important as the West makes it out to be. "Should we be embarrassed because we are near the bottom of the ladder in the ranking?" said former prime minister Goh Chok Tong of the RSF survey. "Should we be worried that investors may be put off? Not at all. What then-Prime Minister Lee Kuan Yew said in 1959 is still our position today. He told a foreign correspondent then: 'You are not going to teach us how we should run the country. We are not so stupid. We know what our interests are and we try to preserve them.'"[4] The ruling People's Action Party (PAP) argues that elected leaders must be empowered to make decisions in the national interest — including those that may be unpopular in the short term. They must not be hindered by media with no mandate to represent the people. The state's freedom *from* the press has therefore been entrenched as a key pillar of good government.

Singapore's political system has been categorised as everything from a semi-democracy[5] and an illiberal democracy,[6] to a hegemonic electoral authoritarian regime[7] and a dictatorship.[8] The PAP itself has referred to its system as a kind of democratic trusteeship in which citizens freely elect a government to which they entrust full powers to rule decisively.[9] Despite the differences in labels, there is no serious disagreement over the key features of the system. Nobody, not even the PAP, quarrels with Singapore's classification as a non-liberal political system. But, that system deserves closer scrutiny and more nuanced analysis than it is usually given. Although there may be consensus about how to colour-code Singapore on a press freedom map, there is much less agreement about the mechanisms and processes that have produced and sustained the system. Myths, assumptions and the occasional fact swirl around the subject of the media. For example, otherwise authoritative sources refer to the news publishing behemoth Singapore Press Holdings as "government-owned" when it is not. And, even individuals within the press or the government may not be able to ascertain which stories in an issue of *The Straits Times* were influenced by pressure from officials and which were determined by the independent professional judgment of editors.

Pinpointing causes and processes may be unimportant to the polemicist who seeks an aesthetically pleasing argument. However, sound explanations are what help us to understand, predict and control the things around us. Whether one wants to reform or consolidate Singapore's system, explanatory precision matters. A reader of

The Straits Times turned off by what he perceives as propaganda may complain that he is getting no better service than Soviet citizens did from *Pravda*, but insisting that they are no different makes it hard to explain why one is the most profitable media property in the region while the other could not survive market reforms. At the opposite end of the political spectrum, inexperienced officials who want to preserve the *status quo* could unwittingly knock the system off balance if they fail to understand that the current equilibrium is based on something more delicate than bully tactics alone. Singapore and Mexico are jointly ranked 136 in RSF's 2010 Press Freedom Index, but there is little resemblance between the two country's media systems. Malaysia, ranked 141, is similar to Singapore in terms of history, culture and legal tradition. But even between these two neighbours are deep differences that help explain why, for decades, a journalist was more likely to be detained without trial in Malaysia than in Singapore, or why alternative media are more vibrant north of the Causeway than in the island republic.

This book tries to fill a gap by offering a detailed account of Singapore's media controls, going beyond rankings and colour codes. I focus mainly on newspapers. This may strike the reader as anachronistic considering how much talk there is about the imminent death of print media. In fact, newspapers in Singapore — as in many Asian countries — are in strong economic health, still making profits that are well above average among manufacturing industries. Singapore Press Holdings continues to achieve profitability ratios twice as large as reported by Singapore Airlines, one of the world's most admired companies. However, newspapers' central place in this book is not based on their profitability but on the fact that they remain, for the foreseeable future, the main institutional home for professional journalism. The central question posed in this book is how the state has tamed that profession. Singapore's broadcast media hardly feature in the following pages because, unlike newspapers, they have never exhibited significant professional autonomy requiring special ingenuity to control. Starting out as a government propaganda department, the national broadcaster MediaCorp is now commercially-driven but remains government-owned, fluctuating between entertainment and civil service values. The government's control of broadcasting is, thus, fairly straightforward and less intriguing than its management of newspaper journalism. Internet policy is another key focus of this book. Alternative online media have challenged the PAP's media model and chipped away at the influence of the mainstream national press. However, their impact should not be overstated. Online-only media have yet to develop a business model that would allow them to hire a large workforce, leaving newspaper companies as still the major employers of professional journalists. While amateurs make an important contribution to media diversity through their blogs and other citizen media, professionals are still relied upon to provide regular news and analysis of current events. Furthermore, the fragmented and polarised conversations of cyberspace mean that newspapers remain the closest thing to a public sphere — a common space where citizens with different interests and perspectives can engage in deliberation and seek conciliation. Therefore, the health of newspapers continues to matter more to Singapore's democratic life than many think and hope.

An Overview

The impulse of the powerful few to shape the minds of the many is timeless and universal. What is remarkable about Singapore is the manner in which such power has been exercised. It is less crude and more refined than what is commonly found in restricted media systems. If the only point of this book was to restate the obvious — that Singapore has less press freedom than liberal democracies — it would not have been worth my writing or your reading. What I aim to do here is to go beyond description and offer explanations of the mechanisms and processes that have sustained Singapore's media system for the past four decades. I approach this subject from different angles, borrowing lenses that have been developed by various fields, such as the sociology of media, political sociology and comparative politics. Together, these pictures reveal a form of media control that is more sophisticated and possibly more resilient than most critics assume. Overt censorship has been largely replaced by self-censorship, achieved through economic disincentives against non-cooperation with the state. Chapter 2 examines how the PAP has harnessed the dominant global trend of media commercialisation to tame journalism's democratic purpose. This "political economy" perspective is central to the book, but cannot fully illuminate the dynamics of press and politics. Chapter 3 borrows from other sociological perspectives to look more closely at the inner workings of Singapore newsrooms. It argues that while political pressure has been internalised in the form of what is colloquially called "out of bounds" or "OB" markers, the way the media works is also heavily influenced by the organisational habits that the Singapore press shares with professional journalism around the globe. These routines include selecting stories through the filter of "news judgment" and the ritualistic application of "objectivity", which has turned journalists into scribes for the *status quo*, shedding their historical role as campaigners for causes.

The Singapore media system is sustained through hegemonic processes. Social theorists understand hegemony to be a kind of political domination in which coercion is masked by consent that has been manufactured through ideological work. Chapter 4 analyses PAP ideology, which has justified state control of media as an integral part of Singapore's success formula and a necessary response to the country's exceptional vulnerability. After 40 years of repetition and reinforcement, elements of this ideology appear to have reached a supremely powerful status in the Singaporean mind — that of unquestioned common sense — despite demonstrable flaws in reasoning. But hegemonic domination requires more than a compelling ideology: states also need occasional recourse to coercion. Authoritarian regimes often overdo their use of force, provoking a political backlash that ultimately weakens them. The Singapore government has been particularly skilled at applying the right doses of force — just enough to contain competition, but not enough to provoke widespread moral outrage. It has also understood that public support is a moving target. In response to Singaporeans' rising expectations, the government has not only ratcheted down its use of force, but also adopted incrementally more open and transparent approaches to governance. These aspects of its hegemony, which I call "calibrated coercion", are explored in Chapter 5.

PAP hegemony has not been totalising enough to wipe out all resistance. In recent decades, the most obvious challenge has come mainly from liberal values promoted by Western media. The PAP has enjoyed framing its enterprise as a nationalistic battle with the West. Its official narrative portrays media controls as being in line with "Asian values" of harmony and consensus. Yet, as related in Chapter 6, the PAP once had to face opposition from a radical, Asian-language press as well. Today's media system has been shaped partly by the PAP's run-ins with the Chinese press, in particular. Although these historical roots of contentious journalism have since been snipped off, the PAP's hegemonic project remains incomplete. The press may be strikingly bereft of any reform movement, but other practitioners in

Singapore's creative industries have pushed publicly for more space. Chapter 7 examines the interventions of artists, dramatists, filmmakers and internet producers in censorship debates. The contrast with professional journalists helps to clarify the factors that keep the press conservative.

The internet has enabled the most radical and unpredictable challenges to the PAP system of media control. It is the only medium of public communication for which producers are not required to obtain a government permit. This has opened a regulatory loophole for alternative media, notwithstanding the fact that they must still contend with laws such as defamation and contempt of court. Chapter 8 looks at the resulting rise of citizen journalism, which has challenged the PAP's authority in setting the national agenda. Citizen journalism projects have not, however, been able to transcend the structural limits on democratisation, such as Singapore's weak civil society and its demobilised public. Some activists have attempted to awaken the public through their campaign of civil disobedience. Chapter 9 describes how they have used the internet to amplify their modest experiments in non-violent protest. So far, online dissent has frayed the edges of PAP dominance without compromising its core. Therefore, this book ends on a similar note as it starts with. While the conventional critique of the Singapore model claims that it is patently unsustainable, I take seriously the possibility that the PAP may have found a viable formula for combining high economic capacity with low democratic performance. In Chapter 10, I suggest that the regime has attempted to keep itself open to the flow of ideas and responsive to change even as it forecloses political competition. This approach, which I term "networked hegemony", has so far spared Singapore the kind of rigidity and decline usually associated with authoritarian regimes. Networked hegemony challenges conventional wisdom about the kind of openness required of a high-functioning modern state.

It is unclear whether the PAP has fully resolved the contradictions of being simultaneously open and closed, or that its formula is sustainable. The 2011 general election punctured the PAP's aura of invulnerability. By insulating itself from public opinion, it had allowed simmering discontent with its policies to boil over, resulting in historic losses at the polls. What remained unclear was whether this represented the beginning of the end for the PAP's longstanding formula, or whether it would be able to respond adequately to public demands without discarding its fundamentals. Most critics assume that Singapore's system is unsustainable because it is undemocratic. This book is less certain about the inevitability of a quantum leap in democratisation. I start with the premise that the PAP model may not be merely transitional or destined to converge with liberal democracies. Mine is not a unique point of view. There is growing recognition that the historical path of the West may not be trajectory of the rest. The scholar and journalist Martin Jacques, for example, has written of "multiple modernities".[10] And George Soros — perhaps the only political philosopher able and willing to put millions of dollars where his mouth is — has in recent years moderated his stand on open society by acknowledging that theorists cannot blithely ignore the good work done by non-democratic governments such as China.[11]

Perhaps, therefore, the "Singapore Paradox" is not so paradoxical. The contradiction could be an artifact of the widely held but erroneous belief that market-driven economic growth always goes hand-in-hand with democratisation — the so-called modernisation hypothesis. Viewed from a different perspective, like that of the "critical" tradition in social science, Singapore is not an anomaly but an archetype of a large and growing group of states marked by having ruling elites that promote capitalism precisely by dampening democracy. When Singapore is viewed through such lenses, awkward questions surface about liberal democratic systems as well. To argue, as I do, that capitalism has aided and abetted authoritarian rule in Singapore is to challenge the liberal democratic faith in the supposed bond between free markets and free media. This, in turn, compels us to look askance at the democratic credentials of the commercial news media that dominate liberal societies and the global news agenda.

The geographer and social theorist David Harvey is one Western scholar who has been prepared to see past the clichés to spot similarities between Singapore and the liberal West. In his powerful monograph *A Brief History of Neoliberalism*, Harvey treats Singapore as part of a growing family of neoliberal regimes.[12] Spearheaded in the West by Margaret Thatcher and Ronald Reagan, neoliberalism spoke the language of freedom but, in reality, was "profoundly suspicious of democracy", preferring "governance by experts and elites" and requiring the state to discipline labour and other radical threats to the power of the elite — all ideas that had already taken root in Singapore. Harvey identifies Singapore as a prime example of an Asian "developmental state", a key variant of the neoliberal state that relies heavily on the public sector and state planning.[13] Harvey suggests that "neoliberalization in authoritarian states such as China and Singapore seems to be converging with the increasing authoritarianism evident in neoliberal states such as the US and Britain".[14]

Let's return for a moment to the Newseum in Washington D.C. One of the most impressive permanent exhibits is the News History Gallery. It contains fascinating artifacts from the history of the American press, including the pamphlets that campaigned for independence from England and a notebook used by the Watergate reporters who brought down President Richard Nixon. There is also a telephone set once used by Rupert Murdoch, history's most powerful news media mogul. The phone has an array of more than 30 speed-dial buttons labelled with the surnames of top executives in his media empire, ensuring that each was just a button-push away from his master's voice. The names you can spot on that phone include that of Roger Ailes, head of Fox News. Murdoch's use of his media organisations to promote politicians who were friendly to big business is well documented.[15] Fox News, in particular, has bastardised the best principles of journalism in order to further a neoconservative agenda, routinely misleading the American public on key issues such as healthcare reform. Across the Atlantic, long before Murdoch's tabloids were discovered to have engaged in criminal phone-hacking, it was public knowledge that they were at the very least grossly unethical, using shameful news-gathering tactics to satisfy prurient interests. Journalists working in higher-quality media may have admired Murdoch's business acumen and the creativity and craft skills of his popular media, but few regarded Fox News, *News of the World* and *The Sun* as paragons of professionalism in the public interest. None of this is mentioned in the write-up next to Murdoch's telephone at the Newseum. This could be because of American political culture, which tends to be sensitive about government control but blind to the dangers of corporate power. Or, perhaps the omission is simply due to the fact that the Newseum's News History Gallery is sponsored by Murdoch's News Corporation. Either way, it's a reminder of how the liberal perspective has tended to downplay capitalism as a threat to the values that a free press is meant to embody.

The concept of calibrated coercion raises equally unsettling questions for democracy. It suggests that although state violence and overt censorship are the most salient symptoms of authoritarianism, regimes can act in subtler ways to subvert freedom of expression and to entrench their power. It recalls the century-old notion of hegemony, which the communist writer Antonio Gramsci used to explain why unjust capitalist orders in the West managed to endure.[16] Freedom from government control does not guarantee that journalism will always play its role effectively. Other impediments — such as market pressures and ideological blindspots — can get in the way of truthful reporting. The single most consequential failure of journalism in the 21st century so far was the American mainstream media's uncritical acceptance of President George W. Bush's baseless case for going to war against Iraq in the crucial months before the invasion, when public opinion was being shaped. This was not because the press was not free enough to probe White House claims but because — as the editors of reputable publications later admitted — journalists had slipped into the lazy habit of relying on establishment sources, rendering themselves unprepared for the neoconservatives' propaganda machine.

I don't mean to suggest that there is no meaningful difference between Singapore and freer societies. One favourite retort of defenders of authoritarian press systems is that there is, after all, no country with absolute freedom. Singapore, one could claim, lies on a continuum of political systems, each trying to resolve the eternal tension between rights and responsibilities according to its particular history and context. True, media freedom everywhere faces constraints, both justified as well as unjustified. Thus, the difference between the Singapore system and liberal democracy cannot be expressed in absolutes: unfree versus free, or falsehood versus truth. But that doesn't make the difference insignificant. The probability that government failures will be investigated, exposed and put on the agenda for public discussion in liberal democracies is not 100 per cent — but it is significantly higher than in societies such as Singapore. In Singapore, a publisher must obtain government permission every year to continue putting out a newspaper; the information minister can refuse or revoke the permit at any time. In liberal democratic systems, governments are typically banned from exercising such "prior" censorship — which gags someone before he utters a word and before courts can judge whether what he would have said crossed any line. As for defamation law, this exists in liberal democracies as well. But in order to give freedom of expression sufficient breathing space, the law, the courts and the wider political culture there generally expect politicians to rescue their own reputations without much help from the law. In Singapore, in contrast, the reputations of elected leaders are accorded special protection through strict policing of defamation, even if this contributes to a culture of fear. Such differences are not trivial: they separate governments that answer to people from governments that dominate their societies.

The subtlety of the PAP's methods means that one is sometimes at a loss for words when trying to describe the government's relationship to the media. Thus, in Parliament in 2011, new opposition MP Pritam Singh referred to the "PAP government's politics of indirect control", adding that many Singaporeans had "perceptions" that "the mainstream media operates with the long shadow of Government firmly cast upon it". Chiding him for hiding behind public perceptions, Law Minister K. Shanmugam challenged Singh to say what he really thought: "Does the member believe mainstream media is controlled, purveys lies and dishonest opinions?" Singh flinched, replying only that he felt the government could do better. The debate ended there.[17] This book's short but potentially misleading answer is yes: the media in Singapore are government-controlled. The longer and more informative answer depends on one's notions of control, truth and honesty. If one goes by a narrower standard, equating control with government censors vetting articles before publication and the media deliberately inserting lies into the public mind, the answer, fortunately, is no. In this book, however, I apply a more comprehensive benchmark. According to this standard, media that are *not* subject to government control are those that are free to exercise independent professional judgment when deciding what to cover and how, constrained only by clearly inscribed legal limits and by voluntary accountability mechanisms such as codes of ethics. Such media are able to forge a direct relationship with the public that they serve. Through that relationship, the media develop a sense of what constitutes the public interest and decide how best to ensure that they are accountable to the public. When I say that the Singapore media are government-controlled, I mean that the state uses its power to intervene in the relationship between the news media and the public, most powerfully by dictating whether a publication can start and when it must stop. The government's intervention goes deeper than the influence that other groups in society try to exercise on the press, because it is backed by force. The fact that this force is often nothing more than an implicit threat does not negate its looming presence. The net effect is to distort the relationship between media and public, making accountability to government more salient than accountability to people in editorial decision-making. As a result, people's access to facts and opinions is limited in a way that could compromise their ability to participate in their country's democratic life.

Of course, whether such a democratic standard should matter at all is a separate question altogether. Democracy has emerged as a universal value and is mentioned in Singapore's national pledge and symbolised by one of the five stars on the state flag. However, the PAP has rebuffed all attempts to assess Singapore according to any global democratic yardstick, arguing that such standards carry a Western liberal bias and are inappropriate for Singapore's exceptional circumstances. Similarly, journalism's democratic mission is taken for granted in most discussions about the press, but not in Singapore. The PAP is suspicious of democratic rhetoric being used to smuggle in the Western ideal of an adversarial, check-and-balance press. It prefers to speak of the media's role as being to secure the conditions for good governance. The contested relationship between journalism and democracy merits some discussion in this introductory chapter.

Journalism and Democracy

In the summer of 2011 in Istanbul — one of the few cities with an even greater pedigree than Singapore as a civilisational crossroad — around 80 academics from around the world packed into a sweltering seminar room for a panel discussion titled, "Must journalism be defined in terms of democracy?" The speakers were Western-trained scholars, but all reflected a deep skepticism with the tendency to treat Western norms as universal. John Nerone of the University of Illinois, for example, referred to "hegemonic Western journalism" as a pastiche of norms that emerged from particular historical developments in the United States. Barbie Zelizer of the University of Pennsylvania argued that democracy's central position in journalism studies had passed its shelf life, contributing to insular and myopic research. After all, while journalism had been historically necessary for democracy, democracy was not necessary for journalism, she noted. The running theme in the 90-minute session, part of the annual conference of the International Association for Media and Communication Research, was the need to be sensitive to multiple ideals and practices in journalism.

Such skepticism about the liberal perspective may be partly a function of the news media's economic woes in developed democratic countries. It is hard to promote the liberal press as the saviour of the world when it cannot even save itself. However, the intellectual roots for less parochial research go deeper: for several decades, scholars have been comparing different societies' press systems. This has generated a large body of cases relating the news media's particular features to the wider society, culture and political system in which they operate. Done properly, comparisons direct the analysts' attention to important features of a media system that had seemed "natural", or so familiar that they escaped notice entirely.[18] Of course, there are more and less open-minded ways to engage in comparative enquiry. The history of European encounters with difference is replete with examples of how the Other was stereotyped and objectified, to render it fit for condescension and colonisation. Within media studies, this was the problem with the classic work, *Four Theories of the Press*, which continues to be assigned as a text in mass communication courses (including in Asia).[19] This Cold War treatise analysed national ideologies in order to construct caricatures of Western and communist press systems. It spawned an industry of comparative work that similarly confined itself to legal frameworks and official statements, making no attempt to study how the press worked on the ground.[20] More recent research, thankfully, has added to our understanding of actually-existing journalisms around the world. Through surveys and qualitative interviews — increasingly conducted by researchers who understand the local context — media scholarship has highlighted similarities and differences in the way the press works, including how journalists perceive their roles.[21]

Still, there is always the risk of a work such as this one being unduly influenced by the overwhelmingly Western — or, more precisely, Anglo-American — professional and academic writing on the press. Since it is not possible to be perspective-free, I should at least try to be transparent about the values and assumptions underlying this book. I contend that there are indeed different journalisms in the world, varying from one another in significant ways due to the different contexts within which they operate. However, they also share an irreducible core: a set of defining attributes without which they should not be called "journalism". I describe journalism as a special kind of storytelling that: (1) is built on observation, investigation and interpretation; (2) provides reporting and commentary on current events; (3) serves a diverse and anonymous public; and (4) helps people engage in collective self-determination. The first and second limbs of the definition say something about the "how" and "what" of journalism, respectively. The third limb positions the public as the "who" of the enterprise. If it is intended to serve newsmakers, it should be called public relations or propaganda, not journalism. The fourth limb adds a normative dimension to the definition, answering the "why" question. Journalism has a social purpose. It is an activity that people care about because it helps them make decisions as a society. To that extent, my lowest-common-denominator definition of journalism incorporates democratic first principles. Journalism matters because it helps people learn about their surroundings and form opinions, and this is important because a society where people collectively determine their future is a better society than one where people don't count. This is, of course, a value judgment. But, as Amartya Sen notes, it is hardly a contentious claim now. "While democracy is not yet universally practiced, nor indeed uniformly accepted, in the general climate of world opinion, democratic governance has now achieved the status of being taken to be generally right," Sen observes. A century ago, colonised Asians and Africans had to struggle to make the case for collective self-determination. This is no longer the case. "The ball is very much in the court of those who want to rubbish democracy to provide justification for that rejection."[22]

The global spread of democratic values — the simple, powerful idea that even the weak should have a say over their society's destiny — has been accompanied by the proliferation of certain professional journalistic norms. It is now widely accepted that journalism's public role requires professionals to rise above private interests and stay independent of those they cover. This is not to say that the press anywhere has achieved the lofty standards demanded of democracy, unblemished by various shades of venality. It is simply to make the point that the best journalists everywhere increasingly share the same aspirations and speak the same basic professional language. Audiences — whether in Canada or China — also seem to be converging around certain shared expectations. In particular, they believe that journalists serve society best when their professional judgments are insulated from possible subversion by the rich and powerful.

Beyond these core democratic principles, there are significant variations in norms and practices. For example, some countries (like Britain) have a tradition of strong, independent public service broadcasters while others (the Philippines) do not. Some societies have public subsidies for private newspapers (Norway); others rely on the free market (Hong Kong). In some countries (Malaysia), many newspapers have open party affiliations; in others (the US), they adopt a neutral stand. To promote media accountability, some have a press ombudsman (Ireland), others a national press council (Indonesia), while others lean on government regulation (Singapore). Speech that insults religious beliefs is protected in some democratic countries (Denmark) and banned in others (India). In some countries, journalists do not name an accused person until he is convicted (Germany), while in most others, they don't even wait for a suspect to be charged. It is relatively simple to describe these national differences, but more of a challenge to explain them. It is even harder to evaluate their strengths and weaknesses fairly. There are two mental traps awaiting those who try. On one side is the tendency to judge others according to the standards that one is most comfortable with. For example, until quite recently, American scholars and journalists found it difficult to grasp the concept of public service broadcasters that are state-funded but politically independent, even though this model is considered normal in Western Europe and north of the border in Canada. The idea was too alien for a political culture that equated the profit motive with freedom. Only since capitalism proved unable to support enough jobs in high-quality, general-interest daily news has there been serious mainstream contemplation of non-profit journalism in the US.

Trying to avoid the pitfall of ethnocentrism, however, can push one into the opposite trap of extreme relativism, such that all differences are rationalised as arising from the local context. This plays into the hands of authoritarian states, which are fond of justifying their restricted media systems by reference to exceptional circumstances, such as social instability or a cultural preference for order. In Singapore, the PAP has used such rhetoric to erect a wall of ideological protectionism; any criticism of its media system is declared foreign and quarantined. Leading Asian communication theorists Georgette Wang and Eddie Kuo have warned that when we attempt to break free from eurocentric universalism — the practice of applying Western theories uncritically to non-Western contexts — the end goal should not be balkanisation into culture-specific relativism.[23] "While no single community should apply its criteria to others, the absence of agreement on criteria would mean that nothing is comparable and that little can be said of competing claims," they note.[24] They propose a "yin-yang" mentality instead of an either-or approach. Researchers should investigate the particularities of the local context for an in-depth understanding of its historical, cultural and social features. But just because contexts are not the same does not mean they are incommensurable or beyond comparison, they say. It is still important to pursue the unachievable goal of universal theories, and to try to reach consensus on what should be valued. In addition, it would be ridiculous to reject or accept concepts purely on account of their origin: by that token, we shouldn't even speak of "Asia", since that itself is a European construct, Wang and Kuo note wryly. While these scholars are concerned with communication research, their arguments could be said to apply to journalism as well. Striking a balance between universal principles and local context is something that journalists the world over understand implicitly. On the one hand, local knowledge is greatly prized, and the press everywhere is intimately tied to its own market. On the other hand, journalism education, training, associations and awards are increasingly global, showing that professionals share certain core values and standards. The baseline democratic values that I've sketched above form a key part of this common core.

Since I do not reject Western theories simply because of their origin, this book draws extensively on American and European scholarship, which offers much insight and wisdom on the subject of journalism and its relationship with the modern state. To resist the inappropriate use of imported concepts, however, I've tried to apply three antidotes: grounding my analysis in the local context; looking for the rationality behind apparently peculiar aspects of Singapore's media system; and constructing what Clifford Geertz has called "actor-oriented descriptions".[25] First, I do not study the press in isolation, but as an institution enmeshed with others and shaped by historical, cultural and economic forces. It is often said that newspapers reflect their societies. (Note that the name *Mirror* can be found on the masthead of papers in Britain, Sri Lanka, South Africa, Myanmar and many other countries.) While postmodern sensibilities no longer permit us to believe that the news media's stories offer an objective looking-glass image of the society they surveil, it is certainly the case that the way journalism operates anywhere is moulded in part by the forces around it. In lay terms, societies get the newspapers they deserve. Or, as the cultural theorist Pierre Bourdieu would put it, journalism is among the least "autonomous" of all cultural practices: it is deeply embedded in and dependent on its economic and political milieu.[26] For example, we cannot understand the paucity of investigative journalism in Singapore — even compared with more authoritarian societies — without reference to the power structure and the information it yields. Even in liberal democracies with a high degree of press freedom, most investigative exposés are not generated entirely by isolated reporters but are built on details received from elite institutions, such as opposition parties, think tanks, lobby groups, judges, civil servants and factions within the executive. Thus, even reporters who lack the luxury of a liberal media regime are able to do hard-hitting investigative journalism if their society's power structure is sufficiently fragmented — as is the case in China.[27] Singapore's relatively tame newspapers are, therefore, not only a function of strict press laws, but also due to an exceptionally cohesive elite.

In the same vein, explaining the low political status of Singapore's press requires an appreciation of the republic's history. In many societies, newspapers sealed their exalted place in their countries' founding narratives by playing key roles in glorious revolutions or independence struggles. Such newspapers earned the right to sit at the victors' table in perpetuity. From henceforth, their moral authority could never be completely negated by governments. In Singapore, however, a quirk of history resulted in the *de facto* national newspaper, *The Straits Times*, being headquartered in the Malaysian capital, Kuala Lumpur, for several years before and after the island separated from Malaysia on 9 August 1965. The leading Malay-language paper, *Utusan Melayu*, also left for Kuala Lumpur. Other non-English papers such as *Nanyang Siang Pau* were too focused on the interests of their respective linguistic communities to grasp fully the PAP's multi-racial nationalist project. If the new republic had chosen to sanctify the anti-colonial struggle of the 1950s as its defining moment, the press could have basked in glory, for many newspapers were at the forefront of that movement. Instead, the national narrative emphasises separation from Malaysia and the subsequent nation-building years. Within this narrative, the PAP could reasonably claim that it succeeded in spite of the media, justifying its philosophy of freedom from the press.

Second, it helps to start with the assumption that people may be acting rationally — even when their behaviour seems alien at first. A good example is the approach advocated by Daniel Hallin and Paolo Mancini, two leading exponents of comparative research into press systems. They propose that we pay heed to the phenomenon of "functional differentiation", or how institutions can evolve separate, specialised roles based on their societies' needs and the behaviour of other institutions.[28] Journalistic values and practices can therefore vary from country to country due to the different functions that particular circumstances require them to perform. Applying this perspective can add texture to our explanation for the undeveloped state of investigative journalism in Singapore. One of the most important functions of watchdog journalism is to check official corruption, but the Singapore press plays no such role. Most journalists say they don't consider this a big part of their job (see Chapter 6). One could attribute this unusual attitude to apathy or cynicism. But the concept of functional differentiation prompts us to ask first whether the watchdog job is being done by some other institution, rendering journalists redundant in this role. And, indeed, Singapore has an exceptionally effective anti-corruption agency in the form of the Corrupt Practices Investigation Bureau. The PAP's decades-long track record as one of the most graft-free governments in the world means that there is no great public push for the press to perform a corruption-watchdog function. Again, the contrast with China is illuminating. Despite the official communist ideology that the press must serve as the propaganda mouthpiece of the party — an ideology enforced with formidable restrictions on media freedom — rampant corruption has propelled journalists into the role of watchdogs on government. Indeed, in an 18-country survey that included several liberal democracies, China was the only country where journalists ranked the watchdog role as their number one function.[29]

One problem with functionalist perspectives, though, is that we risk finding rationalisations for the inexcusable. Just because the *status quo* is able to reproduce itself does not make it right in the eyes of all who live in its shadow. This is why a third check is helpful as we feel our way between universal principles and local contexts. This involves considering the perspectives of relevant actors, including journalists. Several studies have suggested that Singapore and other Asian countries represent a distinct paradigm based on "Asian values" such as harmony, communitarianism and consensus. Typically, these scholars and commentators analyse the statements of government officials and connect them with particular strands of thought buried deep in Asian traditions. Surprisingly, though, most of these works do not include the perspectives of journalists, perhaps assuming that they cannot be anything other than vessels for official ideology. Having convinced themselves that Singapore is structured as a communitarian, consensual society, analysts fail to look for signs of difference and dissent. I do not underestimate the weight of the PAP system around the media's necks, encouraging compliance. But neither do I wish to discount the possibility that Singapore journalists may have their own ideas about their roles, adding their imprint on the media system. As social scientists would put it, our accounts of social structure need to make room for human agency — the ever-present possibility that people can still make choices.

An Insider View

This book is written primarily for readers who are interested in the relationship between media and power in Singapore, including fellow Singaporeans who research, produce or consume journalism, and non-Singaporeans who are deeply curious about this anomalous system and what it says about the relationship between media and power. I am under no illusions, however, that the book will meet with the approval of all such readers. Singapore's political system and its media have been debated for decades, resulting in sharply polarised views. At one end of the political spectrum, most PAP politicians are unshakeable in their conviction that their press system needs no reform. Although priding itself in being open and pragmatic, the PAP has grown increasingly certain that key governance principles — including the subordination of news media — are critical to Singapore's survival and success. It has a reflexive response to critical questioning of the press system (as this book engages in): it automatically assumes that any criticism is aimed at mindlessly mimicking the West and that this betrays ignorance of Singapore's special circumstances. Such views are dismissed as "stooging for the Western media and their Human Rights groups", as Lee Kuan Yew has put it.[30]

Equally dogmatic are those at the opposite end of the political spectrum, in whose eyes the PAP and its instruments are corrupt usurpers of the people's freedom and dignity. This group includes foreign critics with a barely concealed contempt for Singapore and its people. It also includes some Singaporeans with a libertarian streak, who believe that the country's vitality is sapped by arrogant, self-serving politicians and their spineless propagandists in the press. The voices of these critics dominate the discussions on some popular internet forums. In their eyes, any attempt to analyse the press system in anything longer than a single, colourful, expletive-deleted (or not) sentence is at best a waste of time and at worst a smokescreen for the simple truth. To this group, only a PAP lackey or an apologist for its press would claim (as this book does) that Singapore is not as closed or repressive as many other authoritarian regimes, that there is some intellectual justification for its political system, or that its stability is maintained partly by genuine support from many Singaporeans as well as tacit buy-in from the very cynics who fancy themselves as untainted by the regime.

Many of the arguments in this book have been rehearsed in previous writing, in journal articles, book chapters, newspaper and magazine features and my blogs. They have received exactly the kind of resistance I've described above. In response, I have tried to refine my arguments. But I must realistically and regretfully acknowledge that no amount of logic and reason can settle all contentious issues. Fortunately, most readers whom I have encountered have been intellectually curious about media and power in Singapore. While they may not be fully persuaded by my work, they have engaged it with open minds, challenging me to develop and clarify my ideas. The mental image of such sceptical and sincere interlocutors — including scholars, journalists, media activists, students and other questioning minds in Singapore and abroad — has kept me company through the long and lonely writing process. It is for them and others like them that I have worked on this book.

It is not a disinterested analysis. Journalism, for me, is not some activity separate from my own identity as a researcher. I have been consumed by journalism most of my life. When I was nine, I spent my holidays producing a newspaper for my family members, handwritten on paper extracted from my exercise books. Named after the street where we lived, *Woodsville News* had headlines like "Mother goes to the market" and "Sooty taken to the vet". I was hooked on the high of playing with words, and also discovered the social value of holding a mirror up to my community (though I'd find out later that not all audiences are as indulgent as a doting family). I would go on to spend ten years in the national press, starting out as an intern during breaks from college. I married a colleague, making journalism as routine a topic of household conversation as family or food. When I started my second career as an academic, I knew I would not be able to suppress the journalist within me, so I found outlets in the form of blogs as well as an independent monthly newspaper for schoolchildren, co-published with my sister.

Some readers may question how my critique of Singapore's media system squares with the fact that I spent ten years in the mainstream press. It could seem to cynics that I have fed at the trough before spitting into it. I can only say that I was critiquing the press long before moving from journalism to academia. My undergraduate thesis on government-press relations, which analysed suppression of the media during the 1988 general elections, was researched while I was an intern and driven by a desire to understand the profession I was entering. As a *Straits Times* journalist, I continued to believe in subjecting my own institutional setting to critical and public scrutiny. Early in my career, I accepted an invitation to write an insider perspective on the Singapore press for a book published by the American organisation, Freedom Forum. The article was titled, "Inside Singapore's Successful, Self-Satisfied and Sometimes Smug Establishment Press". The title wasn't mine but it was only a slightly sensationalised summary of the article's content. It was more naivety than courage that made me disregard the possibility that it might annoy my bosses and co-workers (if it did, none ever mentioned it).

Being a media insider offers invaluable insights to a researcher, but also complicates his position. It creates a dog-eat-dog situation, notes Nick Davies, a *Guardian* journalist who penned the devastating critique of Britain's quality journalism, *Flat Earth News*.[31] The unwritten rule of journalism, he says, is that journalists are supposed to dig everywhere — except in their own back yard. Davies goes ahead and breaches this protocol in order to investigate what he calls a corrupted profession, but even he draws the line at betraying confidences. He does not draw on personal knowledge of journalists' foibles, gleaned from his former insider status. Similarly, for ethical reasons, I have avoided directly using information that has drifted my way via fellow journalists, unless it is already in the public domain or with their express permission. This is not to say that I have disregarded my own professional experience and that of other journalists in writing this book. I have tried to ensure that my analysis is not inconsistent with my lived experience, even if the latter is not explicitly cited.

My approach means that any reader hoping for a kiss-and-tell exposé will be disappointed: I've tried to avoid finger pointing. This is not only because of a sense of professional solidarity, including with people close to me who have similarly poured their lives into the profession, or because I am reluctant to embarrass individual newsmakers. The main reason is that the blame game is too easy. It goes without saying that in any institution, including government and the press, bad things happen when actors are irresponsible, unethical or negligent. What I find more intriguing is the proposition that good people who are trying their best can produce bad outcomes, due to systemic flaws that are larger than any one person or institution. Sustaining a profoundly undemocratic media system does not require corrupt politicians and dishonest journalists. Indeed, this is a key reason why the Singapore system has proven so resilient: it attracts its share of talented, sincere and loyal Singaporeans who believe that working within the national press allows them to serve their society. Many government officials, similarly, genuinely believe they are doing their best for Singapore. The system's inadequacies are more structural. Explaining this deeper structure has been, for me, a more intellectually stimulating challenge than nitpicking at day-to-day media performance.

There is another sense in which this book is an insider perspective. I was born Singaporean and have lived outside of the country only for my university education. My criticism is tempered by the sense — shared with most Singaporeans — that one has, overall, benefitted from the system. I tried explaining this to a visiting journalist over lunch at a restaurant at the Botanic Gardens, with its blend of priceless natural heritage and meticulous human planning. I told him that I probably enjoyed a higher standard of living and more life choices than my peers in journalism or academia in many other countries. The gap was certainly not because I was more deserving. I neither worked harder nor possessed more talent. It was entirely due to my good fortune of being in Singapore. The city-state has benefitted from a strategic location, which turned it into one of the world's great ports and commercial hubs by the early 20th century. And then — probably less than state propaganda claims but more than critics acknowledge — the PAP wrested Singapore from a number of dire possibilities and thrust it towards a more promising future.

Singapore's economic success is well known and does not need detailed reiteration. The United Nations Human Development Index — a composite indicator that includes health and education as well as living standards — ranked Singapore a respectable 27th in the world and 4th in Asia in 2010.[32] Another way to assess the relative strength of a society in fulfilling the full range of human needs might simply be to ask where people would like to live. While critics have pointed at the seemingly large number of Singaporeans who are happy to emigrate to greener and perhaps freer pastures, the country's emigration rate is in fact lower than some more democratic nations, such as Britain, Ireland and New Zealand.[33] A Gallup poll found that Singapore's population would more than treble if everyone in the world could move wherever they wanted to. Indeed, Singapore topped Gallup's Potential Net Migration Index in the survey of almost 350,000 individuals in 148 countries.[34] To an outsider, the recital of Singapore's successes can sound like national arrogance. For me as an insider, however, it would be hubris to deny Singapore's achievements, as if the slices of it that I have enjoyed were completely of my own making.

Singapore has serious flaws. Compared with countries at a similar income level, it is backward in the inclusiveness it offers to people with disabilities. It is a relatively safe country to raise a family — but an innocent person who is wrongly suspected of a crime has more reason to fear in Singapore than in countries that treat more seriously the rights of the accused.[35] Loyal citizens who care enough for their society to stand up and criticise it have to be prepared to be treated as opponents by an all-powerful government, enduring harassment and threats to their livelihoods. As a writer on Singapore media and politics, I find the system's faults painfully obvious. But, one common form of critique in which I am unable to indulge is caricature, reducing Singapore to a society ruled by dictators, served by a uniformly pliant media, and populated by lobotomised automatons. Such essentialised accounts of government, media and people may satisfy the unengaged, but they generate too much cognitive dissonance for me. The Singapore I know — like any human society — is diverse and complex, and I have tried to reflect that reality in the following account of its media system.

CHAPTER 2

Journalism Tamed: The Mechanics of Media Control

The People's Action Party government of Singapore has never been bashful about its determination to discipline the press. It believes that media freedom cannot be allowed to obstruct the government in its mission to secure better lives for Singaporeans. However, while PAP rhetoric is familiar to most observers, the actual mechanisms with which it controls the media are less well understood. The knowledge void is filled most enthusiastically by critics of Singapore's mainstream press. One eloquent informant was a foreign journalist who worked for *The Straits Times* for some nine months in 2004. Leaving the company on a sour note, he penned a damning critique of the paper. It was widely circulated on the internet and continues to be quoted by others:

> The paper is run by editors with virtually no background in journalism. For example, my direct editor ... was an intelligence officer. Other key editors are drawn from Singapore's bureaucracies and state security services. They all retain connections to the state's intelligence services, which track everyone and everything.[1]

Days before he was to leave the country, I happened to meet the writer at a party and asked him about this statement. He replied that it was common knowledge that the editors were tied to the state's intelligence services. I knew that the direct supervisor he mentioned, who was then the editor of the op-ed pages, was an Oxford-educated scholar who had indeed been recruited from the Internal Security Department (ISD). And, yes, the editor of *The Straits Times* and the group's managing editor had each spent ten years in the administrative service. However, they had worked in economic-related ministries, not the security apparatus. By that year, they had each chalked up at least 15 years of journalism experience. The editor-in-chief at the time, Cheong Yip Seng, had been a journalist since 1963, when my interlocutor was probably still in high school. Other key editors, including the deputy editor, night editor, news editor, political editor, money editor and foreign editor were career journalists who had spent practically all of their adult lives in the newspaper business. The statement that editors had "virtually no background in journalism" did not square with the facts. However, the writer stuck to his position. With the condescending air of someone whose adult musings are being interrupted by a naïve child, he irritably swept aside my inconvenient questions. His final word on the subject was that the editors are all part of the System, so they might as well be intelligence agents. He may have felt that he was entitled to some poetic licence after an unhappy stint at Singapore's national newspaper. So, apparently, did those who gleefully circulated his insider view. Many critics of Singapore's political system do not want to miss the wood for the trees — nor, to borrow an expression from the newspaper trade, to let the facts get in the way of a good story.

The obvious objection to the allegation that editors are nonprofessionals with intelligence agency links is that it is unfair to the journalists who have been so defamed. More importantly for our task at hand, they underestimate the sophistication and resilience of the PAP model of press control. It is quite possible that Singapore newsrooms are under both electronic and human surveillance by the ISD. But, it would be simplistic to believe that the ISD relies on plants with ISD written on their resumés. The induction of several former civil servants into the newsroom from the late 1980s was not prompted by the need for state surveillance or control. The trend was instead part of the national newspapers' effort to keep up with both establishment newsmakers and the public by hiring better-educated journalists. Increasingly, the press looked to the same pool of talent as the civil service, which had a policy of creaming off the brightest young Singaporeans through its bonded scholarships to top universities overseas. The media launched their own scholarship schemes to compete for young talent, and also hired mid-career civil servants to speed up the process. One outcome was indeed to align the press with the broader establishment, but this important difference in interpretation shifts the focus away from cloak-and-dagger machinations typical of unstable authoritarian regimes, towards the ways in which a hegemonic ruling party has succeeded in internalising its ideology of elite governance within key national institutions.

By misidentifying the ways in which the government controls media and politics, analysts have arrived at erroneous conclusions. According to some, Singapore's unfree media system was supposedly incompatible with an open economy and First World standards of living; it would soon crumble beneath the weight of its own contradictions. Most of these predictions have been based on crude misconceptions about how the press is kept in check. They generally overestimate the degree of direct government intervention through censorship and coercion, and overlook the power of ideology, and especially economic incentives, as tools of cooptation and control. They also tend to look at the media in isolation, as if a freer press, on its own, could drive Singapore down the road to full democracy. Yet, one key reason why the media system has been so resilient is that it is not an anomaly by Singapore standards. It is organically embedded in a total system that limits the roles of all those institutions that might otherwise be supportive of political pluralism in a democratic society. Singapore's courts, for example, have no tradition of judicial activism of the kind that has been instrumental in enlarging and protecting freedoms in the United States, Canada, India, Hong Kong, the European Union and elsewhere. Universities, trade unions, the legal profession, religious institutions, civil society organisations and other potential seedbeds of organised dissent have all been politically sterilised as well.

Furthermore, one cannot deny the degree of genuine support for the government within the press, which makes it easier for many journalists to see past the restrictions under which they operate. Take any random group of Singaporeans and you will find among them those who appreciate life in PAP-run Singapore and who support strong, decisive government as an integral part of the formula that has provided security and high standards of living. Therefore, it should not be surprising that the spectrum of political views among journalists includes those that conform with fundamental PAP positions — even with the position that Western-style press freedom is ill-suited to Singapore. "Who, after all, can argue with wanting Singapore to succeed?" a *Straits Times* editor, Han Fook Kwang, has noted.[2] Chapter 3 explores the values and attitudes of journalists: according to a 2009 survey, government controls do not appear to be foremost in their minds, adding credence to the view that the press system is underlain by a high degree of consensus. On the other hand, the claim that the media's domination by government is purely consensual is demonstrably false. If it were voluntary, there would be no need for restrictive laws. After more than 50 years of nation-building and relentless campaigning to re-educate the press, the government has yet to repeal or liberalise any press law. The option of industry self-regulation through an independent press council was surfaced in the early 1970s but rejected in favour of regulation by ministerial fiat. Clearly, the theory that Singaporean journalists and their audience would willingly accept the *status quo* even without coercion is mostly aspirational — something the government wishes were the case, rather than a prediction it is prepared to bet on.

This chapter offers a detailed account of the controls that keep Singapore's media in its subordinate position. It describes the sweeping laws that give the government virtually unchecked powers to punish media that challenge its authority, similar to those found in non-democratic states such as China, Myanmar and Zimbabwe. There are also controls that are more unique to Singapore. These cleverly use the news media's business model against itself: they exploit journalism's reliance on markets for their sustenance, forcing publishers and professionals to choose between editorial freedom and economic success. This layer of controls is a key part of the explanation for why the mainstream press is simultaneously politically conservative and highly profitable. (Professional journalism's economic realities also help to explain why expatriate journalists schooled in free press traditions are willing to suspend their condescension for as long as they need to accept pay checks from Singapore's conformist but cash-rich press.)

Unlike those who see Singapore's media system as a giant contradiction, I would go so far as to say that the PAP has been on the right side of history. By "right", I do not mean "good" in the moral sense. I mean that PAP leaders were correct in gauging the world-historic forces shaping nations and institutions, including the press. Nobel Peace Prize laureate Shimon Peres once said "history is like a horse that gallops past your window and the true test of statesmanship is to jump from that window onto the horse".[3] It is in that sense that Lee Kuan Yew and his key lieutenants demonstrated their statesmanship. Despite their own centre-left leanings, they spotted the irresistible advance of global capital and knew Singapore would have to ride it to survive. They differed from other post-colonial leaders who associated capitalism with neo-imperialism. But they were equally sceptical of democrats who believed that capitalism and democracy worked hand-in-hand and that the free market would deliver free media. They understood the amorality of markets. If the state acted on behalf of capitalist interests, capitalism would repay the favour and support the authoritarian state. Thus, the PAP grasped neoconservatism long before the neoconservatives arrived. While it did not give the market free rein, the PAP was prepared to regulate the press in a way that respected, and richly rewarded, media owners' desire for profit. When faced with publishers who claimed that editorial freedom was sacrosanct, the PAP called their bluff. In some cases, publishers stuck to their principles, and felt the brunt of the PAP's coercive might. But in many other instances, media owners and executives — both in Singapore and overseas — discovered within them a capacity for compliance that belied their professed love for freedom.

The National Media: Censorship 1.0

Singapore's unique press controls were set in place from the mid-1970s to the mid-1980s, but current laws include provisions dating back to the British colonial period. That these instruments were designed by an arrogant imperial power to tame subjects that it believed could not govern themselves did not seem to put off the same subjects when their turn came to govern Singapore. The PAP's attitude to media restrictions has been that of a hoarder, never wanting to dispose of seemingly archaic tools just in case one might come in useful one day. The colonial legacy includes the power to ban a wayward newspaper. To launch a newspaper, a would-be publisher must apply for a licence, which must be renewed annually and can be revoked at any time.[4] Anyone who disregards the licensing requirement risks a two-year jail term and a fine of $50,000. Licensing systems are not unheard of in liberal democracies, but these are generally for the allocation of scarce broadcast spectrum, not for newspapers. Furthermore, international norms recommend that any registration system be implemented according to transparent criteria and by bodies that are independent of the government of the day. In Singapore, however, licensing decisions are wholly at the discretion of the relevant minister. The law does not set out the criteria to be met for granting a permit, or require the minister to give reasons for refusing one. The only avenue for appeal is to the President, who, under Singapore's Constitution, is required to act on the advice of the Cabinet in such matters. A government could, within the law, force a newspaper to close simply because it supports an opposition party. However, the PAP has not used its licensing powers in quite so scandalous a fashion. It has granted publishing permits to opposition party organs such as the Workers' Party's *Hammer*.

In 1991, the government suspended the publishing permit of a women's lifestyle magazine, *Woman's Affair*, saying that it had strayed outside its licensed objectives by commenting on politics. However, licensing has been used mainly to deal with newspapers perceived as having divided loyalties. In 1969, the Malaysian-based *Utusan Melayu* was told to publish a separate Singapore edition if it wanted its permit renewed. The company declined and ceased circulating in Singapore in early 1970. In 1971, the government took action against two new English-language dailies. It accused the *Eastern Sun* — launched in 1966 by the Aw family of Tiger Balm fame — of being a kind of communist sleeper. Although it had been supportive of the government thus far, the publisher had received Chinese communist funds that would ensure the paper's loyalty to outside interests when the time came, the government alleged.[5] These accusations of so-called "black operations" were too intense for *Eastern Sun*'s editorial staff to bear. They walked out and the paper collapsed before the government needed to use its licensing powers. The *Singapore Herald*, launched in 1970, was also found to have overseas backers that the government considered suspect. Its licence was revoked and its senior expatriate executives expelled from Singapore. Although the paper had a "lively, entertaining, refreshingly irreverent approach", in the words of historian Mary Turnbull, it was already in serious financial difficulty and may not have lasted long had the government left it alone.[6] "Lee Kuan Yew chose to make an example of the *Herald* by withdrawing its licence, rather than just letting it fade away," Turnbull writes.[7] She notes that evidence did emerge eventually of foreign slush funds infiltrating the regional press. "While there was no indication that either the *Eastern Sun* or the *Herald* were being influenced by their backers, the financial instability of such newspapers made them potentially vulnerable to external pressures," she acknowledges.[8]

The prime target of the May 1971 crackdown was the leading Chinese-language newspaper, *Nanyang Siang Pau*. The paper had reacted brashly to the prime minister's warning that it should not play up Chinese language issues (see Chapter 6).[9] The government neutralised its leadership by arresting four senior executives without warrant and detaining them without trial. The government was empowered to do this by a piece of legislation that was by then all too familiar to critics of the regime, and that continues to fill Singaporeans with dread: the ISA or Internal Security Act.[10] Like the press permit system, the ISA is a legacy of the colonial period, when preventive detention was seen as an essential emergency measure against communist insurgency. Under the ISA, a person can be detained for up to two years "with a view to preventing that person from acting in any manner prejudicial to the security of Singapore or any part thereof or to the maintenance of public order or essential services therein".[11] Detention orders can be extended by further periods of two years at a time.

Such shock-and-awe tactics have gone out of style as a means of media control. And every year that passes without an ISA detention or newspaper ban raises the bar for leaders contemplating their use, making it harder for them to justify why a threat is so exceptionally serious that it requires a once-in-a-generation remedy. Nevertheless, the laws remain in the books and the PAP is unrepentant about their past use. Films chronicling detainees' sides of the story decades after their arrest and release have been banned, on the grounds that "individuals who have posed a security threat to Singapore's interests in the past" cannot be allowed to "make baseless accusations against the authorities, give a false portrayal of their previous activities in order to exculpate their guilt, and undermine public confidence in the Government in the process".[12] Even if it is difficult today to picture a national newspaper being banned or its editor being detained, the government's past actions are embedded in the institutional memory of media organisations. The enduring lesson from those harsher years is that the PAP is an irresistible force. A former editor of *The Straits Times*, Leslie Fong, has noted: "The press laws and political culture are such that the Government, with a vast array of powers at its disposal, will not countenance the press taking any determined stand against it on any issues that it considers fundamental."[13]

Censorship 2.0: The 1974 Press Law

The government's powers to lock up journalists and close down newspapers — entirely at its discretion and without having to go through the courts — ring-fence the outer limits of media autonomy. They are not, however, the means through which control is exercised on a routine basis. For that, the PAP has depended on provisions in the press law that turned Singapore's newspapers into the collaborative and non-adversarial establishment institutions that they have been for more than three decades. These unique powers moved government-press relations backstage. In this regard, the press law, notes legal scholar Jothie Rajah, is one of Singapore's "'rule by law' controls and constraints enveloped within administrative and regulatory mechanisms; an enveloping that ensures the state's controlling measures do not enter the public domain with the same dramatic flourish as court proceedings or detention without trial".[14]

The law in question is the Newspaper and Printing Presses Act (NPPA) of 1974.[15] The government retained the old licensing rules and added a ban on the foreign ownership of newspapers — a move that was neither uncommon nor surprising, considering the 1971 allegations of "black operations". But, the NPPA also included radically new requirements. First, the Act says that no newspaper can be published in Singapore except by a public company.[16] This legislative innovation, which enshrined the stock market as the rightful place where newspaper companies belonged, set Singapore apart from other authoritarian regimes that chose instead to nationalise their media. This was a counter-intuitive stroke of genius by Lee Kuan Yew. He understood that capitalism as such was not a threat to government. The real risk came from headstrong and ideologically-driven publishers who might be willing to prioritise their ideals ahead of profits. The solution, he realised, was to ensure that no individual or corporation held a controlling interest in newspapers. Therefore, under current rules, no person can control 12 per cent or more of a newspaper company without the government's permission. As at October 2010, Singapore Press Holdings had more than 50,000 ordinary shareholders. The largest five were all financial institutions, with Citibank at the top (13.43 per cent). The others in the top five were the government-linked DBS Bank (10.27 per cent) and its subsidiary DBSN Services (4.11 per cent), HSBC (8.99 per cent) and United Overseas Bank (2.59 per cent).[17] With ownership spread so thinly, the diverse motives of individual shareholders are reduced to their lowest common denominator — the pure pursuit of profit. Stock exchange rules exert their own discipline: directors of a public listed company have a fiduciary responsibility to protect the commercial health of the firm from quixotic impulses.

The second major feature of the NPPA reveals the government's interventionist intent more plainly. It requires every newspaper company to have two classes of shares, namely, ordinary shares and management shares. Both types have the same cash value, but management shares have more voting power than ordinary shares — 200 times more, to be precise — on "any resolution relating to the appointment or dismissal of a director or any member of the staff of a newspaper company".[18] Management share systems are not unknown in the newspaper business. The family owners of the *Wall Street Journal* and the *New York Times*, for example, held "Class B" shares with ten times the voting power. The twist in the NPPA is that it is the government that decides whose shares are to be given supervoting status. "No newspaper company shall refuse to issue or to accept the transfer of management shares to any person who has been granted the written approval of the Minister to purchase or hold the shares except for reasons to be given in writing acceptable to the Minister," the law says.[19] In October 2010, SPH had 19 management shareholders. They had a combined entitlement of over 3.25 billion votes on appointments of directors and staff — more than double the number of votes for all ordinary shareholders combined. Great Eastern Life Assurance topped the list. Great Eastern is a subsidiary of OCBC Bank, which was itself the second largest holder of management shares. Neither is a government-linked company. Others holding more than 1 million management shares each were NTUC Income Insurance Cooperative, Singapore Telecom, DBS Bank and United Overseas Bank. While NTUC Income, SingTel and DBS all have close government links, the more telling trait of management shareholders is that most are financial institutions deeply invested in Singapore's political stability.[20]

After the devastation of May 1971, the press had feared nationalisation. After all, most authoritarian regimes believed that taking over ownership was the best way to exercise control over the media. Often, this had the bonus of adding richly to government or party coffers. This was the approach taken not only in communist states, but also in neighbouring Malaysia, where national newspapers found themselves owned by ruling parties or their cronies.[21] In Singapore, radio and television had started as government services. Broadcasting was gradually corporatised to make it more market-driven, but it remained in state hands — showing that the PAP was certainly not allergic to government ownership of media. However, while broadcasting had never been a private sector enterprise, Singapore's newspapers had always been owned by businessmen. Nationalising private firms would spook foreign investors at a time when Singapore was trying hard to build a business-friendly reputation.

Besides, Lee Kuan Yew understood that government control did not require government ownership: media corporations focusing on their commercial self-interest would voluntarily cooperate with a government that had shown itself utterly committed to political stability, industrial peace and policies that favoured big business. By taking a government-friendly editorial stance, a company could even turn the licensing system to its advantage. A newspaper's permit would not be at risk as long as it cooperated with the government; furthermore, the permit system assured monopoly profits, since it effectively kept out potential competitors. A publishing permit looks unfair to those who do not have one; to those who do, it is — to borrow an expression used by one media mogul[22] — a licence to print money.

While the government did not wish to nationalise newspapers, it was not above intervening in the business in other ways. It has forced major restructuring of the industry, in the name of establishing stable and responsible national media. The first such exercise was initiated by the Malaysian government. After Singapore's expulsion from the Federation in 1965, the Straits Times group (like the national airline) spent several years in the odd situation of straddling two sovereign countries. It was headquartered in Kuala Lumpur while still being 70 per cent Singapore-owned.[23] Both governments may have found this untenable, but it was Malaysia who acted first. In 1972–3, the company's Malaysian operations were absorbed into a holding company of the ruling UMNO party. This created the New Straits Times group in Malaysia, while the Straits Times company at last planted roots in post-colonial Singapore.

The PAP government's own interventions in the industry structure were focused mainly on the Chinese press. As described in Chapter 6, these eventually led to the founding of Singapore Press Holdings in 1984. When the Tamil-language daily *Tamil Murasu* was brought under the SPH umbrella in 1996 — again to ensure the survival of a vulnerable Asian-language title — SPH incidentally secured a total monopoly of domestic daily newspapers. This monopoly was broken in 2000, when the government permitted its wholly-owned national broadcaster, MediaCorp, to launch a free daily newspaper, *Today*. To be even-handed, the government gave a broadcasting licence to SPH, but the newspaper company proved unable to profit from its television channels. In 2004, the government declared that the experiment had shown that Singapore was too small to have full-blown competition in media (a conclusion that would have been more persuasive if investors other than SPH and MediaCorp had been given the opportunity to try). The government's faith in SPH as a dependable corporate citizen was such that it allowed the company to take a 20 per cent stake in MediaCorp, the first time since launching as a radio service in 1936 that it had non-government shareholders.

The Gatekeepers

Through the NPPA, the PAP government gained control over key appointments in Singapore's newspapers. How exactly it would use this power was, for the press, a matter of anxiety and tense negotiation. As related in Chapter 5, the government ultimately settled on the practice of parachuting trusted former senior officials into the role of publisher, while leaving the editors' jobs in the hands of experienced professionals. In 1982, S.R. Nathan became executive chairman of the Straits Times group shortly after retiring as permanent secretary of the Foreign Ministry. According to Turnbull, Nathan was more "bridge-builder" than "censor-in-chief" during his six years at the newspaper group.[24] This probably set the tone for his successors, who similarly avoided day-to-day interventions that would shatter the long tradition of professional management of the press. Lim Kim San, a Cabinet minister for 17 years before he retired in 1981, was appointed chairman of the newly formed Singapore Press Holdings from 1988–2002.[25] Tjong Yik Min, a former permanent secretary and before that a chief of the fearsome Internal Security Department for seven years, was appointed head of SPH's management team in 1995. Alan Chan took over that post in 2002. A President's Scholar, Chan had more than 24 years' experience in the civil service, including as Principal Private Secretary to Prime Minister Lee Kuan Yew. Tony Tan, a heavyweight Cabinet minister until his retirement in 2005, took over as chairman of SPH the same year, resigning in 2011 to run for election as the Republic's President. He was replaced by another former Cabinet minister, Lee Boon Yang. Also on the board in 2011 were former Cabinet minister Yeo Ning Hong and the former Chief Justice, Yong Pung How, an old friend of Lee Kuan Yew.[26]

As for newsroom leadership, the government continued to recognise, perhaps reluctantly, that this was best left in the hands of experienced journalists. "I say that one of Mr Lee Kuan Yew's wisest decisions as Prime Minister was to abort a plan to send in a Government team of officials to run Times House," says Peter Lim, who was editor-in-chief of the Straits Times group for nine years from 1978.[27] Lim and his two most senior colleagues in the 1980s and 1990s — Cheong Yip Seng and Leslie Fong — were high-flying editors before the NPPA era: their professional competence is rarely disputed by those who have worked with them. However, Lee Kuan Yew made plain his disdain for journalists' intellectual credentials. "The not so bright go into political science and sociology. When they cannot get a good job, they go on to journalism," he said at an election rally in 1972.[28] Lim, Cheong and Fong — not unusually for men of their era — had not received the luxury of a university degree. From the 1970s, even without the goading of the prime minister, they and others in senior management were acutely aware that their newspapers' competitiveness depended on attracting, developing and retaining high-quality editorial talent. The public sector — Singapore's biggest employer then and now — was a potential pool of talent that newspaper executives could not overlook. Thus, several Singaporeans who started out as relatively anonymous civil servants were able to find their true calling in the press. Some young public sector high-fliers proved harder to prise out of their government jobs. This was partly because, at the time, the press did not pay competitive salaries and also because the government held on jealously to its own.

In the mid-1980s, however, both these obstacles were lowered and the press succeeded in drawing from the same talent pool as the bureaucracy. In a sign of the PAP's growing ideological hold on the Singaporean mind, newspapers began to adopt yardsticks for measuring journalistic talent that were strikingly similar to those that the government used when choosing the administrative elite. Stratospheric A-level grades and degrees from Oxbridge and Ivy League universities became the credentials of choice. In the late 1980s, SPH became one of the first non-government corporations to start an overseas scholarship system modelled on that of the Public Service Commission. SPH also got the government's blessings to recruit mid-career inductees from the elite administrative service. These moves helped push the profession firmly into the establishment. The trend was not unique to the Singapore press. In the United States, for example, it has been observed that journalism has been transformed from a working class occupation to an elite profession, with editors and journalists now in the same social circles as the government and corporate decision makers they cover.[29] Once again, the PAP was riding a global trend, rather than working at odds with the media industry's own trajectory.

Significantly, the mid-career inductees from the civil service were not given senior positions straight away. Several proved ill-suited to the newsroom and left the profession. However, three eventually rose to the top. Shaun Seow, a President's Scholar, moved to the national broadcaster, where he rose to head MediaCorp. Han Fook Kwang, who had worked in the communications and labour ministries, joined the *Straits Times* in 1989 and became editor in 2002. Patrick Daniel, recruited from the trade and industry ministry in 1986, succeeded Cheong Yip Seng 20 years later in Singapore's most powerful journalism post — editor-in-chief of SPH's English and Malay newspaper group. According to press folklore, his staff gave Daniel the symbolic gift of a "plant" when he became the *Business Times* editor in 1992, as a good-natured hint that he would need to live down his government ties. A few years into Han's tenure as editor, Warren Fernandez was identified as his likely successor. Fernandez, the first beneficiary of SPH's own scholarship scheme, had a First Class from Oxford as well as a Masters in Public Administration from Harvard's Kennedy School — the favoured post-graduate credential of the administrative elite. He replaced Han as *Straits Times* editor in 2012.

Regardless of their backgrounds, editors — whether an ink-in-his-veins veteran like Cheong or former civil servants like Han and Daniel — would require both professional journalistic competence to run newspapers, as well as the political skill to maintain the trust of top government leaders. Peter Lim notes wryly that the job would have been much easier if the government just told the press what it wanted and editors simply obeyed. Instead, it was not the *Straits Times* culture to take the path of least resistance; nor did Lee Kuan Yew want the papers to become a government news agency. "Thankfully, the Prime Minister wanted to have his national media cake and eat it too," Lim says. "Mr Lee wanted a national press that would think the way he did about national imperatives, yet a press that could report, interpret and analyse like the best newspapers in the most developed and the freest countries."[30] In the same vein, Lee's successor, Goh Chok Tong, said he did not want the Singapore press to be a "government mouthpiece".[31] "I do not favour a subservient press," he said. "An unthinking press is not good for Singapore."[32] Goh asked editors to be mindful of their "larger responsibilities" and "Singapore's uniqueness as a country, our multi-racial and multi-religious make-up, vulnerabilities and national goals". "By this," he added, "I mean that our editors and journalists must be men and women who know what works for Singapore and how to advance our society's collective interests."[33]

Thus, the government allows the press considerable day-to-day autonomy. Often, editors deviate deliberately or unwittingly from the government's preferred script. Officials may signal their displeasure either publicly, through the newspaper's own letters page or in speeches, or privately through phone calls or in meetings with editors. For reporters, the erosion of political capital could result in loss of access or, in rare cases, a transfer out of one's beat. For an editor, the loss of the government's trust could result in being eased out or sidelined. Since editors are well paid, there is no doubt a pecuniary interest in holding on to one's position for as long as possible. However, it would be unfair to impute purely selfish motives to editors' preparedness to bend to the government's will. Editors know that the alternative is not necessarily better for the press or the country. If they exhaust their political capital, they would obviously be replaced not by bolder and more independent colleagues, but by those whom the government believes to be more compliant. Indeed, the government's management of its national broadcaster is hardly suggestive of great respect for media professions: in the early 1990s, it handed the top two positions in television news to administrators with no journalism experience — one a former civil servant who was heading the broadcaster's corporate development division, the other a high-flying mandarin seconded from a government ministry. The PAP leadership has shown, at best, a grudging and conditional acceptance of the value of professional journalists.

Foreign Media in the Spotlight

By the early 1980s, Singapore's domestic media had been neutralised as a force that could potentially challenge the PAP's legitimacy and its control of the national agenda. However, the government remained prone to attack by foreign publications. As it had done with the national press, the government turned to the draconian ISA but later introduced more sophisticated legislative innovations to encourage self-censorship. The government was particularly sensitive to foreign publications which treated Singapore as a key market and which therefore devoted regular space to political and economic coverage of the country. With domestic media no longer able to satisfy the tastes of more critical Singaporeans (a state of affairs mirrored in several other Asian markets with restricted media freedoms), these offshore titles enjoyed a strong competitive advantage, attracting high-end readers with their fiercely independent reportage. The most incisive was the *Far Eastern Economic Review* (*FEER*), a newsweekly based in Hong Kong. In 1977, two Singaporeans who had written for *FEER* were detained. Arun Senkuttuvan was released after eight weeks (after which he was stripped of his citizenship) and Ho Kwon Ping after seven — but only after they had confessed on television to slanting their reports. "In my articles I deliberately sought to portray the Singapore Government (which I considered to be virtually synonymous with the PAP) as elitist, racialist, fascist, oppressive and dictatorial," Ho was recorded as saying. He added that he "saw the *Review* as a vehicle through which he could create issues and propagate his 'pro-communist ideals'".[34]

The government seemed to be building its case against *FEER*. In the mid-1980s, Lee Kuan Yew was preparing to hand over the reins of government to a new generation of leaders and warned *FEER* editor Derek Davies that he would not countenance meddling by foreign media.[35] However, the outright banning of a high-profile newsmagazine seemed too extreme a measure even for the PAP. "[W]hen you ban, the newspapers have the satisfaction of knowing 'Ah, I hurt you and therefore you can't stand my criticisms and therefore you banned me'," Lee said.[36] He wanted a way to deny editors like Davies the right to interfere in Singapore politics "without giving him the moral high horse of having been banned", he said.[37] Such a mechanism was grafted onto the NPPA in 1986, two years after a general election that witnessed a historic 13-point drop in the PAP's share of the popular vote. Under Section 24 of the amended NPPA, the government could "declare any newspaper published outside Singapore to be a newspaper engaging in the domestic politics of Singapore" and impose a cap on the total number of copies that could be sold or distributed in the country.[38]

The first to drift past the government's crosshairs was *Time* magazine. It was gazetted less than two months after the new NPPA provisions came into effect. The government ordered that *Time*'s circulation was to be halved to 9,000 the following week and cut again to 2,000 the following year.[39] The offending article, titled "Silencing the Dissenters", was highly critical of the state's treatment of opposition leader J.B. Jeyaretnam. However, the government said that the magazine was being punished not for the article's content but for its mishandling of subsequent correspondence from the prime minister's office. *Time* was refusing to publish unaltered a letter from the prime minister's press secretary. The letter detailed errors that the government had spotted in the original article. The government had told *Time* it could publish a rebuttal to the letter if it wished, but that the letter had to be run unedited. "The amendment to the Newspaper and Printing Presses Act is to discourage foreign publications from biased reporting on Singapore. Persistent refusal to publish corrections is an example of bias," the government statement said.[40]

Other foreign publications circulating in Singapore did not realise immediately that business as usual was no longer an option. They were like drivers on a highway reacting too slowly to a crash right before their eyes. A pile-up was inevitable. The *Asian Wall Street Journal*, *Asiaweek* and *Far Eastern Economic Review* were all gazetted in 1987. When Goh Chok Tong became prime minister in 1990, some anticipated a new era of openness — but in 1993, *The Economist* was gazetted. In all these cases other than *FEER*'s, the test of whether a publication was engaging unlawfully in Singapore's affairs was not the extremity of its criticism, but how it handled the government's responses. The government demanded nothing less than the right of completely unedited reply. (A government booklet giving its side of the story was accordingly titled, *The Right to be Heard*.[41]) In the *Time* case, the publisher initially insisted that it was standard practice to edit all letters. A fortnight later, *Time* went ahead and printed the reply in full, adding that it did "not agree with all the corrections cited ... but prints this letter in the spirit of full discussion of issues".[42] Its circulation was restored nine months later. As for the *Economist*, the newsmagazine gave in swiftly enough to limit the damage: instead of slashing its circulation, the government merely capped it at its current numbers. It was de-gazetted after five months.

Of course, in liberal eyes, a regime that chose to choke offending titles' circulation *in lieu* of banning them could hardly be described as tolerant of criticism. But the government insisted that it was not trying to censor the foreign press or to restrict the flow of information. It went to tortuous lengths to live up to its rhetoric of reasonableness. If a gazetted publication were prepared to distribute complimentary copies without advertisements, there would be no cap on the quantity, the government declared. It even changed the law to allow third parties to reproduce such newspapers without the publishers' permission. They could be sold on a cost-recovery basis, minus the ads.

Under this scheme, facsimile copies of *FEER* circulated for a while in Singapore, with blank pages where the ads should have been. The government even offered to subsidise the printing cost if *FEER*'s publishers wanted to do this themselves. It explained the political message it wanted to deliver:

> [W]e do not want to leave any of your supporters befuddled with the idea that you were defending the freedom of information. You want the freedom to make money selling advertisements. If our offer helps to dispel this myth, it has served its purpose.[43]

The prime minister seemed to relish the prospect of calling the Western media's bluff and exposing the commercial motives behind their democratic pretensions: "You can write what you will and you'll make no money out of it, and we will see whether you're interested in upholding great freedoms, or whether you are interested in your advertising revenue.... We'll prove it."[44]

When dealing with offshore publications, as with their Singapore counterparts, Lee banked on his conviction that commercial news media's commitment to press freedom was less steadfast than their desire for profit. The foreign media railed against his government's actions, but were ultimately not immune to financial pressure. Singapore represented the single largest market for the likes of the *Asian Wall Street Journal* and *Far Eastern Economic Review*. Of various measures used on the foreign media, writes Garry Rodan, "None was more strategic than the pressure applied to media organisations' bottom lines through official control over access to domestic circulation and advertising markets — a strategy that produced remarkable results."[45] Studying foreign media coverage of political controversies in the 1990s, Rodan concludes that they had gotten the message that there was "a range of sensitivities to be very carefully navigated, or avoided completely".[46] Despite editors' claims that there would be no compromise in their reporting, major news organisations adopted "a decidedly restrained reporting approach in Singapore".[47]

Mopping up: Defamation and Contempt

The government's decades-long campaign to get journalists to anticipate and adjust to its thinking has not been 100 per cent effective. Editors are given enough freedom to exercise their own judgment and make mistakes. Sometimes, they may err on the side of caution, frustrating those who believe that the available acreage for critical journalism is not being tilled. In other cases, the national newspapers' misjudgments have swung the other way. Although famously conservative, they have occasionally been judged to merit the threat of old-style punishments using Censorship 1.0 laws. One instance in which self-censorship failed involved *The New Paper*'s reporting of a military helicopter crash in 1991. Furious that the paper had enterprisingly gone beyond the official statement, the defence ministry threatened prosecution under strict military secrecy laws.[48] In 1994, when I was a political journalist for *The Straits Times*, I was accused of contempt of Parliament for writing that the Speaker was overly strict in his timekeeping during the Budget debates. Possible punishments included jail and a fine, but I was given the chance to retract before proceedings against me began, which I accepted.[49]

The severest action against the domestic press since the 1990s involved the publication by the *Business Times* in 1992 of seemingly innocuous flash estimates of Singapore's economic growth figures before their official release. The *BT* editor and another of its journalists, together with two private sector economists and a senior civil servant, were convicted under the Official Secrets Act and fined.[50] The episode was an oddity. The government seemed motivated mainly by a desire to signal to public servants that it had zero tolerance for leaks, rather than any firm belief that the men being prosecuted had criminal minds. While the 20-month-long investigation and trial was undoubtedly traumatic for the five men, the final verdict did not terminate the career of *BT*'s editor at the time, Patrick Daniel, who eventually rose to head the newspaper group. The civil servant found guilty of mishandling economic data, Tharman Shanmugaratnam, eventually became finance minister and deputy prime minister.

Major lapses of self-censorship that provoked the wielding of sledgehammer laws against the national press were extremely few in the 1990s and practically non-existent by the 2000s. The rough edges of the foreign media, on the other hand, proved harder to smoothen. This was partly due to structural and organisational factors. In a large international news organisation with multiple platforms such as print and online, not all Singapore stories would be handled by an editor sensitised to the PAP government's idiosyncrasies. Furthermore, even for old hands, the government's sensitivities could be notoriously difficult to predict. The classic example was a case against the *International Herald Tribune*, sparked by an article that referred to "intolerant regimes in Asia". Although Singapore was not mentioned by name, the government charged that the article defamed Singapore's prime minister and scandalised its courts.

These two laws — defamation and contempt of court — have been the most regularly used instruments against foreign media, next to the government's gazetting powers. The defamation suits have been triggered by two main types of unsubstantiated allegation. The first has to do with the meteoric rise of Lee Kuan Yew's family members. His son, Lee Hsien Loong, became Singapore's third prime minister in 2004. The younger Lee's wife, Ho Ching, headed government-linked corporations, including ultimately the government's investment arm, Temasek Holdings, one of the world's most powerful sovereign wealth funds. Any brazen claim that Lee family members owed their positions to nepotism rather than merit has been treated as an unconscionable attack on their reputations. Two news organisations that crossed this line were the *International Herald Tribune* in 1994 and 2010, and Bloomberg in 2002. A second category of statement that has provoked swift civil action is any suggestion that Singapore's leaders are corrupt, including unfounded allegations that critics have been silenced in order to conceal wrong-doing. Among those that have been sued for such claims were Malaysia's *Star* newspaper in 1987 and the *Far Eastern Economic Review* in 1988 and 2006.

Defamation law is universally recognised as a necessary means of protecting people's reputations. In liberal societies, particularly the United States, public figures are expected to stomach a large dose of even unfair criticism in the interest of preserving space for critical scrutiny by the press and public. However, the "public figure" test does not apply under Singapore law. Singapore courts have accepted plaintiffs' arguments that officials have greater reputations to defend, that degrading their integrity will affect their ability to govern and deter other honest men and women from entering politics, and that unfounded attacks thus merit higher damages.[51] Allegations that judges lack independence have resulted in a string of prosecutions. Under

Singapore law, remarks that scandalise the court or damage the credibility of the judiciary's independence constitute contempt of court.[52] Foreign publications that have fallen foul of this law include the *Asian Wall Street Journal* in 1985 and 1990, and the *International Herald Tribune* in 1994.

Just like the domestic media, foreign news organisations have, over the years, become less combative and quicker to accept their fate when ruled offside by the state. Thus, in 2010, the *International Herald Tribune*, the global newspaper of the venerable *New York Times*, apologised and paid up before a defamation action reached the courts. The public editor of the *New York Times* noted,

> Some readers were astonished that a news organization with a long history of standing up for First Amendment values would appear to bow obsequiously to an authoritarian regime that makes no secret of its determination to cow critics, including Western news organizations, through aggressive libel actions.[53]

The *IHT* explained itself thus:

> Singapore is an important market for The International Herald Tribune. There are more than 12,000 I.H.T. readers who shouldn't be deprived of the right to read the paper in print or online. In addition, getting kicked out of Singapore would also make it more difficult for others in the region to get the I.H.T. since we print in Singapore for distribution there and in the neighboring areas.[54]

Similarly, Bloomberg's editor explained to his staff that the company's swift settlement with the government in 2002 was necessary to protect the welfare of 180 employees and 2,695 customers in Singapore.[55]

Critics of the PAP had predicted that Singapore's ambitions to be a media hub would be thwarted by its lack of respect for press freedom. Instead, like investors from other industries, media corporations found Singapore's location, communication links, infrastructure, stability and liveability to be a winning combination when deciding where to site their Asian or Southeast Asian operations. For media focused on business and economic news, Singapore's status as one of the financial, commercial and maritime capitals of the world added to its allure. Once these corporations planted stakes in Singapore, there was added incentive to avoid unnecessary controversy. Rodan cites the example of the Foreign Correspondents' Association, which ceded to the government's request to abandon a forum that was to involve Indonesian opposition leader Megawati Sukarnoputri. The government's ally, Suharto, was still in power in Indonesia at the time.[56] By the late 1990s, therefore, foreign media had moderated their criticism of Singapore. "This was not just in response to the negative sanctions imposed on publications deemed to have 'engaged in domestic politics'," says Rodan. "It was also a measure of the seduction of Singapore as both a market in its own right and reporting base for servicing other markets in the region."

The most ironic and telling example of how capitalism could thwart hard-hitting journalism must be the story of the *Far Eastern Economic Review*. Founded in 1946, the illustrious publication died in 2009, while embroiled in a defamation suit brought by the Lees. However, it was not Singapore but New York that killed the *Review*. The magazine had been acquired by the Dow Jones media conglomerate in the 1980s. When it lost a defamation suit in 1989 and had to cough up S$230,000 in damages, the new owners took notice. According to former *Review* editors David Plott and Michael Vatikiotis, the suit raised concerns at Dow Jones headquarters "that this feisty little news magazine may have started to become a problem for a company that was raising its profile in Asia as a source of business news, not political controversy".[57] Plott and Vatikiotis accuse Dow Jones of mismanaging the business side of the *Review* and gradually treating the Asian edition of its flagship *Wall Street Journal* as its favoured vehicle in the region.[58] To cut costs, the two publications were made to merge their reporting staffs in 2001. The *Review* was closed as a weekly newsmagazine in 2004 and reformatted as a monthly with a fraction of the staff. Dow Jones finally pulled the plug in 2009. It was not an isolated case. *Asiaweek*, born in 1975 and purchased by AOL Time Warner a decade later, suffered a similar fate in 2001. By closing *Asiaweek*, the parent company eased the competitive pressure on the Asian edition of its favoured child, *Time* magazine. Thus, *Far Eastern Economic Review* and *Asiaweek*, two proud Asian titles that had had their share of run-ins with the PAP, provided the ultimate vindication of Lee Kuan Yew's faith in the profit motive as a counter to firebrand journalism.

Market Censorship

This chapter has argued that the strength and longevity of Singapore's press model has a lot to do with its compatibility with the market.

Fashioned in the early 1970s, the PAP approach ran counter to the dominant liberal view, which considers profitable market-driven media as the best watchdogs on government. There is, of course, plenty of evidence that capitalism is liberty's best friend. Not for nothing do communist states — the antithesis of free societies — choose to insulate their media from the market by placing them under party ownership. There are many examples of media becoming more responsive to the public when they start answering to the market instead of to government officials. Even in China, where all media remain ultimately in the hands of the Communist Party, those publications mandated to seek profits have moved to the forefront of critical commentary and investigative journalism, compared with those not exposed to the market. Thus, it is certainly not the case that profit-seeking publishers are less keen on journalistic independence than are authoritarian governments. However, the capitalist commitment to freedom is not absolute or unconditional. Business is itself a site of power. It can act as a countervailing force against the state, as liberals argue. But it also has interests of its own that it will protect against democratic forces. Profit orientation imposes its own constraints on press freedom — constraints that can reinforce government control.

This non-mainstream perspective has been explored by scholars working within what has been called the political economy or, simply, "critical" tradition. In the United States, one of the best known is Robert McChesney, who notes that journalism there has been increasingly subjected to an "explicit commercial regimentation". He argues that "the market will very effectively push the content to more politically acceptable outcomes, without the need for direct censorship".[59] Garry Rodan has arrived at similar conclusions. "Fears of access to lucrative domestic and regional markets being withdrawn by governments, and of other forms of commercial pressure, have resulted in media organisations and publishers engaging in extensive forms of self-censorship," he says.[60] In the standard liberal view, Singapore is a paradox: it is open for business, but restrictive in its media policies. From a critical perspective, however, there is nothing contradictory about Singapore's combination of free markets and unfree media. Singapore and other authoritarian regimes can instead be seen as "viable alternative political models for capitalist development", as Rodan puts it.[61] David Harvey has a broadly similar view of Singapore and its place in the world. He argues that it is part of a growing family of neoliberal regimes, in which the state creates and preserves a conducive environment for private property rights, free markets, and free trade — even at the expense of democracy.[62] The PAP's introduction of the NPPA in 1974 showed its intuitive grasp of neoliberalism, even before the phenomenon had been identified and named.

Leaving newspapers in the hands of commercial owners, the Singapore government had to live with a certain amount of dissonance from a press torn between two masters, the market and the government. Yet, the government was confident that the deviations would be within certain bounds, not only because of its own formidable reserve powers, but also because publishers focused on profitability would see it in the company's own interest to rein in journalists too consumed by their democratic mission. Critical studies of the press tell us that owners do not need to intervene directly in day-to-day newsroom operations in order to blunt journalism's democratic edge. They do so indirectly, by shifting the balance of power between editorial and marketing departments, ensuring that the needs of advertisers get more attention when setting editorial priorities and allocating resources. Thus, journalism has focused increasingly on "lifestyle", entertainment and personal finance, cultivating the public as consumers and investors rather than citizens. The trend is most visible in the proliferation of advertiser-friendly lifestyle sections and supplements — the *Business Times*' meatiest annual supplement, with more than 50 pages in good years, is devoted entirely to high-end watches. Even front pages of the *Times* of London and news bulletins of the BBC — once high temples of serious news coverage — have grown more entertainment-focused.

Most critiques of the Singapore press — such as the visiting journalist's diatribe quoted at the beginning of this chapter — fail to recognise the multiple pillars on which the media system rests. Antonio Gramsci compared hegemony to the way currency was backed by gold reserves that the authorities might never be called upon to touch. Similarly, the government's coercive power underwrites its politest requests for cooperation. As for the public, liberal Singaporeans may be highly critical of their unfree press, but there is no evidence that they would go out of their way to support a freer one. That was the lesson from 1971, a *Straits Times* editor Han Fook Kwang has said. "These actions showed how far the Government would go in removing any roadblock that might get in the way of its nationhood project," said Han Fook Kwang. "They also showed that the Singapore electorate was by and large prepared to allow the Government to do so."[63] The dilemma that such realities pose for the everyday practice of professional journalism will be examined in the next chapter.

CHAPTER 3

Inside the Press: Routines, Values and "OB" Markers

In 2009, *The Straits Times* broke the story that Singapore's main feminist organisation had been taken over by a group of conservative Christians. Initially coy about their identity and intent, the insurgent faction eventually let it be known that they were opposed to AWARE's liberal agenda, especially on homosexuality.[1] AWARE's stalwarts eventually roused themselves from their slumber and reasserted themselves, theatrically reclaiming the leadership of the organisation at a general meeting that truly deserved its "extraordinary" billing. *The Straits Times* led the coverage of the unfolding drama with its considerable news-gathering muscle and newspaper acreage. Perhaps inevitably, the newspaper became part of the story. One of the burdens of being a monopolistic national institution is that readers are quick to suspect it of abusing its power. In this case, supporters of the failed AWARE coup and other conservatives alleged that the newspaper had sensationalised the story in a way that favoured the liberal old guard. Several blogs and forum postings accused the journalist who was at the forefront of the coverage of letting his own homosexuality colour his reports.[2] A widely circulated e-mail, which was even quoted in Parliament, claimed that he had been seen "hobnobbing with the homosexual fraternity" at the EGM.[3] Other journalists sympathetic to the gay cause were also influencing the newspaper, critics alleged. "I believe there might be some gay activists in ST that want to make use of the media to force the new team out," said one.[4]

Some tried to divine the presence of the government's hand in all this. To these observers, it was inconceivable that the national daily could act independently of its political masters. They did not revise their theory when Home Affairs Minister Wong Kan Seng ticked off the press and accused it of coverage that was "excessive and not sufficiently balanced" and "even breathless".[5] Instead, they suggested that the *Straits Times* editor had misread the government. One commentator wrote that the editor must have assumed that the government wanted to "beat up religious fanatics" who were putting at risk Singapore's attempts to attract the pink tourist dollar and "all those creative types". "Next time ask the right ministers first," he added sarcastically.[6]

A detailed analysis of *The Straits Times*' AWARE coverage would take us beyond the scope of this book. What is relevant to this chapter, though, is the kind of hypotheses that were floating around to explain the newspaper's reportage. Those unhappy with the coverage sniffed conspiracies, whether masterminded by the gay lobby or the government. This was not an isolated case. Typically, if people do not like what they read, the instinct is to blame the agendas of the individual journalists and their corruptibility by power, profit or personality traits. Social scientists refer to a "fundamental attribution error" — the habit of reaching for individual-level causes instead of more contextual and systemic explanations. Similarly, when celebrating or vilifying journalism, there is a tendency to single out heroes and villains. Media organisations give out awards to their professionals; media critics paint scarlet letters on the reporters they think are responsible for failures; and the government opens files on journalists they suspect of harbouring political agendas.

The truth is more complex. Media scholars have identified various interconnected influences shaping news content, of which the values and attitudes of the individual journalist is only one. According to the widely cited work of Pamela Shoemaker and Stephen Reese, journalism is shaped by several dimensions of influence acting within the media and from the outside: individual factors, newsroom processes, organisational pressures, external forces and society-wide ideologies.[7] Most of this book looks at external influences (mainly the state) and their interactions with organisational structures (especially the commercial priorities of media businesses). In this chapter, the focus is on processes within newsrooms. Although these have been subject to a major line of journalism research, they are less familiar to the layman. And even professional journalists themselves tend to take some of their practices for granted, failing to reflect on how seemingly innocuous routines affect their quest for truth. These practices include what journalists regard as commonsense news judgments, their understanding of their professional role, and the standards they try to apply when they want to pursue "good" journalism. Such frameworks for making editorial judgments are not unique to Singapore. They are broadly similar to professional practice elsewhere in what is increasingly a global enterprise.

There are also some criteria for editorial decision-making that are more peculiar to Singapore, having been inserted into the establishment media's operations by their political masters. They include boundaries of political acceptability that do not appear in formal regulations, but loom large in the calculations of anyone engaged in sustained public communication in Singapore. Referred to colloquially as "out of bounds" markers, these will also be discussed in the following pages. In keeping with one of the central themes of this book, this chapter will argue that the government has not shepherded the press in a direction that is completely opposite to journalism's own modern trajectory. Just as the PAP harnessed the commercial thrust of the news business (see Chapter 2), it has also been able to exploit certain conservative tendencies that can be found embedded within professional practices, even in more liberal societies. In particular, professional journalists' love affair with "objectivity" and their rejection of journalism's more activist past has made it easier for them to be turned into scribes for the *status quo*.

Within the web of interconnected forces that influence journalism, there is no denying that the values and idiosyncrasies of the individual journalist do matter, particularly if that individual is the editor or publisher. However, the impact of the individual is usually exaggerated, since mainstream journalism is a collaborative enterprise with several professionals handling each story. One of the main jobs of sub-editors and editors is to iron flat any individual kinks apparent in the reporter's copy before it goes to press. Indeed, a common complaint of rookie journalists everywhere is that their editors rob them of their voice. Journalists may be driven partly by the ego gratification of seeing their bylines in print, but they quickly learn — and the good ones soon appreciate — that the best journalists are those who can suppress their own egos long enough to understand and incorporate the multiple perspectives of their sources and their readers. Those with an activist bent or a self-conscious ideological mission usually do not last long or are never attracted to mainstream journalism in the first place.[8] Even when the individual journalist stamps his or her personal imprint on a story, it is not always reducible to bias. Readers tend to underestimate the degree to which plain screw-ups account for problematic content. A daily newspaper creates a new product every 24 hours — an intensity of research and development that few manufacturing industries can match. In this compressed production cycle, human error infects operations far more often than conspiracies get in the way. Yet, newsmakers and readers often jump to the conclusion that hidden agendas are the real reasons for journalists' missteps.

Ken Kwek was one *Straits Times* journalist on the receiving end of such suspicion. In 2006, he wrote up a seemingly straightforward interview with the deputy prime minister, S. Jayakumar, about racial and religious harmony in Singapore. On whether schools should do more, Kwek's story quoted Jayakumar as saying, "I do not like to load Tharman (Shanmugaratnam, Education Minister), my Tamil brother, with more, because everyone is telling him the Ministry of Education should do this and that."[9] It was not unusual for Cabinet ministers to refer to their ethnic backgrounds when trying to show their more human sides: George Yeo occasionally referred to his Teochew heritage and Khaw Boon Wan to his Buddhist upbringing, for example. To Kwek and his editors, Jayakumar seemed to be adding a warm, collegial touch to his reference to his younger Cabinet colleague. Unfortunately for Kwek, the deputy prime minister did not say "my Tamil brother". He actually said, or meant to say, "Shanmugaratnam". In a letter to the Forum page, Jayakumar accused Kwek of making an "inexcusable" error. Behind the scenes, officials questioned the intentions of a journalist who had already earned a reputation as a headstrong liberal. Through his editors, Kwek had to assure the government he had no agenda. He told me that, in the midst of the dispute, many colleagues listened to the notorious audio clip, straining to catch Jayakumar's words and arriving at different conclusions about what the minister was saying. I have no trouble believing Kwek because my own biggest howler as a reporter was also the result of mishearing a Cabinet minister. In 1994, I reported George Yeo, who was then the information minister, as saying that "an initial cable service with 2,000–3,000 channels could be ready in two years' time". That's what I heard him tell me; when I played back the tape, that's still what it sounded like. I had no reason to disbelieve my ears, as I was covering the minister's study trip to the United States where media giants were briefing him about the incredible potential of new broadband technologies. Thousands of channels did not seem a technological impossibility. The next day, though, my office informed me that Yeo's ministry had called to say that I'd made a mistake. I was filled with indignation at first, pointing out that I had him on tape. On listening to it again, though, the awful truth sank in. What he'd actually said was not "two or three *thousand*" but "two or three *dozen*" channels.

In any newsroom, insiders would be able to cite almost daily instances where the best intentions are waylaid by snafus, leading to outcomes that they acknowledge in hindsight could have been better. In addition to individual error, mistakes can result when a reporter with deep background knowledge happens to be on leave when a complicated story breaks, or when relevant information is not passed on when one shift of editors takes over from another. News organisations constantly create and reinforce protocols to prevent the recurrence of particularly serious gaffes, but it is impossible to achieve zero defects, since the permutations and combinations of possible errors are as endless as the news itself. Of course, when journalists get the story right, there is still no guarantee that it will please all its readers. One classic definition of news is that which somebody somewhere wants to suppress; the rest is advertising.[10]

Singapore's media system is designed to maintain the press as a separate institution, while aligning editors' judgment with government thinking. Nobody denies that this occasionally requires editors to accept government input that is implicitly or explicitly backed by its coercive might. "There have been many occasions when something published or not printed was exactly what the Government wanted but not really what the editors judged to be right," admits former Straits Times group editor-in-chief Peter Lim, asking only that we accept that such decisions are not taken lightly. "Such deference — euphemism for surrender — came with much agonising and followed considerable exercise of journalistic skills and editorial judgment to try and minimise the restriction on information flow."[11] Government control is an omnipresent reality in Singapore, and much of this book is devoted to tracing its contours. However, government pressure cannot be credited or blamed for every article that is out of the ordinary. The relationship between media and power is subtler and more multi-faceted. Furthermore, social structures never remove entirely the potential for humans to act differently from what is expected. This ever-present potential, which social scientists term "agency", requires that we try to understand better what makes journalists tick, even as we acknowledge the constraints on their autonomy.

Journalistic Excellence

One place to start is on the high ground, where the profession is at its most noble. Journalists as well as their critics believe that journalism is more than just a job. In the news media everywhere, there is a hunger to discover and share the news, driving individuals to both quotidian and quixotic acts of self-sacrifice. In the lobby of the Reuters building in Singapore's Science Park, there are two large bound books containing obituaries of the global news agency's staff who were killed in the line of duty. Other than the uniformed services, few professions wear their ethos of altruism so plainly. It is easy to be cynical, and cynical journalists would be the first to say that a selfish desire for professional glory explains their pursuit of excellence at least as much as their public service ideals do. However, the effort and risk taken by reporters and editors often cannot be explained by the prospect of any financial reward or career advancement. The history of Singapore journalism includes, for example, the extraordinary tale of how *The Straits Times* was revived at the end of the Japanese Occupation: as soon as Changi Prison gates were thrown open by the surrendering Japanese, staff who were interned there and others across the island instinctively gravitated to the newspaper's premises in Cecil Street to publish their first post-war edition, undeterred by the fact that their printing press was inoperable (they "borrowed" another company's machine), the uncertainty of receiving any pay for their work and the risk of upsetting British military censors who were on their way back to the island.[12] The context may have been exceptional, but that gut instinct to share the news is not unfamiliar to journalists in less tumultuous settings, including contemporary Singapore.

Beyond the workaday task of pouring stories into newspaper pages, journalists the world over strive to live up to the highest standards of professional excellence — if not daily or weekly, at least regularly enough to sustain their passion for their calling. A key question that needs to be asked of Singapore journalism is whether it aspires to the same benchmarks of excellence as professionals elsewhere. One popular theory is that Singapore follows a different model, which some have called "development journalism"; others refer to it as "Asian values" journalism.[13] These terms refer to a preference for stories that support good government and emphasise consensus and harmony. Certainly, many stories in the national media show these tendencies. But are these examples of excellent journalism in the eyes of their producers? Answering this question is trickier than it first appears. Determining what journalists stand for by analysing their published work mistakes the empirical for the normative — confusing what is with what should be. Given the multiple pressures that newspapers are under — not least the tyranny of the deadline — most editors would readily admit that not everything they publish makes them proud. On a good day, every story would pass minimum standards of accuracy and relevance, while a handful would, in an exacting editor's eyes, be worth the paper's cover price. In a politically controlled media environment such as Singapore, there is the additional problem of trying to distinguish content that reflects journalists' own values from that which has been shaped by political pressure that is beyond their control.

Furthermore, journalism is not like, say, the automobile industry, in which the required standards are made explicit on the factory floor as well as by industry bodies and government regulators. In journalism, much of the decision-making is implicit and not based on any codified procedures that can be independently analysed. Journalists are notoriously poor at explaining to non-journalists why their stories come out in a particular way. Many feel that their output is already so public that it speaks for itself; they wrongly assume that the accessibility of their products amounts to accountability for their processes. It could also be because of what cultural studies scholar John Hartley observes as a "strong culture of separation between insiders and outsiders" — so much so that journalists can be thought of as a tribe or an ethnicity, he muses.[14] The challenge for researchers is to penetrate that cultural divide and listen carefully to journalists' conversations about their craft.

One such opportunity is provided in the awards that journalists give to their peers. This is where journalists declare to one another what they consider to be excellent journalism. In Singapore, there are no national press awards like the Pulitzers in the United States. However, news media organisations do hand out their own prizes for excellence. Singapore Press Holdings' English and Malay Newspapers Division (EMND) gives monthly and annual awards for the best news story, feature, news picture and work in other categories. The awards are highly coveted by EMND journalists and the competition among sections and newspapers can be intense. The awards are decided by the Newspaper Committee (Newscom), which is chaired by EMND's editor-in-chief and includes the chief editors of the division's various newspapers and senior section editors. I received my first Newscom award, a special award for excellence, when I was an undergraduate interning with *The New Paper*. As a geography student, I was thrilled that MPH Bookstore had chosen to celebrate National Day by publishing a large satellite map of Singapore — a novelty in the late 1980s, long before the era of Google Maps. When I got a copy, I saw that several parts of the map were concealed with green patches of ink. I then noticed that these patches could be easily scratched off, revealing air force runways and other military installations. I contacted MPH and the Ministry of Defence. The maps were recalled, and I got a page one story and an award — despite Mindef's preference that the story not run at all. I treated the award as an early signal of the kind of enterprise that SPH editors wanted to see more of.

When I joined the organisation full time, I had my share of practising what others might label as "developmental" or "Asian values" journalism, serving as a partner of good government. I wrote editorials supporting government policies, news reports amplifying ministers' speeches and human interest stories that served as parables for various on-going official campaigns. I did not consider such work to be unrespectable, as I generally agreed with my editors who felt that one of the legitimate roles of *The Straits Times* was to help communicate sound policies to the public, at least until they were proven unsound. However, even if the collaborative role accounted for a large proportion of one's time as an SPH journalist, it seemed clear that journalistic excellence lay mainly in the scoops, features and columns that dealt with controversial topics and got people talking. Overwhelmingly, Newscom awards seemed to reward such work, even those that might not please the government. For three years in the late 1990s, I was a member of Newscom and was privy to its discussions about good journalism. I do not recall "Asian values" ever entering our deliberations. There was no apparent anti-government tendency either; once in a while, one would hear members cite praise from a government official or other respected source as an added testimony of a story's worth, but this was neither a necessary nor sufficient condition for winning. In general, the definitions of "good journalism" being used in Newscom seemed to be no different from what I had learnt at Columbia Journalism School, the high temple of American journalism education and home of the Pulitzer Prizes.

These casual, insider impressions can be tested more systematically. Awards come with citations, which can be analysed for insights into the selectors' thinking. Citations for two of the most prestigious awards in American journalism — the Pulitzers and the American Society of Newspaper Editors (ASNE) Awards for distinguished writing — show a preference for impact, enterprise, analysis, emotion and style.[15] Impact is recognised in stories that bring about positive change, by prompting investigations that led to policy reforms, for example. Enterprise is demonstrated by reporters who overcome practical hurdles, ranging from uncooperative sources to the destruction of the *Wall Street Journal* newsroom in the September 11 attack on the World Trade Center next door. Judges appreciate analysis that makes complex topics accessible through clear, expert writing. Award-winners are also cited for moving readers at an affective level, finding human interest in ways that are powerful and riveting. As for style, citations compliment articles that are well crafted, with story-telling that brings the reader to the scene with compelling narrative.

Do Singapore journalists define excellence any differently? Their thinking can be divined from the monthly Newscom citations as well as the commemorative books that SPH publishes every year, compiling the previous year's annual award winners together with comments from their supervisors.[16] It should not be surprising to find that Newscom, like the American awards, recognises stories with analysis, emotion and style — such attributes are not necessarily in conflict with "Asian" values such as harmony and consensus. However, if it were true that the Singapore press subscribed to the "development journalism" model, Newscom would not value enterprise and impact in the way that the American awards do. Yet, contrary to the cynics' view that the Singapore press is content with reproducing government handouts, Newscom citations encourage journalists to dig for exclusives and overcome barriers, including obstructive government officials. In citations for 1999–2005, most of the winning news stories are described as "scoops" or "investigative journalism". Several recognise reporters' efforts in prising stories out of reticent official sources. The citations for the Young Journalist of the Year praise the nominees' enterprise, resourcefulness, tenacity and "intense desire to beat the competition", among other qualities.

As for the impact of the award-winning work, there is again no evidence that the benchmarks being applied in Singapore are fundamentally different from those used elsewhere. One award winner was a human-interest story about a Thai couple — the woman was a visa overstayer — so fearful of being caught by the authorities that they lived, and even had a baby, in a rat-infested canal. Homelessness being almost non-existent in Singapore, the story was front-page news for the tabloid *New Paper*. The citation claimed that the story succeeded in influencing public opinion and in turn the immigration authorities: "It resulted in a flood of calls and letters, with offers of help for the family. It culminated in the authorities, well-known for being hard on immigration offenders, here releasing husband, wife and Baby Nook." The citations for two other winners the same year noted that the articles, both healthcare stories, prompted officials to be more forthcoming with answers and explanations.

It is hard to find any trace of "consensus" or "harmony" being applied as touchstones for journalistic excellence. The closest any citation came to this was for a feature on traditional Chinese "Hungry Ghost" Month rituals, which was described as "a good example of community news". However, the supervisor's citation also lauded how the feature reported on "the lower strata" of society "as the income-gap widens further". Such highlighting of the class angle suggests that the supervisor did not expect reporters to help construct Singapore's preferred self-image as an egalitarian, middle-class society. Similarly, a community reporter who won the Young Journalist of the Year award in 1999 was praised for her "commitment to constantly track life in the raw in squeaky-clean Singapore". Several of the citations highlight elements of conflict in the winning stories, using words and phrases such as "controversy", "scandal of the highest order" and "a potential political hot potato". One annual award winner "raised a host of issues, not all of which have been resolved". For one winning story about the sacking of the national bowling coach, the reporter was congratulated for being "sharp enough to highlight a controversial point". Citations note approvingly that stories triggered calls by "irate customers" to a newsmaker. Even "a stream of hate mail" against the reporter was cited in support of the nomination, presumably because it showed that moral courage had been required to report unpleasant truths.

Singapore journalism is supposed to disavow the Fourth Estate — the adversarial role that the press plays within liberal democratic political systems. Instead, it should play a supportive and subordinate role. In this regard, the evidence from the citations is mixed. Among those studied, none of the winners were explicitly cited for being helpful to the government. Some of the articles themselves, though, could be read that way. For example, one monthly award went to a reporter who merely followed up on a speech by the minister for home affairs that mentioned that the Internal Security Department had thwarted a fund-raising scheme by the Sri Lankan separatist group, the Tamil Tigers. The reporter, the citation said, "swung into action" immediately, seeking elaboration from official sources. His follow-up "made many Singaporeans sit up and realise that fund raising for the Tamil Tigers was going on in this country" — which was probably the effect intended by the minister when he revealed the plot in his speech. On the other hand, several award winners were not quite so supportive of the political system and government policy. The most explicitly political story among the 24 monthly award winners studied focused on a negative side of Singapore's one-party dominance: the growing number of walkovers during general elections. The citation said that the article highlighted a trend that spelt "a loss of the sense of ownership over the political process which could translate to a loss of commitment to Singapore". The story about the Thai family referred to earlier described the drama as a "cruel game of hide-and-seek" rather than framing it in law-and-order terms. This was at odds with the government's hard-line stand on immigration offenders. The best feature for 1999, according to the citation, raised a "wrenching issue — the lack of opportunities to pursue tertiary education in Singapore". The same year, a columnist received a special award for a series of commentaries on Parliamentary sittings that "packed the most wallop". "Along the way, she tussled with some of the MPs," the citation added.

These citations are not generally written for public consumption. They are crafted by journalists for journalists. Any EMND journalist can nominate a colleague for an award, although in practice most nominations come from the nominees' supervisors, including Newscom members. The citations provide probably the most authentic indicator of what Singapore journalists consider to be "good journalism". Overall, there is nothing in the citations to suggest that Singapore journalists view their profession through an "Asian values" lens. They do not seem to equate good journalism with support for the government or total submission to its agenda. They laud peers who stir controversy, raise critical points and make a difference to people's thinking or conduct. Usually, the impact of such work is admittedly shallow. None of the award-winning stories during the period covered in this study were claimed to have forced "reforms" or "overhaul" of policy — terms one finds routinely in Pulitzer citations. There are two possible explanations for this. The "Asian values" explanation would be that Singapore journalists do not believe that it is the rightful role of the press to engage in such journalism. Another reason could be that they do not have the opportunity to produce such high-impact work because of limited information and access. The explanation that is least palatable to critics is that high-level scandals are difficult to find in what has been, by most accounts, an extremely well-run country. Even American intelligence reports have arrived at this assessment. "The biggest challenge to the development of the opposition in Singapore is the PAP's highly successful track record," stated a leaked confidential diplomatic cable from the US Embassy in Singapore. "Even without the checks that a vibrant press or opposition would provide, the PAP has also been able to avoid the pitfalls of corruption, which would tarnish its reputation."[17]

Newsroom Routines

Through awards, journalists celebrate the profession at its best. Everyday journalism, however, is a different proposition. It may be more than just a job, but it is also that. Scholars have coined the term "newswork" to capture those mundane but vital aspects of professional journalism. In *Flat Earth News*, a stinging critique of the state of quality journalism in Britain, Nick Davies finds that the most destructive force within the news media is not pressure from politicians or advertisers, nor any erosion of professional ideals, but an organisational emphasis on raising productivity, which has left reporters with no time to carry out even basic checks to verify information churned out by newsmakers. Although journalists may be termed knowledge workers or creative professionals, their activity is also embedded in a prosaic manufacturing industry. Newswork has some factory-like characteristics that are far removed from the glamour and heroism that is honoured in professional awards. To understand the inner workings of Singapore newsrooms, we also need to come to grips with these workaday practices of the profession.

These include what media scholars call "routines": the standard operating procedures that make it possible for a newspaper to pull off the daily miracle of creating a new product from scratch. Except that it is not really from scratch. The trick in daily journalism is not to start each day with a blank slate or enter each decision via a discussion of first principles. There is simply no time. Instead, many decisions are routinised. One example is the beat system. Editors pre-assign reporters to cover the substantive areas or places that are most likely to generate desired stories, such as crime, politics, sports, business and selected foreign capitals. The pre-allocation of a news organisation's scarce journalistic manpower to various areas of coverage is one of the most consequential decisions editors make, but rarely attracts scrutiny. Specialised beat reporters are more likely to break news and to report stories in depth. When a subject or place is not covered by a dedicated beat reporter, stories may be missed and issues under-researched. On the other hand, beat reporters tend to develop symbiotic relations with their sources that tend to compromise their independence. Journalists may pull their punches in order to preserve their working relations with reliable sources. Probably the best-known example of this is the fact that the Watergate scandal that brought down President Richard Nixon was exposed not by the White House press corps but by two crime reporters. Similarly, it is probably no accident that celebrity athletes' sordid sex lives — think Tiger Woods and Ryan Giggs — are rarely exposed by the sports reporters who cover them most closely.

Also highly consequential is the way editors divide the paper or broadcast bulletin into more or less fixed sections that are delegated to different teams to fill. Such divisions — into local, world, sports and so on — structure the news in a way that the audience tends to find helpful. In addition, by delegating different sections to different teams, the production process is rendered more manageable. However, what is rarely questioned are the value judgments behind a news medium's particular configuration. The allocation of space and time within commercial news media all over the world reveals overwhelming evidence of editorial judgments being skewed to accommodate advertiser-friendly consumer values. Serious newspapers do not allow any individual advertiser to influence how they cover a particular story. But, even the proudest journalistic institutions no longer resist the pressure to create an ambience that encourages consumption. Thus, even though most readers do not buy cars on a weekly basis — and, in Singapore, most households do not buy cars at all — even downmarket newspapers have weekly car review sections, to present themselves as worthy recipients of motor traders' advertising dollars. In addition to — and, some would say, at the expense of — its democratic mission, the commercial news business worldwide has taken on the responsibility of cultivating a culture of consumption that supports the advertisers on which it depends for much of its income. Such tendencies are not subject to daily self-reflection within the newsroom because they have been routinised as part of workflows and production calendars that are now taken for granted.

However, the most impactful routine is probably the way journalists apply "newsworthiness" criteria to filter an infinite number of potential stories and decide how to tell them. The benchmarks are strikingly similar across the world. In general, stories are treated as more newsworthy if they are current and unusual, have a direct impact on readers, occur locally or close by, and involve people who are already well known. Some stories lacking these elements may be treated as newsy if they have a "human interest" quality — some compelling x-factor that readers can connect with. This list of criteria is published in journalism text books for the benefit of students — usually in introductory chapters with titles like, "What is News?" — but the profession has internalised the knowledge so well that it requires no formal codification. The definition of news is not found in staff manuals or codes of practice, for instance. Its global power arises from having evolved through trial and error over some two centuries of practising journalism for a mass market. Journalists have harnessed this knowledge to help them predict which stories are most likely to interest their large and diverse audiences. In applying the newsworthiness checklist, editors believe that they are working with a force larger than themselves. Indeed, according to historians, this operational definition of news has much deeper roots than newspapers and can be found even in pre-literate societies. It is part of a social system of sharing information and gossip that predates the profession of journalism by millennia.[18] Other scholars have argued that news performs the modern function of myths, not in the sense that news is untrue, but that it helps societies make sense of a complex world by drawing on a set of stock themes or meta-stories — about heroes, villains, disasters and so on.[19] These meta-stories are another example of routines.

None of this is to suggest that there will always be a consensus within a news organisation on how to treat the day's news. Professional disagreements are an everyday occurrence. For example, there is no set formula for deciding whether the top story should be the collapse of a big international bank, or a major natural disaster in a neighbouring country, or a change in government rules for property purchases, if they all happen on the same day. Each of these events has a different kind of impact and appeal, and editors will debate their relative merits at editorial meetings. How a newspaper handles these grey areas and competing claims to prominence defines its identity. Some — like *The New Paper* and *Shin Min Daily News* — give more weight to human interest and oddity when assessing newsworthiness. Others, such as *The Straits Times* and *Today*, lean towards national and international impact, in line with their more serious image. However, even upmarket newspapers would not deny the newsworthiness of a sensational crime story. They would simply relegate it to a lower position on page one or to an inside page.

Editors have a great, if sometimes reluctant, respect for newsworthiness criteria. Intellectually, they may know that a story about a celebrity's sex life is trivial in the larger scheme of things, but they believe that they have little choice but to run it, given its "newsworthiness". Being able to apply such knowledge astutely on a day-to-day and intuitive basis is regarded as a fundamental professional skill, along with writing and fact-gathering. Journalists with this skill — with a knack for spotting a newsy angle within a story — are respected by their peers. News judgment is also appraised by editors when deciding promotions and salaries. Conversely, lay people who cannot fathom why a particular story is treated the way it is are likely to be dismissed by the professionals as betraying their ignorance of what news is all about. Journalists are under no illusions of infallibility. They recognise that their decisions are made under severe time constraints and with incomplete information, and therefore carry a high risk of failure. But, they typically seek validation first from their in-group — fellow journalists — rather than from the lay public.[20] Often, readers' hasty accusations of bias or other unprofessional conduct — such as in the AWARE controversy cited at the beginning of this chapter — only serve to confirm in journalists' minds that outsiders simply do not understand the first thing about journalism.

Professionals have been known to apply their rituals uncritically, mistaking their procedures for their principles. Newsworthiness criteria are certainly a tried and true formula for spotting interesting stories, but they do not measure importance. While intuitive news judgments speed up the workflow of a busy newsroom, they also produce blindspots and distortions. For example, the news media tend to perform poorly when confronted with long drawn-out processes. Global warming, water shortages, malnutrition and the tobacco industry will, over the long term, kill more people than earthquakes, tsunamis and terrorist attacks — but the latter set of events will always receive more prominent coverage because their compressed, episodic quality gives them more currency and generates newsier images. Journalists perform at their best when the interesting stories are also the important ones and vice versa — but this is often not the case. Therefore, the challenge for meaningful journalism is to make the important, interesting. With enough commitment and creativity, they can do it. Too often, however, even serious news media follow the example of the tabloids and other entertainment outlets, covering the merely interesting as if it were also hugely important.

Another ritual that has taken on a life of its own is that of "objectivity". Journalistic objectivity was never meant to be an end in itself, but rather a means of truth-seeking. It is about excluding one's own values from one's work, in order to be open to empirical evidence and the perspectives of others. Professional detachment from a story is an important antidote against the potential abuse of media power. For large news organisations, objectivity is coincidentally a useful management tool. It provides a neutral quality-control benchmark that can be rolled out across the newsroom, sparing editors interminable debates with reporters and among themselves over values. It also generates a more marketable product, for reports that do not take sides are less likely to offend various segments of the population. Wire agencies such as the Associated Press and Reuters played a key role in institutionalising journalistic objectivity because, as wholesalers of news, they realised that their copy had a higher chance of being picked up by diverse newspapers if it was perceived to be free of ideological slants.[21] China's aggressively expanding Xinhua agency, striving to establish itself as a global force, is trying to take the same tack.

Media sociologists have also observed that objectivity offers the strategic advantage of limiting professional accountability for controversial stories.[22] Journalists armed with objectivity do not need to claim to give you the truth of the matter — whether, for example, a person really did commit a crime, whether a government policy has actually worked or whether a particular industrial project is safe for the community — but only that someone who should know really did express a judgment about it. Getting at the truth may be difficult or even impossible within the time available. The ritual of objectivity allows the journalist to quote sources without necessarily checking their veracity. The journalist does not vouch for the truth of what is said, but only for the fact that the source said it.

This critique of objectivity is not some trivial philosophical matter. The ritualistic application of this principle can have life-or-death consequences. Consider the failure of journalism in the run-up to the American conquest of Iraq (backed by a coalition that included Singapore). The United States administration was supported by public opinion that, it is now known, had been fed untruths by its free press. On the eve of battle, when diplomatic options were still the favoured path of most of its NATO allies and United Nations Security Council members, President George W. Bush persuaded his country that the matter could not wait, because Saddam Hussein's regime possessed weapons of mass destruction that posed an imminent threat, and that it was somehow implicated in Al Qaeda's terrorist attacks of 11 September 2001. Both were empirically testable statements that one might have expected a free and truth-seeking press to investigate at any cost, given that its citizens' lives were at stake. If America's journalists had done so, they might have exposed these statements for the lies they were, saving more than a hundred thousand lives.

What accounts for such catastrophic failure of the free press? Disciples of Noam Chomsky would be inclined towards conspiracy theories, pointing the finger at media institutions that willingly serve as the propaganda tools of the American empire.[23] While this may be a correct diagnosis of certain sections of the media such as Fox News, the wider problem was the unthinking application of professional routines. The main side effect of journalists' suppression of their own voices is their dependence on sources. Their choice of sources must also be "objective": they quote sources that society already regards as credible or authoritative, such as people in positions of power or experts with credentials.[24] This dependence on elite sources can be sufficient to produce balanced and well-rounded stories in plural societies, where the elite is internally competitive and does not speak with one voice. Thus, this approach to journalism normally serves the American public reasonably well. However, in the run-up to wars, the American elite tends to close ranks behind the president and flag.[25] The press objectively reports these multiple sources, all echoing the same lies. Post-mortems of their coverage by major American newspapers acknowledged that they had relied too much on too few sources — US officials and Iraqi exiles with an agenda — a realisation that came a year and thousands of lives too late.[26]

Journalists' dependence on diverse elite sources should not be underestimated. Pick up any major Western newspaper with a reputation for fearless journalism — say, Britain's *Guardian* — and you will find few if any stories that are entirely the work of investigative reporters digging independently for the facts. Instead, most exposés and critical stories originate from within the elite: major opposition parties, leaks from within the civil service or even Cabinet ministers, whistleblowing by members of the establishment, comments by judges, reports from independent commissions, studies by non-government organisations, trade unions and watchdog groups, and so on. In the United States, it takes a war to silence dissenting voices within the establishment. In Singapore, the establishment has been characterised by strong cohesion at all times. Even in comparison with other authoritarian regimes, Singapore's elite is remarkable for its lack of factions and fractures. This is partly because the power structure is simple and centralised, unlike the fragmented and internally competitive administrations of, say, China and Malaysia. Furthermore, the centre monopolises official data; there is no right to information law with which facts and figures can be prised out of the hands of officials. The government established in the mid-1990s its zero tolerance for leaks, by prosecuting journalists and civil servants for a seemingly minor breach of the Official Secrets Act (see Chapter 2). Meanwhile, its readiness to use the Defamation Act and contempt of court provisions encourages journalists to stick to the facts in hand rather than risk going out on a limb to speculate and comment on controversial matters. Journalists are fully aware that, in the Singapore environment, not all truths are easy to tell. Perversely, the professional ethos of objectivity helps assuage their conscience, for it demands telling only those truths that are backed by verifiable facts and attributable opinions, both of which are scarce commodities in Singapore. If Singapore journalism too often sounds like an echo chamber for the government, it is not only — or even mainly — because journalists lack the freedom to be objective, but because that is what objective journalism sounds like in the absence of political pluralism.

Singapore journalists' comfort with a reportorial rather than activating role comes through clearly in a 2009 survey conducted by my colleague Hao Xiaoming and me.[27] Almost 60 per cent of the SPH and MediaCorp journalists surveyed said it was extremely important to get information to the public, compared with only 35 per cent who felt that way about investigating government claims and statements, and only 10 per cent who believed it was extremely important to be constantly sceptical of government actions. Less than 6 per cent said that it was extremely important to set the political agenda for the society. Journalists recognise their potential impact on society — and are uneasy about it. When asked how much influence the media had on the formation of public opinion, they gave an average score of 7.3 on a scale of 0 to 10. However, when asked how influential they thought the media *should* be, the average score was 6.7. In other words, their desired influence is less than their perceived influence.

This pattern is not unique to the Singapore press. In one analysis of 242 codes of ethics in 94 countries, researchers found a broad consensus in favour of a more neutral, detached and defensive role, rather than promoting an adversarial stance towards centres of power.[28] Another major international study, covering 1,800 journalists on five continents, again showed more support for the informant role.[29] The 18 countries included the United States, Australia, China, Indonesia, Brazil and Israel. The journalists were asked how important various roles were for the news media. In all but one country (Bulgaria), they rated setting the political agenda and influencing public opinion lower than being an absolutely detached observer and giving citizens the information they need to make political decisions. Acting as a watchdog on government was rated lower than the informational role in 15 of the 18 countries; only in China did journalists rate being a watchdog highest among the 12 suggested roles. While some of the differences may be small and not statistically significant, the overall pattern is clear. Globally, this is a profession that is uncomfortable with the same powers that, ironically, it celebrates through its professional awards. This discomfort encourages a routinised approach to day-to-day newswork. The aspiration to make a difference to society by revealing truths about things that matter, fearlessly and fast, makes journalism inconvenient to those in power. Yet, journalism's threat to the *status quo* is blunted by the time-pressed, routinised nature of newswork — including going through the motions of "objective reporting" in lieu of dogged truth-seeking. As a result, mainstream journalism is rarely as revolutionary as its own mythology suggests, even in countries with a high degree of press freedom. Around the world, the press tends to get most energised and activated when wider social forces are in motion.

OB Markers

If benchmarks of excellence and standard operating procedures are broadly similar across the world, Singapore journalism's attention to "OB markers" is more endemic to the city-state. These "out of bounds" markers are informal rules of engagement. The term comes from golf and refers to the boundaries of political acceptability. OB markers delineate a field of play that is narrower than what is legally permissible. In other words, there are areas that the government believes responsible players should treat as off-limits even though they are not prohibited under any written law or regulation. While not punishable by imprisonment or fines, a breach of OB markers invites political retribution: individuals and organisations risk losing political capital. This is not a daunting prospect for those who do not depend on government resources or blessings. Thus, OB markers are irrelevant to most independent bloggers and opposition websites. Singapore's media companies, though, cannot afford to be cavalier about these political no-go areas. In the extreme, a news organisation that has lost the government's trust could also lose its permit to publish or broadcast. Senior editorial positions are also vulnerable. On the level of day-to-day operations, an errant journalist or news organisation can lose access to officials — not a small matter in a country where the government is the number one newsmaker.

In many countries, including some that are more authoritarian, media are less dependent on the state. With enough support from their audiences, businesses and other alternative power centres, the media can engage in running battles with the government in that zone of contentious politics that is on the wrong side of the authorities but still on the right side of the law. In Singapore's more monolithic system, however, the trust of the top leadership is indispensable for any establishment institution, including the news media. Showing respect for the OB markers, and not just the law, is one of the key ways in which mainstream media gatekeepers earn that trust. For this reason, editors are expected to internalise OB markers, applying them alongside their news judgment and standards of excellence in their day-to-day decision making.

The most frequently mentioned OB markers are those to do with racial and religious sensitivities. Extreme and inflammatory speech is already regulated under sweeping laws such as the Sedition Act. In addition, OB markers discourage the media from initiating debates on matters that could stir ethnic passions. Reporting on events and controversies with racial or religious dimensions is also muted. These OB markers are by now internalised both within the press and the general public. There is a high degree of consensus that discussion of race and religion carries a great risk of causing offence and should be moderated.

Therefore, even without active government policing, national newspapers are unlikely to cross this particular line. More contentious is the OB marker protecting the authority of individual officials. The PAP believes that public service is already onerous enough and should not be made less attractive by a prying and disrespectful press. The government has been powerless to impose this standard on cyberspace, where netizens routinely pillory politicians. But the mainstream media are expected to uphold the Confucian norm of respect for authority. As a result, national newspapers do not carry political cartoons that caricature the country's politicians. Singapore's leading editorial cartoonist, Heng Kim Song, focuses on international politics, not Singapore. Another talented Singaporean political cartoonist, Morgan Chua, could not find work locally after the *Singapore Herald* was closed down, and spent the rest of his career with the *Far Eastern Economic Review* in Hong Kong.

There are also OB markers that reflect the government's belief in the power of the press to define society's norms and shape a national identity. The issue of class is particularly challenging for journalists to deal with. On the one hand, the government wants better-off Singaporeans to understand that they have a social obligation to help the down and out. The country's levels of voluntarism and philanthropy are low relative to other developed countries. The press can contribute to developing a more caring society by informing readers about the plight of less fortunate citizens — a role that many socially-conscious journalists embrace whole-heartedly. On the other hand, the government does not want coverage of the disadvantaged to emphasise the growing underclass. This would undermine Singapore's official self-image as a country where all benefit from economic growth, either directly through better jobs or indirectly through redistribution policies. Nor does the government want too much coverage of the swelling ranks of super-rich, as this might stoke up what it calls the "politics of envy".

OB markers to do with societal values and norms are especially sensitive when the government perceives foreign groups to be pressuring Singapore's policy makers. Debates on homosexuality and the death penalty fall into this category: the press is expected to reflect mainstream Singaporean norms and not become a proxy of western pressure groups. Such OB markers tend to shift gradually over time. The existence of homosexuals was not reportable in the past, but this restriction has eased: now, the government expects the press to help maintain an uneasy standoff between gays and the religious right, a balance that would be upset if the gay lobby were given too much coverage. As for the death penalty, former chief minister and human rights champion David Marshall complained bitterly in 1994 that *The Straits Times* refused to carry his letter arguing for the death penalty to be reviewed.[30] In more recent years, however, the paper has reported the rise of a domestic lobby group opposed to the death penalty. While coverage is spare, the cause is not entirely blacked out.

OB markers also apply to foreign news. The government is fiercely protective of its authority in representing Singapore in international dealings. Indeed, it is probably in foreign relations that it is least tolerant of alternative views within the national media. Since perception is everything and foreign analysts perceive the Singapore media to be a mouthpiece of the government, the media are expected to act accordingly. The national media are required to reinforce — or at least never contradict — the government's diplomatic stands, especially in bilateral disputes. For example, it would not be acceptable for a newspaper columnist to urge a conciliatory stance towards Malaysia while the two neighbours are in the midst of fraught negotiations. Given the complexity of managing its relations with both China and Taiwan (where Singapore has military training facilities), the government is also sensitive to how cross-Straits relations are reported in Singapore media.

Many other OB markers are topical, relating to particular political controversies of the day. These could relate to a new government policy, increases in various public sector fees and charges, apparent mismanagement by a government agency, or some politically insensitive statement by an official. Editors have to use their journalistic and political judgment to make a series of decisions, usually without any explicit signal from the government. First, at what point and in what form should the criticism be surfaced: should the paper be pro-active in highlighting flaws in the government position, or wait for independent signs of public disquiet, such as in letters to the editor, statements by civil society organisations, and blogs? When critical views are reported, what weight should they be given, relative to statements from the government? Should the newspapers' columnists contribute independent views, and how forcefully? Should the newspaper itself weigh in, through its leader column? When the government responds with a statement from the prime minister, should that be treated as the last word, or should the paper continue to highlight unresolved issues?

Sometimes, professional rivalry with colleagues and competitors is enough to stiffen the spines of journalists who come under pressure from newsmakers. However, such competitive instincts are often blunted when covering government and politics, since OB markers are applied more or less uniformly across the mainstream media. Journalists may not welcome instructions to play down a controversy or not report an open secret, but there is at least some comfort in knowing that one's competitors are subject to the same rules. While foreign media have greater freedom, they are not a key reference group for the Singapore press, since their attention to Singapore politics is too sporadic and shallow, and their reach too limited. The path of least resistance may seem irresistible. However, even without significant commercial competition, the national newspapers know that their audiences would reject them if they were nothing more than a mouthpiece of the government. This reality has become all the more salient with the emergence of alternative online media, which are regularly the first to register public discontent with government moves, and to report rumours, news and trends that the establishment would prefer to ignore.

Multiple Pulls

The special requirements of operating in Singapore have been institutionalised within the press but not necessarily internalised by individual journalists, notes former editor Peter Lim.[31] This subtle distinction helps to explain how newsrooms try to get the best out of their staff, while staying within the OB markers. Media scholar Beate Josephi, who interviewed young journalists and their supervisors at *The Straits Times*, found both groups "caught in the conundrum of global awareness and local restrictions". Singapore journalists, she found, cope with this situation through "accurate reporting of authoritative voices, and treading a fine line between curiosity and criticism".[32] Thus, between the passion for professional excellence, the pressures of newsroom routines and the pull of PAP power, the Singapore press is subject to conflicting influences. In trying to understand how the media work, there is no tidy way to resolve this tension or to predict which tendency will rule the day when journalists deal with any given story.

In American journalism scholarship, James Ettema and Theodore Glasser have investigated a related contradiction, between journalists' moral engagement and their method of objectivity.[33] In *Custodians of Conscience*, they observe that award-winning investigative journalists in the US are, on the one hand, driven by an adversarial instinct to empower the powerless to speak, force the powerful to account for themselves, and stoke righteous indignation in the public. On the other hand, the same journalists are reluctant to attribute their work to an exercise of conscience or moral discourse; they claim instead to be using only rigorous empirical methods to supply information to the public. Ettema and Glasser point out that such separation between values and facts is philosophically suspect. Selecting what is important in public affairs surely involves judgments about what is right and wrong. They suggest that journalists are coy about operating in the realm of values because this would entail accepting responsibility for what citizens and policy makers do or don't do with the information they are given. Perhaps, they add, the tension is a necessary one: in an age of science, only a strategy of rigorous disinterest would give journalism the credibility to unearth scandals and cultivate righteous indignation.

What, then, of the tension between political imperatives and journalistic ideals? Conventional wisdom holds that the PAP — a regime armed to the teeth with the powers of coercion — completely overwhelms any professional norms and ideals that the Singapore press may have once possessed. Critics view journalists in a state of unconditional surrender to the government. "They are running dogs of the PAP and poor prostitutes," said David Marshall in 1994.[34] Such comments reflect the tendency among some free press proponents to write off media that sometimes act like willing collaborators instead of out-and-out adversaries towards an authoritarian regime. It also results from an intellectual short-circuiting: an impatience with the idea that people could hold contradictory thoughts simultaneously, and a preference for a binary free/unfree categorisation of media. The daily reality in Singapore newsrooms is one of constantly trying to strike that uneasy balance between journalists' own sense of professional duty, the exigencies of news production, readers' expectation of credible coverage, and the government's demands for obedience.

Just as Ettema and Glasser argue that the values-facts paradox may have been necessary for the development of American journalism, it could be said that the tension between professional and political judgment has been vital to the endurance of Singapore's press model.

The PAP's calibrated use of its coercive powers (see Chapter 5) has allowed the press to perform within internationally recognised professional norms in many circumstances. Journalists are able to serve enough of the people enough of the time to keep their products relevant and profitable, sparing the PAP the embarrassment of mass boycotts of the national media. The profession, though weakened, is not completely gutted: it is able to attract bright and highly mobile young Singaporeans to spend at least a few of their years working as journalists. At the same time, editors know that whatever autonomy the press enjoys is not theirs by right. It has been bestowed as a special dispensation by an all-powerful regime that the public has shown no great desire to oust. Singapore journalism's room for manoeuvre is based on neither the power of argument nor the letter of the law, but on trust. The media's occasional acts of independence and impertinence are tolerated only as long as, overall, they enjoy the confidence of top leaders in government. Paradoxically, therefore, the internalisation of OB markers may be not just inimical to, but also a precondition for, the practice of professional journalism in Singapore.

CHAPTER 4

Government Unlimited: The Ideology of State Primacy

For the People's Action Party, winning the battle for power has never been enough. It has needed to believe that it has won the intellectual argument as well. The result is a paradox. On the one hand, the state routinely forecloses debate on a wide range of issues, claiming the unilateral right to declare when the time for decision has arrived and when further contention is not in the national interest. On the other hand — and unlike most authoritarian governments, which prefer to bark less and let their bite do the talking — spokesmen for the Singapore way seem incapable of keeping a low profile in debates about democracy and freedom. This is one reason why Singapore has achieved such iconic status in such discussions. It is not only because, among rich countries, it has the widest gap between its socio-economic and democratic indicators, but also because its ruling elites have not had the grace to stay quiet about it.

Many traits of the regime can be traced back to its larger-than-life founder, Lee Kuan Yew, and this particular PAP habit may be no exception. His background as a lawyer gave him an appetite for argumentation. In addition, having been a victim of colonial condescension, Lee was not going to allow his young independent nation ever again to play the role of the obedient but under-achieving student. "Please remember, we're not kindergarten pupils," he shot back when one foreign correspondent questioned Singapore's press freedom.[1] More typical authoritarian leaders chorused the West's liberal lines even as they acted undemocratically, whereas Lee decided to talk the walk. Having decided on his political system, he would defend it vocally and unapologetically. For Lee, press policy was more than a matter of shaping Singapore's state-media relations; it was part of an ideological, geopolitical struggle that he dedicated his entire adult life to. He was sensitive to what he perceived as the West's attitude of cultural supremacy — an attitude that he detected even when the American media praised Asian countries that were democratic. "It is praise with condescension, compliments from a superior culture patting an inferior one on the head," he said. "And it is this same sense of cultural supremacy which leads the American media to pick on Singapore and beat us up as authoritarian, dictatorial; an over-ruled, over-restricted stifling sterile society. Why? Because we have not complied with their ideas of how we should govern ourselves."[2]

A less Lee-centric explanation for the PAP's insistence on explaining itself is its hegemonic intent. While not shy about using coercion to discipline the minority who stray, it wants the majority to cooperate voluntarily, not out of fear but out of sincere belief that the PAP is right. The government considers it extremely important to attract into public service the most able and accomplished Singaporeans of every cohort. Therefore, even if it cannot convert external critics or opposition supporters, it is helpful to have a coherent and compelling justification for its political system — including its press controls — in order to maintain the loyalty of its supporters and satisfy the conscience of its most intelligent inductees. This chapter reconstructs in detail the ideology around the system, drawing on the public statements of Lee and other government leaders. The approach taken here is to address that ideology at its strongest, making the best possible case for the system, before considering possible counter-arguments.

There is no better place to start than the Finnish capital, Helsinki, in June 1971. The International Press Institute (IPI) had invited the prime minister of Singapore to speak to its general assembly. The timing could not have been more sensational. The Singapore government had just crushed three newspapers (see Chapter 2), leading to calls for IPI to protest by withdrawing its invitation.[3] IPI kept the door open, if only to expose Lee directly to the opprobrium of 300 editors from across the globe. The chairman of IPI was none other than Sally Aw Sian, a financial backer of the *Singapore Herald*, one of the papers that Lee had just killed. Any modern-day spin doctor or public relations minder would have advised Lee to invent some excuse and stay away. Fortunately for headline writers and media scholars, Lee was not one to allow himself to be handled by media consultants, even if he had them.

His speech would set out the principles behind the PAP government's management of the press for the following decades. Lee scanned the globe and discussed the choices faced by new nations as they dealt with the power of the media to mould public opinion.[4] Referring to the controversy in the United States over press opposition against the Vietnam War and the Nixon administration, he noted that "even in highly developed countries, objectivity was the subjective views of the owners and commentators of the mass media". Leaders of new countries were wary of the Western "laissez-fair system" because of its apparent association with "chaos", "confusion" and "dissensions", he said. But, Lee was also dismissive of the "closed and controlled" Communist model, which paid a heavy price for isolation: "The incessant exhortation to progress, the constant stress on conformity in ideology, ideas and action, they lead to drab uniformity." Speaking at the height of the Cold War, Lee suggested that the realistic choice was neither of the extreme poles on offer, but "some intermediate point between the two, depending on the level of education and sophistication of their peoples and the political traditions and style of the governments".

While defending new, small countries' right to choose their own paths, Lee was also anxious to distance Singapore from the *hoi polloi*. He noted that many African nations had opted for one-party states, while in several new countries in Asia, "every election is an exercise in auctioning the country's non-existent reserves and future production". Ceylon was censoring all editorials and threatening to nationalise newspapers, he added. In contrast, Lee presented Singapore as an open and progressive state — not as an ideological choice but as an unavoidable fact of life. Singapore even allowed the Pill. (In the United States, oral contraceptives were legalised for unmarried women in all states only the following year.) Lee said he hoped that traditional Asian family values would counter Western sexual mores associated with the Pill, but he could not be sure. "We are an international junction for ships, aircraft and telecommunications by cable and satellite," he noted. "People from the richer countries of the West, their magazines, newspapers, television and cinema films, all come in. We are very exposed. It is impossible to insulate Singaporeans from the outside world."

Many people are "uncritically imitative" of the media, he added. Fads and fetishes of the West were not relevant to the circumstances of developing countries and could confuse the young, he said. Then, there was Singapore's special problem as a heterogeneous society with various ethnic groups. Some were connected by ethnicity to political forces beyond Singapore, he said. He noted how the country's Chinese population could be influenced by different political forces in Greater China, and the small Sikh community had been caught up in the struggle over the Indian city of Chandigarh. Lee also related the events of inter-racial riots of 1950 and 1964, pointing out that inflammatory media reports had helped to spark the unrest. "I used to believe that when Singaporeans become more sophisticated, with higher standards of education, these problems will diminish. But watching Belfast, Brussels, and Montreal, rioting over religion and language, I wonder whether such phenomena can ever disappear," he said.

Returning to the geopolitical, Lee portrayed Singapore as a target of great-power propaganda. As they jostled for maritime dominance in the Indian Ocean and the South China Sea, these powers were prepared to expend resources on influencing the strategically-located Singapore towards policies that suited them. Radio stations such as Voice of America and Radio Peking were beaming in, he said. Foreign agencies were even using local proxies to set up or buy into newspapers that could shape domestic public opinion. "My colleagues and I have the responsibility to neutralise their intentions," he said.

Lee ended his speech with words that would be quoted several times in the coming decades: "In such a situation, freedom of the press, freedom of the news media, must be subordinated to the overriding needs of the integrity of Singapore, and to the primacy of purpose of an elected government. The government has taken, and will from time to time have to take, firm measures, to ensure that, despite divisive forces of different cultural values and life styles, there is enough unity of purpose to carry the people of Singapore forward to higher standards of life, without which the mass media cannot thrive."

Much was to change in the following decades. The end of the Cold War would eliminate the threat of Communism as an ideological force. And while part of Lee's 1971 speech was devoted to Western cultural influences — "urban guerillas, drugs, free love and hippieism" — the government grew less uptight over time. However, what is more striking is how much the government's position would remain fundamentally unchanged. The image of Singapore as a society facing immutable and unique constraints; the principle of the press as a subordinate partner in nation-building; and the rejection of foreign critics' moral authority to shape Singapore's destiny — these and other core ideas would be reiterated through the years by Lee and his successors as prime minister, Goh Chok Tong and Lee Hsien Loong, and other thought leaders in Cabinet and the foreign service, such as Kishore Mahbubhani, Bilahari Kausikan and K. Shanmugam. In the following pages, I analyse the main pillars of the PAP philosophy on the press.

Choice of System: A Matter of Sovereignty

For the PAP government, the choice of media system, like the rest of the political system, is a domestic matter for a country's citizens to decide through their elected government. There is no universally applicable formula. According to senior official Bilahari Kausikan,

> What we have argued consistently is that diversity is an empirical fact — countries have different histories, cultures, values, and problems — and thus each nation must find its own best social and political arrangements by means of a pragmatic and continuous process of experimentation.[5]

It is easy for outsiders to express opinions about how Singapore should be run because they do not need to live with the consequences of any decision, the government argues. "We are responsible for our survival. If that survival is jeopardised, we can expect no Santa Claus, no Lone Ranger, to come to the rescue," Lee Kuan Yew has said.[6] This principle was articulated even before the PAP swept into government in 1959. Threatening to charge with subversion any newspaper that soured relations between Singapore and the Malayan Federation, he later clarified that he was referring only to foreign-controlled media.[7] "If locally owned newspapers criticize us we know that their criticism, however wrong or right, is bona fide criticism because they must stay and take the consequences of any foolish policies or causes they may have advocated," he said. "The folly of allowing newspapers to be owned by people who are not citizens or nationals of the country, is that their sense of responsibility is blunted by the knowledge that if the worse came to the worst, they could always buzz off to some other place."[8]

Decades later, Lee was still using this nationalist line to question the credibility of foreign critics. At a press conference during the 2001 elections, a Caucasian correspondent for Hong Kong's *South China Morning Post* questioned whether Singapore had a free press. "I believe we've got a responsible press," Lee replied. "You may want to make them ashamed, but I believe you are a mercenary. You don't represent Hongkong. Your future is not in Hongkong. If you are a Hongkong Chinese and you are going to stay in Hongkong as part of China in 50 years and you believe that's your way out, then I'll take you seriously."[9]

The PAP's stout defence of Singapore's sovereignty over its media system may appeal to many Singaporeans' sense of nationalism, but risks slipping into a kind of ideological protectionism, with the national origin of critics cited as a rhetorical strategy to delegitimise inconvenient questions and criticisms. The government's argument fudges the distinction between foreign ownership of domestic media and the ideas of foreigners. While the former may indeed require regulation, the latter could be countered with better ideas rather than restrictions on media freedom. The PAP's counter to this has been that the marketplace of ideas is imperfect — legislation is required to compel foreign media to honour the government's right of reply. Its policy has been forcefully and controversially institutionalised in the press law, which empowers the government to declare a foreign newspaper to be "a newspaper engaging in the domestic politics of Singapore" and then restrict its circulation if it fails to give Singapore officials the right of unedited reply (Chapter 2).

Also problematic is the use of the "foreign" label to marginalise domestic critics. Lee had indicated in 1959 that criticism from locals would be treated as "bona fide", but Singaporean media would find that they were hardly exempt from punishment. If they crossed the government's path, they could be accused of being proxies for foreign interests, which would then justify their being treated as harshly as any foreign-owned media. Take, for example, the 1971 crackdown on *Nanyang Siang Pau* for campaigning against the government's language policy. Many Singaporeans would eventually come to accept that the relegation in status of the Chinese language was an inevitable cost of Singapore's economic development and the necessary promotion of English as a unifying working language. The Chinese press may indeed have been too emotional, shortsighted and even chauvinistic in its opposition to the government's language policies. Nevertheless, the unhappiness reflected by *Nanyang Siang Pau* represented genuine grievances among its readers. Indeed, the issues championed by the paper continued to simmer decades later. Rather than do battle with its Chinese ground, however, the government dealt with *Nanyang Siang Pau* as a vehicle of foreign interests, and thus as an enemy of the state (see Chapter 5). As for English-educated liberals, they are categorised as "pseudo-Western".[10] Lee said in 1995, "In order not to let people be confused, we must debunk those who echo the American media line that we will only prosper and progress if we dismantle our practices and institutions ... and become free like Taiwan or Thailand or Korea or the Philippines. Those who peddle this line to our people are stooging for the Western media and their Human Rights groups."[11] Thus, what started as a valiant assertion of national sovereignty by a small state evolved into a rhetorical bulldozer for sweeping aside alternative viewpoints arising from an already-weak citizenry.

What Counts: Good Governance

To the PAP, a healthy political system is one that creates the conditions for a government that can deliver. "While democracy and human rights are worthwhile ideas, we should be clear that the real objective is good government," Lee said.[12] PAP leaders have defined "good government" in different ways, but their emphasis is mainly on material progress and social order. Lee has described good government as one that is "honest, effective and efficient in protecting its people, and allowing opportunities for all to advance themselves in a stable and orderly society, where they can live a good life and raise their children to do better than themselves".[13] His successor, Goh Chok Tong, described Singapore as a "pragmatic democracy", which gauged its success based on whether it worked for Singaporeans.[14]

As for how to produce good government, the PAP is convinced that good leaders are the critical ingredient. Getting institutions and processes right is futile if the wrong people are in charge. The government tries to induct public servants of "high competence and high integrity".[15] While political leaders must present themselves to the electorate and campaign for support, they should be shielded from the most destructive aspects of competitive politics, such as personal attacks and invasions of privacy. These deter able individuals from public service and erode a good government's authority. Hence,

Singapore's strict policing of defamation. "If you make a personal attack of fact against a person's reputation, for example by alleging that he is corrupt, or that he is a liar, or that he embezzled State funds, then you should be prepared to prove it in court," said law minister K. Shanmugam, defending Singapore's media system at Columbia University in 2010. "We do not believe that public discourse should degenerate to a base level, by allowing untrue personal attacks. We would like to keep political debate focused on issues."[16]

From the PAP's perspective, its results speak for themselves. It does not deny that its policies require constant review and evolution. However, it feels that criticism should be tempered by the knowledge that, overall, this is a system that works. The PAP gets indignant when critics attack its political system as if Singapore were some failed state. As for the press system, the country's leaders regard it as an integral cog in their well-oiled machine. The news media's role is to support the conditions for good government, and not to compete with elected leaders. "The Western idea of the press as the fourth estate of the realm, as an adversarial watch-dog of government, goes against our goal of consensus politics, of getting Singaporeans to row as a team," said Goh.[17] The media should instead help perpetuate the "virtuous cycle of good government, constructive journalism, cohesive society and strong, stable and prosperous Singapore", he said. This does not mean that they must be pro-PAP. Rather, their mission is to get Singaporeans to understand policy choices and the constraints on their society. Lee said, "The mass media can help to present Singapore's problems simply and clearly and then explain how if they support certain programmes and policies these problems can be solved."[18]

Thus, the PAP evaluates press freedom and democracy in largely instrumental terms — what these can do for Singaporeans' material well-being and security. It concludes that since the country has done well for so long by blazing its own trail, it would be unnecessary and even risky to change course and follow countries that may be less successful than Singapore and definitely very different. But, this aspect of PAP philosophy has been criticised as being too focused on the economic benefits of its chosen political system. It neglects the intrinsic value of democracy and freedom of expression. Even if we concentrate on economic arguments, the PAP's position is not wholly persuasive. If the media system should ultimately be judged on Singapore's overall progress, the question that arises is how credible the country's report card can be without an independent and thorough assessment system — the kind that would be provided by press freedom and freedom of information. Of course, there is no reason to disbelieve the macro indicators contained in most international comparisons, such as the Human Development Index, which places Singapore among the world's 30 most developed countries. However, the correctness of individual policies could be exaggerated and mistakes understated. Evidence has been accumulating of policy errors, which have resulted in the under-provision of public transport, hospital beds and university places, for example. A lack of dissent may have allowed the government to push through some unpopular but necessary policies, but it could also have spared policy makers the kind of scrutiny needed to get the best out of them. Some have also argued that greater freedom of expression could strengthen Singapore by developing a culture more conducive to the kind of innovation, creativity and entrepreneurship that is increasingly required in an advanced economy.

Government, Not Press, Represents the People

The PAP challenges the special status that the free press has been conferred in the liberal worldview. It argues that an elected government is the legitimate voice of the people, while the press is an unelected institution that is ultimately accountable only to its owners. The press has no moral authority to challenge the government on equal terms; it has no right to act as the Fourth Estate. Note that, to the PAP, this is not an anti-democratic argument but quite the opposite. Elected leaders have the mandate and the responsibility to govern for the people and cannot allow themselves to be obstructed by undemocratic forces such as the press. "Accurately reporting wrongdoings is a legitimate role. You also help make the government better by fair reporting and providing a forum for readers' complaints and debate on national issues," acknowledged Goh. It was also acceptable "to probe, to ask the inconvenient question, to report fully and fairly what is going on", he added. "But the concept of the press being all powerful and having the last word smuggles in the power that ordinary citizens do not bestow on them."[19] Hence, Lee's bedrock principle that freedom of the press must be "subordinate to the primacy of purpose of an elected government".

Over the decades, Lee found many occasions to substantiate his charge that the press did not really represent the public interest.

Indeed, his mind was probably made up even before he gained power in 1959. Stung by the critical reception of the *Straits Times* to his party's rise, he was convinced that this was due to the fact that the paper was not an organic part of the local community but a vehicle for British commercial interests. Just before the PAP's victory, the *Straits Times* moved its headquarters to Kuala Lumpur. It was a logical decision, given that even the PAP believed that Singapore's postcolonial future lay in a union with Malaya. In hindsight, though, it was probably the greatest strategic blunder by the press in the history of Singapore. Only the English-language press could reach out across ethnic divisions in Singapore, but its flagship had chosen to base itself outside the city-state. "Birds of passage," Lee called them. In 1971, in the midst of his crackdown on the local media, he pressed the point to a gathering of party activists: "Newspaper editors do not owe you a living; they do not owe your children a job. But my colleagues and I do."[20]

Unease about the media's lack of public accountability is not unique to Singapore. It has been a major theme within democratic theory. By the 1940s, the press in the United States had become a power in its own right, leading to the Hutchins Commission Report calling for a new ethos of social responsibility.[21] But while there are sound reasons to be wary of media power, PAP ideology cultivates this seed of skepticism into a thicket that chokes the life out of press freedom. Its argument can be critiqued on at least two separate grounds. First, it exaggerates the relative power of the press. No matter how influential the media are, their impact is of a different order compared with the power of the state. The media can sway people's minds — but unlike the state, newspapers and television stations cannot write laws, tax or seize property, or use violence against citizens. Even if a government is apparently made up of honest people, the sheer scope of its responsibilities — and thus its capacity to inflict real harm either willfully or through honest mistakes — requires constant public vigilance. This is why most societies have come to appreciate that they need media scrutiny of the state more than they need state supervision of the media.

Second, this aspect of PAP ideology overlooks the fact that freedom of expression is one of the requirements for the free and fair elections from which the PAP claims its legitimacy. Note that the party bases its moral authority not on any heavenly mandate but on the support of voters as demonstrated through democratic elections. While there have been no significant complaints of polling irregularities in Singapore, political theorists argue that electoral democracy requires more than just clean voting procedures. It should also include the opportunity for individuals and groups to offer themselves and their ideas to the electorate, and for the public to receive such ideas, discuss the alternatives and form their own opinions and preferences. In any large community, these activities require media that are open and diverse, and not under the control of any one party. Therefore, when a government restricts freedom of expression, it undermines the very legitimacy of the mandate on which it claims to base its restrictions. K.S. Rajah, a former judicial commissioner, has made a similar argument from his reading of the Singapore Constitution. "The concept of representative government occupies a powerful position in the Singapore political system," he noted. "A true choice, with an opportunity to gain an appreciation of alternatives, is only available if voters are given access to relevant information, ideas and views about the functioning of government in Singapore, policies, and political parties and candidates in elections. Freedom of communication on matters of government and politics is an indispensable incident of representative government."[22]

A Vulnerable Nation, Too Small for Democracy

Singapore's sense of vulnerability is seen as a natural response to its unique geographical and social realities. Since years of peace and plenty may have lulled citizens into a false sense of security, the PAP regularly reminds them about what it regards as the immutable facts of Singapore's existence: its small size, its heterogeneous population, and its unstable and unfriendly neighbourhood. These conditions mean that things that may be viable elsewhere — such as free-wheeling democracy and individualism — would be ruinous for Singapore. Asked what the country needed to survive, Lee Kuan Yew said, "[T]he people must be aware of its fundamental vulnerabilities, and willing to pull together to face challenges."[23]

Singapore's small size is undeniable. When they travel, Singaporeans are invariably struck by how puny their homeland is. Its land area of 710 sq. km. makes it slightly smaller than New York City's five boroughs, while its population of 5 million in 2010 is comparable to those of the greater metropolitan areas of Houston, Detroit and Philadelphia. It is smaller in both area and population than the Asian metropolises of Bangkok, Jakarta and Hong Kong. If Singapore were an Indian city, it would rank 5th in population; in China, it would be around 12th. For the PAP, Singapore's size amounts to an inescapable constraint that calls for a prudent and conservative attitude to freedom. Yet, in terms of population, Singapore is not as small as Singaporeans have convinced themselves it is. It is a middle-ranking country, larger than 100 or so other states. Singapore's supposedly limited talent pool is cited to justify the lack of competition in politics, as well as regulators' tolerance for monopolistic government-linked and government-licensed companies in the media and other sectors. Many smaller countries do not feel so constrained.

While being small is a limitation in some regards, it is not necessarily a net liability for governance. In an era of fairly open international trade, Singapore is rarely hobbled by the fact that it is a city-state with a hinterland that lies outside its national borders. Indeed, Singapore's city-state status has spared it from the plight of other dynamic Asian cities, where incessant rural-urban migration strains the infrastructure and creates slums. Singapore can control immigration at its city borders in a way that the authorities in Mumbai and Guangdong can only dream of. Neither India's *laissez-faire* approach to urban overcrowding nor China's attempts to regulate the influx of peasant labour provides an inspiring model for sustainable and humane cities. The various international rankings that are closely watched by the Singapore government cast additional doubt on the idea that countries need heft to succeed. The top three in the World Economic Forum's Global Competitiveness Index 2010–11 were all nations with populations of under 10 million — Switzerland, Sweden and Singapore. Also in the top 10 are Finland and Denmark, with roughly the same population as Singapore, and the Netherlands, with under 20 million people.[24] IMD's World Competitiveness Scorecard, which places Singapore at the very top, has only two economies in the top 10 with populations of over 30 million.[25]

But size is not the only source of Singapore's sense of vulnerability. The PAP sees Singapore as a society riven by internal ethnic differences that pose a perpetual threat to its stability. The country's stability is made more tenuous by its location in Southeast Asia, where it is the only majority-Chinese state and is surrounded by Muslim neighbours. In 1950, Muslims went on a rampage against whites and Eurasians after a controversial custody battle involving a Dutch girl who had been adopted by an Indonesian family and raised as a Muslim. The so-called Maria Hertogh Riots, which claimed 18 lives, were instigated in part by two Muslim newspapers that hijacked the court case as a community cause. Half a century later, religious extremism remained an issue. After the attacks on the United States of 11 September 2011, a cell of the regional Islamic militant group, Jemaah Islamiah, was discovered in Singapore, showing that years of nation-building had not eliminated the risk of religiously-inspired violence.

Few aspects of PAP ideology have been as successfully transferred into the Singaporean psyche as this deep sense of vulnerability, rooted in a distrust of both fellow citizens as well as neighbouring countries. However, Singapore's ethnic mix may not be as explosive as the PAP claims; conversely, societies that are more homogeneous are not immune to violent social conflict. The price of being located in Southeast Asia may also be exaggerated. Take the Global Peace Index, an aggregate of various indicators assessed by the Economist Intelligence Unit, with scores ranging from 1 (most peaceful) to 5 (least peaceful). Singapore's aggregate score in 2007 was 1.673, placing it at number 29 out of more than 140 countries studied. Lee claimed that the relatively low ranking (for a developed country) was not due to internal factors. "It is the external conditions that bring us down to 29," the *Straits Times* quoted him as saying. "We are in South-east Asia. It's a volatile region prone to problems. And you have to remember we cannot take Singapore and tow it away and put it next to Europe so we will have water."[26] Lee's interpretation of the Global Peace Index was inaccurate. Although "relations with neighbouring countries" was scored at 2, this was not the main factor that adversely affected Singapore's score. After all, although Southeast Asia has had a tumultuous history, no war has been fought between members of ASEAN since the association's founding in 1967. Contrary to Lee's claim, internal factors were responsible for dragging Singapore down. The proportion of people jailed, with a score of more than 2.8, was rated as a bigger negative attribute than regional relations. So was the level of distrust between citizens, given a 3. The biggest set of factors that pulled the country's marks down was its level of militarisation, with its military capability/sophistication scoring a 4, arms imports at close to 3 and military expenditure exceeding 2.4.[27]

Furthermore, even if one were to accept that Singapore is exceptionally vulnerable because of its racial and religious mix and its regional situation, it is not clear how this justifies the specific media controls that are currently in place. Many other societies emerging from ethnic strife have not seen democracy as a hindrance to their peacebuilding efforts. While international law allows — and even demands

— limitations on hate speech,[28] this should not justify censorship of dissent, the United Nations' special rapporteur on freedom of expression said in his 2009 report. "Furthermore, resolution of tensions based on genuine cultural or religious differences cannot be achieved by suppressing the expression of differences but rather by debating them openly," he added. "The Special Rapporteur notes that free speech is therefore a requirement for, and not an impediment to, tolerance."[29] Israel, which even the PAP could not deny is in a more vulnerable situation, has allowed itself far greater press freedom and academic freedom than Singapore. Freedom need not mean irresponsibility: news media professionals in Singapore are highly sensitised to the risks of causing offence to the country's various ethnic communities or inflaming their passions. They have internalised these considerations into their editorial judgments; voluntary self-restraint arising from a sense of social responsibility rather than government control is what keeps them responsible. Over the past three decades, most cases of political management of mainstream media have had nothing to do with national security or Singapore's supposed fundamental vulnerabilities. They have instead been directed at shoring up support for policies or protecting the government's own authority.

Against Individualism and Populism

The PAP frames freedom of expression as an individualist value and regards individuals as prone to selfish and shortsighted urges. Freedom of expression is therefore regarded as a right that is in tension with societal interests. The PAP does not deny the universal appeal of this freedom. "I believe that most people, regardless of race, religion or culture will want to live in societies which promote individual liberty and freedom, including the right of free speech," K. Shanmugam has said. However, the PAP treats this individual longing as a luxury. The United States can allow extreme individualism because the country's size and the depth of its resources give it the resilience to bounce back from errors, PAP ideology says. Many other countries, however, need to strike a more conservative balance between individual rights and societal interests. Furthermore, the PAP argues, individualism is prioritised differently in different cultures. Singapore is an Asian society heavily influenced by Confucianism, which emphasises community interests over the individual. "Consensus, not conflict" was adopted by the Goh Chok Tong Government as one of Singapore's five

Shared Values, along with "Nation before community and society above self".[30] Accordingly, Goh said, "The press has a role to forge consensus and not foment confrontation, facilitate nation-building and not fray the social fabric."[31]

The obvious counter-argument to the PAP position is to reiterate the libertarian view: freedom of expression is a sacrosanct individual right that cannot be violated by the collective. It has intrinsic value — it is good in its own right — and needs no extrinsic justification in terms of positive consequences for society at large. This argument, regardless of its philosophical merits, has proved politically ineffective because it allows the PAP to frame the debate in terms with which it is comfortable, as a battle between the individual and society. Not surprisingly, when the choice is framed in this manner, many citizens express their support for societal interest. The libertarian view is also not in keeping with international human rights law, which recognises legimate limitations on free speech.

A stronger but less-heard critique of the PAP position is to point out that press freedom is not just a matter of individual self-expression. It is also required for collective self-determination.[32] Accordingly, senior Singaporean lawyer K.S. Rajah has argued that, even if we de-emphasise the fundamental liberties of the individual, freedom of communication remains necessary for representative and responsible government, which is a core principle of the country's Constitution.[33] Similarly, even in the "individualistic" US, an important strand of thought argues that the First Amendment to the Constitution protects press freedom mainly because of its importance to the community. According to this view, the press deserves its exalted position not primarily because it promotes the interests of individuals but because it allows citizens to deliberate on issues that matter to their collective existence.[34] Thus, the 1948 Hutchins Commission titled its report *A Free and Responsible Press*.[35] Today, the "social responsibility" model that it crystallised is widely accepted by the journalistic profession. A more recent document, the Statement of Shared Purpose of the Committee of Concerned Journalists, opens with the line, "The central purpose of journalism is to provide citizens with accurate and reliable information they need to function in a free society."[36] It is rooted in the social responsibility paradigm, not libertarianism. Denying the well-established connection between community interests and press freedom allows the PAP to justify press control as a stand for Singaporeans' collective welfare against selfish individual urges.

The PAP's suspicion of the individual is also seen in its resistance towards populism. While the people's will is seen as the ultimate source of the PAP's mandate, it believes they should not have a constant, direct bearing on decision-making — which is often better left to experts. The PAP's model of democracy entails citizens voting freely in competitive elections, after which the winning party governs decisively. A responsible and responsive government rules with the consent of the public and in the public interest — but without being slaves to public opinion. Many national challenges can be addressed only by a strong leadership able to push through the occasional unpopular decision. Short-term public opinion can obstruct good government, which requires a long-term orientation. "This is why, in Singapore, the government acts more like a trustee," said Goh. "As a custodian of the public's welfare, it exercises independent judgment on what is in the long-term economic interests of the people and acts on that basis."[37] Although citizens will increasingly be consulted in the formulation of policy, decisions will not be made by referendum or opinion poll. Only over the long term would people be able to assess the impact of government policies on their lives; they can vote accordingly. The implications for the press are clear: the media's primary role is not to champion public opinion but to educate the public. "If Singaporeans do not have an appreciation of the big picture, the challenges they face, the realistic alternatives, the level of public debate falls, populism prevails, and the difficult decisions will never get taken," said Goh. "Then the big forces changing the world will overwhelm us, and we wouldn't even know what hit us."[38]

This philosophy is not alien to Western democratic discourse. Several respectable theorists have taken a dim view of the capacities of the public and argued that the only realistic vision for democracy is an elitist one in which day-to-day government is left to specialists.[39] The American public intellectual Walter Lippmann, for example, was highly critical of the myth of the "sovereign and omnicompetent citizen".[40] "I think it is a false ideal," he wrote. "I do not mean an undesirable ideal. I mean an unattainable ideal, bad only in the sense that is it bad for a fat man to try to be a ballet dancer. An ideal should express the true possibilities of its subject."[41] Holding a similar view, Joseph Schumpeter argued for a more modest but "greatly improved" theory of democracy in which "the role of the people is to produce a government".[42] Samuel Huntington was another illustrious political theorist who argued for moderation in the exercise of democracy.[43] "A value which is normally good in itself is not necessarily optimized when it is maximized," he said.[44] He would go so far as to say that "some measure of apathy and non-involvement on the part of some individuals and groups" was required to avoid overloading the government with demands.[45]

Of course, the theory of democratic elitism is only one view of what we should reasonably expect of democracy. Against it are arrayed competing theories that see a much more active role for the public. One of the strongest critiques comes from the perspective of deliberative democracy. The deliberative ideal rejects the elitist view that people are incapable of rational discussion of issues that matter to them; the problem is that elites have not given them the chance.[46] Jurgen Habermas, the leading light of this school of thought, argued for reviving the "public sphere", which he describes as that domain of life in which "people's public use of their reason" is the medium through which they engage authorities in debate.[47] The deliberative ideal calls for a press that actively engages the citizens and prods them out of their apathy. The influential American media scholar James Carey said, "The public will begin to reawaken when they are addressed as a conversational partner and are encouraged to join the talk rather than sit passively as spectators before a discussion conducted by journalists and experts."[48]

The conflict between democratic elitism and deliberative democracy (not to mention various other strands in democratic thinking) is unresolved. It would appear, therefore, that the PAP is assured of good company, not just among the defenders of authoritarian systems but even within democratic thought. However, the apparent similarity between democratic elitism and PAP's own ideas about leaders and followers is superficial. Go deeper and fundamental differences emerge. First, while democratic elitism is as pessimistic as PAP ideology about the capacities of the public, it is resistant to the over-concentration of power in the hands of leaders. The elite that Lippmann, Huntington and others pinned their democratic hopes on is an internally competitive one with functioning checks and balances, including an effective opposition and a free press. This is a far cry from the supremely powerful executive that the PAP has constructed. Second, democratic elitism does not propose to exclude anyone from the public sphere by force. To Huntington, the problem of an "excess of democracy" was to be solved by "self-restraint" on the part of groups with the right to participate in politics.[49] The PAP, in contrast, ensures non-involvement by curtailing civil liberties.

Both see an excess of democracy as a health risk, but they have different patients in mind. Democratic elitism's concern is the future of the democratic system as a whole. PAP ideology, on the other hand, is consumed by the need to protect the conditions for good government. The two are related, of course: sustained failure to deliver could diminish public support for democracy. But while it would take an extreme overdose of democracy to threaten the system as a whole — Huntington was writing in the wake of the tumultuous protest movements of the late 1960s when social mobilisation was at its peak — even low doses could interfere with day-to-day government. Hence the heightened sensitivity of the PAP to democratic expression despite Singapore's already passive and demobilised citizenry. Seen through democratic lenses, the PAP's fear of unleashing an excess of democracy is akin to denying Sub-Saharan Africa food aid on the grounds that a culture of excess has caused obesity in the West. No objective diagnosis would claim Singapore is at risk of the democratic "overindulgence" that Huntington was warning of.[50]

Singapore Must Be Open

The PAP has been so forthright in its condemnation of Western-style liberal democracy that it could be mistaken for promoting the opposite extreme — the closed authoritarian model. In fact, it has been consistent in disavowing closed societies and one-party states. In his 1971 Helsinki speech, Lee said, "Some governments like China, or the Soviet Union in pre-Khrushchev days, effectively sealed off their people from the outside world. Then the world is what the rulers say it is. And the rulers are unchanging for long years. But there is a heavy price to be paid for such isolation. The incessant exhortation to progress, the constant stress on conformity in ideology, ideas and action, they lead to drab uniformity."[51] He also distanced himself from leaders who had opted to nationalise their media, noting that "many leaders, especially in Africa, have decided against free play and opted for the one-party state with all mass media supporting the one-party".[52] Debating opposition MP J.B. Jeyaretnam in Parliament in 1984, he made a similar point, suggesting that Singapore's model of strictly regulated but commercial media compared favourably with the nationalised press of some other Asian countries: "The Member should ask himself: is Singapore better off with a privately-owned press under strict rules of ownership and self-censorship? Or is it better of where the press is owned by the governing parties, as in Sri Lanka and Malaysia?"[53]

Since most of its critics have come from the democratic rather than authoritarian end of the political spectrum, the PAP has not needed to justify why Singapore is not more closed than it is. Nevertheless, statements about the value of openness do crop up now and then in speeches and interviews. First, there is a characteristically realist argument, that Singapore cannot be anything other than open. Lee said in Helsinki that "in practice, new countries, particularly the smaller ones, cannot altogether insulate themselves from outside news and views".[54] Second, the government has occasionally acknowledged that openness is not just unavoidable, but may even be a good thing. Lee reminded critics that he had personally appealed for the BBC World Service to keep its FM transmission station in Singapore as a service to Singaporeans when the British military pulled out in 1971.[55] In the 1990s, 24-hour international news channels and then the internet were embraced as part of the infrastructure required for a modern economy. "As an international trading centre, our economy is fuelled by information. Our financial markets cannot be a nanosecond behind London, New York or Tokyo," Lee said. This being the reality, "we cannot stop reports which are disagreeable to us". He added, "Governments that try to fight the new technology will lose."[56]

Thus, the need to be plugged into the world is not disputed. PAP ideology also shows a deep commitment to change, based on an endless cycle of trouble-shooting, environmental scanning and timely policy innovation (Chapter 10). Public sector leaders have exhorted officials to keep their minds open and to challenge convention.[57] While this culture of openness is encouraged within the policymaking elite, the signals for the wider society have been far less enthusiastic. The PAP has conceded that it must salve the public's hunger for more consultation and debate, but has not gone so far as to create the conditions generally seen as required for an open society.

The Hold of History

The various strands of the PAP's philosophy link to form an ideological fence around its media system. Each argument has its weaknesses, as outlined above. What is more, there is an internal contradiction in the PAP position: it depends on two diametrically opposing claims about the Singapore public. On the one hand, to justify its elitist and paternalistic version of democracy, the PAP portrays the public as immature, incompetent in the matters of state, and forever prone to disintegrate into warring tribes. On the other hand, to defend its political legitimacy, the PAP holds up the public as rational, responsible and wise, repeatedly returning the party to power out of enlightened self-interest — not, as critics allege, because Singaporeans have been bullied and brainwashed. Singaporeans vote for the PAP and trust their media because they "know better" than to believe foreign critics; they are now "well-educated, sophisticated, and know their rights", according to Shanmugam.[58] Of course, both traits — irrationality and wisdom — are part of being human. What is questionable about PAP ideology is not that it sees both aspects of humanity, but that it tactically recognises one at a time. When faced with appeals for a more deliberative and open society served by a free press, it is dismissive of the possibility that a rational public could be cultivated to discuss sensitive issues peacefully and discern what is in their long-term interest. On the other hand, the PAP denies that its media restrictions help it to dominate over society; suddenly, Singaporeans are too smart to be misled.

Admittedly, there is a certain futility to all the critiques arrayed in this chapter. Powerful ideologies are never built on facts and logic alone, so they are unlikely to be dislodged by academic analysis. Take, for example, Singapore's small-country syndrome. Scholars could carry out rigorous comparative analysis to assess the relationship between a country's size, its political system and its level of economic development. They might then find that Singapore, despite it size, is no worse off and no less fit for democracy. However, such a study would resolve little, since Singapore's size is ultimately a state of mind. History, more than geography, helps explain why the country's leaders — and many of its citizens — are convinced that its smallness is a problem. Had Singapore achieved independence as a result of a long secessionist struggle, it would probably celebrate its city-state status as a precious part of its national identity — you prize what you fight for. Instead, 9 August 1965 was described by Lee Kuan Yew as "a moment of anguish", representing a traumatic failure of Singapore's post-colonial vision.[59] Until then, the republic's founding fathers had assumed that the island city would only be viable as part of Malaya. Singapore's unplanned separation from Malaysia meant that, overnight, Singaporeans' national borders snapped inwards like a vise, enclosing a space that was less than 2 per cent of the Federation's area and with just one-fifth as many people. They would never again be able to regard their country as anything other than small and vulnerable.

While PAP ideology has traceable historical roots, it also undergoes diligent cultivation. Among other strategies, the PAP perpetuates the idea that Singapore's policy choices are limited. Lee has said, "There just is no viable alternative programme for an island city state other than what we have empirically worked out in the last 30 years. This is why the able and talented have not come forward to form a credible alternative team and challenge the PAP. They know the PAP is doing the right thing, and there is no alternative way."[60] Political scientist Chan Heng Chee has recognised the significance of such claims. Lee's "genius" established a governing style of structuring events in such a way that, when politically sensitive decisions had to be made, there appeared to be few other solutions that fit the circumstances. Thus, "the seemingly inevitable option that should be or could be adopted was the one he favoured".[61]

In debates about the press, the PAP has presented the options as a dichotomy, as if the only alternative to the *status quo* is an extreme libertarian position with no limits on irresponsible and destructive speech. If these were indeed the only choices — responsibility versus freedom; order versus anarchy — it should not be surprising that people take the conservative road. What the PAP fails to acknowledge, though, is that this dichotomy does not exist outside of school debating competitions and junior college general paper classes. In reality, democratic societies as well as international human rights law accept that no freedom is absolute. It is not illegitimate to require the individual's freedom of expression be exercised in ways that take into account the rights of other individuals as well as the public interest. People have a right to protect their private lives and their reputations, and there is no right to incite hatred or violence. International standards allow restrictions on speech to uphold public order, public morality and national security.

The problem with the PAP system is not the presence of restrictions as such, but that the forms and functions of these restrictions violate international best practices. There is by now a well-articulated set of principles in international law to help determine what is a legitimate restriction and what constitutes an unacceptable infringement. First, a restriction must not be arbitrary; it must be according to written law that is "accessible, unambiguous, drawn narrowly and with precision so as to enable individuals to foresee whether a particular action is unlawful", to quote the UN's special rapporteur for freedom of expression issues, Frank La Rue. Second, it must be in aid of one of the legitimate aims identified in international law. Third, the restriction "must be proportionate to the aim that is seeks to achieve, or the least restrictive means possible for protecting that aim".[62] The three-part test is geared towards ensuring that restrictions are the exception and freedom is the rule. The desirable end is not absolute freedom, but rules that fulfill a social purpose while not amounting to "a cure worse than the disease", as the Hutchins Commission put it.[63] Within this paradigm, the burden of proof is on the state: it is not for citizens to persuade government that they deserve freedom.

Many of the PAP government's restrictions fail the three-part test. They are over-broad and excessively punitive. As a result, even when they serve legitimate aims, they discourage and dampen citizens' democratic participation — exactly opposite to the intended effect of freedom of expression. PAP rhetoric admits no space for such discussions, which could give Singaporeans the benefits of greater freedom without the costs of unmanageably irresponsible speech. One ironic result is that Singapore has not kept up with advances in media self-regulation around the world. Despite the PAP's emphasis on professional responsibility, Singapore lags significantly in building media accountability systems.[64] There is no press council as you would find in Scandinavia, or press complaints commission like Britain's. To increase transparency and accountability, major Western news organisations make their codes of ethics publicly available; Singapore's two media giants do not. Nor have Singapore's media emulated the *Washington Post* or the *New York Times* in installing in-house ombudsmen as internal watchdogs monitoring their performance on behalf of the public. The introduction of such voluntary mechanisms would, of course, reduce the justification for government intervention. These and other ideas for reforming the media system have been sucked into the ideological black hole that the PAP has created in between authoritarianism and anarchy.

CHAPTER 5

Calibrated Coercion: The State Strategy of Self-Restraint

China's crackdown on the 1989 Tiananmen Square protests is such a taboo topic that the merest hint of a mention online is sufficient to trigger the country's famed internet firewall. However, as a statesman who has been in the game longer than most — indeed, longer than 100-plus current members of the United Nations even existed as sovereign nations — Lee Kuan Yew is often granted the latitude to comment on other countries' most sensitive matters. Thus, at a closed-door meeting with China's then-premier, Singapore's elder statesman went ahead and shared his opinion on Tiananmen. "I said to Li Peng, 'you had the world's TV cameras there waiting for the meeting with Gorbachev, and you stage this grand show,'" Lee later told *Time* magazine. "His answer was: 'We are completely inexperienced in these matters.'" Lee related his own experience with (admittedly smaller) student protests in the early years of his government: "When I had trouble with my sit-in communist students, squatting in school premises and keeping their teachers captive, I cordoned off the whole area around the schools, shut off the water and electricity, and just waited. I told their parents that health conditions were deteriorating, dysentery was going to spread. And they broke it up without any difficulty."[1]

It was not the only time that Lee chided a fellow authoritarian leader's excessive use of state violence. In 1998, Malaysian prime minister Mahathir Mohamed moved to neutralise his erstwhile deputy, the charismatic and popular Anwar Ibrahim. Anwar's arrest under the Internal Security Act and his beating in custody, from which he sensationally emerged with a black eye, sparked protests the likes of which had not been seen for decades. A few months later, Lee met Mahathir at Davos in Switzerland. He related the conversation to *The Straits Times*. "'Why did you arrest him under the ISA?'" Lee recalled asking Mahathir. "And he told me he did not know that Anwar was going to be arrested under the ISA. The Police chief had acted on his own authority. It never should have been that way, it should have been a straight-forward criminal charge." As for the physical assault on the jailed politician, Mahathir pointed out that he would not have obtained any benefit from ordering the police chief to beat up Anwar. "I agreed," Lee told *The Straits Times*, "but these are things that have been done and I am afraid he has paid very dearly for it. My sympathies are with him."[2]

In his accounts of conversations with the leaders of China and Malaysia, Lee did not join the international chorus of condemnation against their use of excessive state violence. Instead, his criticism was grounded in realpolitik: why use physical force when subtler means could get the job done with less political cost? Tanks and men with guns may be a quick way to silence critics, but they also tend to create martyrs and provoke outrage in those watching from the sidelines, unleashing forces that will be even harder to tame in the long run. Lee understood that a state must calibrate its coercion if it wants to consolidate its dominant position.

Calibrated coercion is an important feature of Singapore's approach to managing the media. Draconian powers remain in the statute books. Yet, the government has often left these on the shelf and reached for less visible tools to prod the media this way and that. Over the decades, there has been a shift away from flamboyant punishments such as imprisoning journalists and banning publications, towards more behind-the-scenes controls that create the conditions for self-censorship. Economic sanctions are favoured over those that violate the integrity of the individual. In addition, controls are targeted at limited numbers of producers and organisers of dissent, rather than at the mass of ordinary citizens. Obsessed with the goal of aligning the press with the PAP's vision, there were moments when Lee was sorely tempted to dispatch civil servants to *The Straits Times* to take over the day-to-day running of the newsroom. Lacking neither the power nor the conviction, he nonetheless demurred and opted for subtler controls. Lee's skill at calibrating coercion may be one key reason why his

People's Action Party, together with its media system, has been so successfully entrenched. This is an under-studied aspect of Singapore, and of politics in general. The field of political science has had little to say about the strategies available to authoritarian rulers, perhaps because most political scientists consider authoritarian systems unworthy of in-depth study. They want to believe that authoritarianism is straightforward to execute in the short term and unsustainable in the long run. After the fall of the Soviet empire, hope blossomed that non-democratic regimes represented merely a transitional phase, a detour en route to inevitable freedoms — as argued by Francis Fukuyama in his *End of History* thesis.[3] Besides, there is certainly a greater need to provide fledgling democracies, rather than would-be dictatorships, with the intellectual capital and policy advice that could help them entrench their chosen forms of government. There is thus substantial scholarly literature on democratic consolidation, but no equivalent sub-field called authoritarian consolidation.

Nevertheless, those who have studied authoritarian regimes have made observations that this chapter echoes. Juan Linz, writing about Franco's Spain, noted that persecution alone could not explain the regime's persistence. Instead, an approach of "limited pluralism" or "semifreedom" — the other side of the coin of what I call calibrated coercion — contributed to the "frustration, disintegration and sometimes readiness to co-optation" of opposition forces.[4] Similarly, Israel's security forces tempered their interrogation methods when they realised that not leaving visible scars demoralised their Palestinian prisoners more effectively than martyring them.[5] Closer to Singapore, Indonesia offers a telling case study. In his study of opposition to Suharto's 32-year-long New Order, Edward Aspinall has argued that it was not just repression but "a combination of repression with toleration" that accounted for the regime's durability and success.[6] Although it had the military at its core, the regime's power centres did not rely only on physical might; it also subordinated other groups by co-opting them. As a result, the dominant form of opposition was "semiopposition": groups that did not fundamentally challenge the regime but instead adopted "work-from-within" strategies, pushing for political reform while cooperating with the government.[7] By the 1990s, Aspinall observes, repression was never "entirely unconstrained or indiscriminate": "Instead, coercion was focused on the most overt challenges and aimed to limit societal mobilization and criticism rather than smash it entirely (which, by now, would have required great repression)."[8]

We can also find intellectual signposts pointing to the core of calibrated coercion within theoretical works that put aside the distinctions between democracy and authoritarianism, and instead analyse the essence of state power. For a start, there is Max Weber, the father of political sociology, who observed that the definitive characteristic of the modern state is its monopoly over the use of legitimate violence — legitimate, that is, in the narrow sense of being lawful.[9] Whether the state's use of violence has *moral* legitimacy is a subject that exercised the mind of the Italian journalist and communist party leader Antonio Gramsci as he sat in prison in the 1920s and 1930s. Gramsci observed that although the state's domination is ultimately underwritten by force, violence is not normally the currency that is in daily circulation. Looking at the capitalist societies around him, he remarked that the ruling class dominated without routine recourse to violence, and indeed usually with the consent of the ruled. This blend of coercion and consent, violence and ideology, he called hegemony.[10] Gramsci's hegemony leads us to a counter-intuitive notion: that there is an inverse relationship between violence and power. This idea was developed by the German-Jewish political theorist Hannah Arendt as she contemplated the totalitarian regimes of 1940s Europe. In her essay, *On Violence*, Arendt noted that while power can *use* violence, it cannot be based on violence. This is because power corresponds to the human ability to act in concert; it belongs to a group and exists only as long as the group coheres. "Single men without others to support them never have enough power to use violence successfully," she wrote.[11] What power needs is legitimacy, and legitimacy is what is lost when violence is misapplied: "To substitute violence for power can bring victory, but the price is very high; for it is not only paid by the vanquished, it is also paid by the victor in terms of his own power."[12]

Singapore can be seen as a textbook case of a state that has adopted a long-term view of power, deliberately reining in its use of force in order to build ideological consent. Of course, coercion — calibrated or otherwise — is not an aspect of governance that politicians like to discuss, so one should not expect to find the subject celebrated alongside the other features of the Singapore model, such as the public housing programme, water management and investment promotion. The government's official position, stated in reply to a newspaper op-ed piece I wrote on this topic, is that "the Government does not depend on 'calibrated coercion', but derives moral authority precisely from what Dr George himself acknowledged — 'an outstanding record in delivering the goods, internal discipline, ability to win genuine freely-given loyalty from the majority of Singaporeans'.[13]

Indeed, calibrated coercion cannot be a source of legitimacy, which must be built on electoral success and good governance. However, it can certainly limit the erosion of that legitimacy. Failure to exercise self-restraint in the application of violence is one of the surest ways for a state to provoke the kind of moral outrage that opponents can use to mobilise the public. Grievances may be long term and complex, but revolutions often require catalytic events. Thus, the Arab Spring of 2010–11 has been traced to petty officials who abused a Tunisian vegetable seller to breaking point. His self-immolation galvanised the opposition against the country's dictator Zine El Abidine Ben Ali. In Southeast Asia, the assassination of Benigno Aquino, Jr. on the tarmac of Manila International Airport in 1983 solidified the opposition and sparked the Philippines' first People Power revolution, leading to the downfall of the seemingly unassailable Ferdinand Marcos. Similarly, when troops killed four students at Trisakti University in Jakarta in 1998, it marked a tipping point in the Reformasi movement against the Suharto regime. The main reason why Lee did not follow these Southeast Asian strongmen down the path of disgrace and oblivion is his incorruptibility: he and his family appear to lack a venal bone in their bodies. A relatively overlooked factor, however, has been Lee's relative finesse in the use of force.

Learning from Repression

It was not always this way. Finesse is not a word one would associate with the early decades of PAP government. It was dealing with militant opponents who were perceived to be threatening national security on three fronts. There were communists who infiltrated trade unions and other organisations to foment revolution, opponents of merger with Malaysia, and ethnic chauvinists who whipped up communal sentiments at a time when the fragile foundations of a multi-cultural society were being laid. Most historians agree that these risks were real — although doubts remain over whether every individual identified as a national security threat really was one, or conveniently caught in the dragnet to remove any opposition to the ruling party and its leaders.

Justified or not, the treatment meted out to these enemies was harsh. The main instrument used was the Internal Security Act of

1963 (the same law that Lee Kuan Yew chided Mahathir Mohamed for using against Anwar Ibrahim) and its predecessor, the Preservation of Public Order Security Ordinance of 1955. This empowered the authorities to arrest individuals without warrant and detain them without trial. The largest single sweep was Operation Coldstore in February 1963, which rounded up more than 110 opposition politicians, labour activists and other opponents. Since independence, from 1965 to 2010, approximately 640 people were detained under the ISA.[14] Whether detainees have suffered torture is disputed. However, former detainees' accounts of mistreatment in detention — sleep deprivation, interrogation in icy cold rooms and psychological pressure — have not been contradicted by the government. Former detainees have also alleged that confessions were coerced.[15]

The spectre of the ISA has been so permanent and prominent on Singapore's political stage that it can distract from other significant trends in the PAP's employment of coercion. What is particularly noteworthy is the fact that the government has tried to avoid routinising the use of detention without trial, which it regards as a blunt instrument of last resort. The same is true of other extreme discretionary powers, such as banishment and the banning of newspapers. Although believing firmly in the necessity of such laws, the government prefers to use more precise tools when they are available, and will create them quickly when they are not. Thus, the 1971 crackdown on the *Nanyang Siang Pau*, *Eastern Sun* and *Singapore Herald* (Chapter 2) prompted a rethink of press laws. The public relations cost of the government's threats included a "Save the Herald" fund-raising campaign that attracted university students and other educated Singaporeans. It was not just the young republic's democratic credentials that were sullied by these, but also — and more worryingly for the PAP — its reputation as an investor-friendly economy. The *Herald*'s management pointed out that, on top of violating press freedom, the government had decided "to interfere in a commercial enterprise in an unprecedented manner".[16] Addressing to the Hong Kong Foreign Correspondents' Club, a writer who had been based in Singapore said that some foreign businessmen were concerned about "arbitrary Singapore Government interference in the private sector".[17] The government may have won its battle against the press, but the collateral damage must have been a concern at a time when its business-friendly image was still a work in progress.

Other authoritarian governments may have simply written off this cost to their legitimacy and gone back to business as usual. Lee, however, sought to fix the system to prevent a recurrence. He appeared to recognise that the colonial-era reserve powers over the press were inadequate to the PAP's nation-building project. The power to ban newspapers and imprison editors guaranteed that the government could knock out any offending elements in the press, but what the PAP needed was a way to win without throwing a punch. Its ingenious new press law, the Newspaper and Printing Presses Act 1974, provided exactly that. As described in detail in Chapter 2, the NPPA retained discretionary licensing as its cornerstone, but introduced unique legislative innovations that gave the government more calibrated tools to deal with national newspapers. The NPPA ensured that newspaper companies would focus on commercial success, aligning their interests with a pro-growth government. While never surrendering its most repressive powers as an omnipresent Sword of Damocles, it recognised that the actual use of these powers is often unnecessary, and usually counterproductive. More subtle methods can do the job with less political cost.

This principle has been applied not only to the press but also to practically every power centre with the potential to challenge the PAP. In each of these battles, the sequence has been repeated. First, the government resorts to the ISA to neutralise dissenters by force, and shock and awe their followers into quiescence. Then, it introduces specific legislation to nip further dissent in the bud, thus ensuring that the ISA would not need to be used again. Finally, it co-opts and rewards those who are prepared to partner the PAP in its nation-building movement. The first sector to be subject to this approach was, not surprisingly, organised labour. Militant unions were a powerful political force before independence: their leaders were key targets for arrest. Labour activists continued to be detained when Singapore became independent. However, the PAP also moved decisively to restructure labour relations. Immediately after coming to power in 1959, it amended legislation to empower the Registrar of Trade Unions to refuse registration of unions, thus stemming their proliferation. In 1961, the National Trades Union Congress (NTUC) was created to place relations on a more even keel. In 1968, labour laws were amended to confine the role of unions to dealing with wages, benefits and certain work conditions; other matters such as recruitment, promotions, retrenchments and dismissals were deemed entirely the prerogative of employers.[18] Another major reorganisation of labour unions followed in 1979, when the government perceived that omnibus unions had become potential power bases from which ambitious labour leaders could mount political challenges. Omnibus unions were phased out and replaced with smaller industry-wide unions.[19]

Writing in 1970, political scientist Chan Heng Chee described the PAP's handling of certain labour disputes as "shabby" and even "inexplicable". This, she warned, could push the NTUC to strike out on its own, causing the PAP to "lose one of its levers of control".[20] The PAP evidently recognised this risk as well. It invested more attention to building the NTUC as a key axis in a tripartite system of government-business-labour negotiations.[21] "Admittedly the left's downfall was also due to the NTUC's success," Michael Fernandez and Loh Kah Seng would write in their critical review of Singapore's labour history.[22] Ultimately, the PAP did not deny that workers might have legitimate grievances that required credible representation — but it was not going to allow such representatives to develop as independent power centres that could one day challenge its own authority. Its strategy was not to suppress ground sentiments entirely, but to divert such energies into more manageable channels. Labour leaders were inducted into the PAP as MPs, and PAP MPs were placed into NTUC leadership positions. The old adversarial relationship, with a multiplicity of often unruly unions, was gradually replaced with a symbiotic relationship between the PAP and the NTUC, making it almost inconceivable that any labour union would act in a fashion necessitating the use of the ISA.

Student activism was another political threat that the PAP neutralised within the first two decades of independence. Left-wing student activists were rounded up in Operation Coldstore, but this failed to dampen student movements — which were no doubt emboldened by similar uprisings in other countries. In 1965 and 1966, Chinese-medium students reacted against perceived unfairness towards Chinese education with class boycotts, sit-ins, processions, threats of violence and even an arson attempt. English-stream students joined in to demonstrate against so-called "suitability certificates" that were introduced to weed out university applicants with politically suspect backgrounds. More than 250 students were expelled; many were banished from Singapore.[23] In the mid-1970s, the University of Singapore Students Union adopted a more radical stance under its new president Tan Wah Piow. The union championed the rights of retrenched workers in Singapore and squatters across the border in Johor. Tan was sentenced to a year in prison for causing a riot.[24] Once again, the PAP was not content to be trapped in a cycle of action and reaction. The University of Singapore Amendment Bill was passed in 1976 to overhaul the structure, funding and scope of all campus organisations. There would be eight faculty clubs and three non-faculty associations. One political association, admitting only Singapore citizens, would be the sole student body allowed to engage in politics or issue statements of a political nature.[25] The move dealt a "fatal blow to student politics", said historian Huang Jianli.[26] Simultaneously, the PAP built up a highly competitive exam meritocracy and an attractive overseas scholarship system, encouraging high-flying students to embrace more careerist definitions of a good education.

In the mid-1980s, it was organised religion that appeared on the government's radar. Ten Catholic church workers were among 22 individuals arrested under the ISA in May and June 1987. Supposedly influenced by liberation theology, they were engaged in various forms of social activism, highlighting the plight of foreign maids and other marginalised groups. Understandably reluctant to single out the Catholic Church — one of the few institutions in Singapore that will, without doubt, outlive the PAP — the authorities presented to the public a "Marxist conspiracy" to overthrow the government by force. Notwithstanding allegations of links to the Tamil Tigers, the real target was almost certainly what Michael Barr calls a "subculture of Catholic activism".[27] "The movement did not threaten the state or the nation, but it did threaten the government's capacity to set the agenda for public discourse," Barr contends.[28] Operation Spectrum was the biggest security sweep in more than a decade. Yet again, its aftermath witnessed legislative innovation to prevent a repeat of the problem. The Maintenance of Religious Harmony Act of 1990 empowered the government to place gag orders on religious preachers deemed to be "carrying out activities to promote a political cause, or a cause of any political party while, or under the guise of, propagating or practising any religious belief". Thus, instead of using detention without trial against errant preachers, the government could now apply a more calibrated restraining order.

In May 1988, a prominent critic of the PAP, Francis Seow, was detained under the ISA for allegedly accepting funds from an American diplomat to lead a group of lawyers against the government. To counter the public perception that he was being detained to prevent him from taking part in the coming general elections, the government released him after two months. He duly contested the September 1988 elections, lost, was charged with tax evasion, and fled the country before the trial.[29] Two years earlier, the Law Society of Singapore — with Seow as president — had seen fit to criticise the government Bill introducing circulation caps for offshore publications deemed to be meddling in domestic politics. The government believed it was protecting Singapore's honour against disrespectful foreign media, so the Bar association's intervention was viewed as a betrayal.[30] Once again, the government did not stop at neutralising the individual case: it moved swiftly to close the loophole that its opponent had exploited. In this case, legislative fixes were implemented even before Seow's detention. Lee Kuan Yew's dealings with the communists had taught him to be perpetually wary of political opponents using seemingly innocuous front organisations. The challenge was how to prevent the Law Society turning into pseudo-opposition. The government wasted no time in amending the Legal Profession Act. Under the new provisions, the Law Minister was empowered to nominate up to three of the Society's 22 council members. More importantly, the Society would be allowed to comment only on those Bills that the government submitted to it.[31] In addition, the government instituted a competing organisation, the Singapore Academy of Law. This included judges, members of the government's legal service and in-house counsels, thus diluting the impact of more autonomous lawyers on the organisation's direction. The legal profession's 1986 entry onto the political stage would be a cameo appearance with no encores.

Between 1991 and 2010, there were seven detentions for espionage. In the decade from 2001, 60 individuals were detained for alleged terrorism-related activities linked to the regional group, Jemaah Islamiyah.[32] Francis Seow's 1988 detention marked the last fresh arrest of a non-violent political opponent under the ISA. Since then, the Singapore government has honoured an undeclared moratorium on detention orders as a means of controlling dissent. Malaysia provides an interesting contrast. It continued to use the ISA against opposition members and other peaceful activists. As recently as 2008, Malaysia arrested under the ISA a mainstream newspaper journalist for accurately reporting a ruling party politician's inflammatory outburst. In keeping with the theory of calibrated coercion, Malaysia's kneejerk use of the law delegitimised the ISA in the eyes of a broad swathe of public opinion and made it a political issue in itself, compelling the Prime Minister Najib Abdul Razak to promise its repeal in 2011 in order to shore up his position. In contrast, Singapore's human rights activists have had a harder time building up public support against the ISA, which is widely seen as a necessary national security tool.

Media Detainees

The list of individuals detained since the PAP came to power in 1959 includes several who were involved in media, although many of them were hauled up not for their media work as such, but for their activities in opposition parties, trade unions and other organisations. Targets of the 1963 crackdown included Singapore National Union of Journalists secretary general A. Mahadeva of *The Straits Times* and committee member James Fu Chiao Sian of *Nanyang Siang Pau* (who would later become press secretary to Prime Minister Lee Kuan Yew). Others such as Poh Soo Kai and Tan Jing Quee were involved with the left-wing undergraduate magazine *Fajar*. Said Zahari, jailed for 17 years (the second longest period in detention), was editor of the opposition Barisan Sosialis party's Malay newsletter, *Rakyat*, and before that editor of the Malay daily *Utusan Melayu*. Lim Hock Siew edited Barisan's English organ, *Plebeian*.

In the decade or so after independence, the ISA was used against several individuals working for mainstream Chinese and Malay media organisations. Before the milestone May 1971 crackdown on *Nanyang Siang Pau*, Ngiam Tong Hai of the same paper (1966) and Julius Yeh Sai Fu of *Sin Chew Jit Poh* (1971) were detained. *Nanyang Siang Pau* chairman Lee Eu Seng was detained for five years from 1973. In 1974, three *Sin Chew Jit Poh* staffers were among 31 people detained as alleged members of the Malayan National Liberation Front. In 1976, *Berita Harian* editor Hussein Jahidin and assistant editor Nahar Azmi Mahmud were arrested for allegedly sowing discontent and propagating communist thinking among Malays as part of a plot masterminded by the PAP's left-wing founder member Samad Ismail. In 1977, *Min Pao Daily* journalist Kwok Chong Kwee was detained for ten days in connection with alleged pro-communist activities. In February 1977, the ISA was directed at the foreign media. Arun Senkuttuvan, who wrote for the *Far Eastern Economic Review* and other overseas publications, was detained for two months and stripped of his citizenship. Then, in March, the same magazine's reporter Ho Kwong Ping was detained for seven weeks until 29 April.

Operation Spectrum of 1987 ensnared two individuals who were, among other activities, involved in publishing an underground newsletter that allegedly contained hostile and left-wing views about army life, and two others accused of infiltrating the Workers' Party organ, *Hammer*. There were also two subtitling editors with the national broadcaster and a journalist with the Malaysian daily *New Straits Times* — but these media employees were not accused of using their outlets as part of their Marxist conspiracy. Therefore, Operation Spectrum could not really be characterised as a crackdown on journalism. Instead, the last time the ISA detention was used as an instrument of media regulation was 1977. Ho Kwon Ping, whom the government would appoint 20–30 years later as a statutory board chairman, chairman of the national broadcaster MediaCorp and president of Singapore Management University, would hold the additional distinction of being the last person to suffer ISA detention in the line of professional journalistic duty. Since then, the government has been able to count on the NPPA to create a culture of self-restraint in domestic newspapers. Defamation suits, contempt of court charges, circulation restrictions and work permit controls became the preferred tools for disciplining the foreign media.

There were other signs of a government re-think of its use of the ISA. By the late 1970s, American diplomats were noting that some detainees were being released despite not publicly renouncing communism or armed revolution. Some detainees refused to make such statements on the grounds that this was tantamount to admitting that they had believed in communist revolution in the first place. To break the stalemate, the government was willing to release them with restrictions.[33] As Singapore's security landscape changed, it may have also occurred to the government that overuse of the ISA would strain credibility. As early as 1977, the US State Department's human rights report on Singapore registered the fact that the ISA was originally justified in connection with communist insurgency but that the definition of a "security case" was now being extended to include "those who portray Singapore as a state in which individual liberties are curtailed or the Singapore Government as undemocratic, totalitarian, autocratic and 'oppressive'; and those journalists whose reporting is considered by the Government of Singapore to be slanted and therefore capable of being exploited by communists".[34]

The spread of civil rights norms may have had some effect as well. By 1989, not only was the Soviet empire crumbling, there were also rumblings of a democratic breakthrough in South Africa. If Nelson Mandela were to be released, the ignoble record of housing the world's longest serving political prisoner would suddenly shift — to Singapore. Chia Thye Poh, an allegedly dangerous communist, had been detained in prison and government halfway houses since 1966. On 17 May 1989 — nine months before Mandela's release — Chia was released to Sentosa island. There were still restrictions on his movements, which meant that some sources would go ahead and count him as the world's longest serving prisoner of conscience. The unusual arrangements made for Chia on Sentosa, primarily a leisure development, inspired a *New Yorker* writer to call him a "prisoner in the theme park".[35] Restrictions were loosened in phases so incremental and involved that it was hard for observers to keep track of his status; thus, when they were totally removed in 1998, the event passed almost unnoticed. This was perhaps the point of the painfully long process: it robbed Chia's release of the kind of epic and climactic impact of Mandela's. In so doing, it denied the opposition and civil society the opportunity to turn it into a media event.

Operation Spectrum of 1987 dispelled any doubts that a Cabinet made up mainly of second generation leaders had the stomach for using the ISA. In hindsight, though, the swoop could be said to have crossed a threshold — the point of diminishing returns — causing the government to reconsider its menu of coercion. The problem was not the objections from international human rights monitors, the Catholic church or Singapore's liberals, since the PAP continues to draw a certain macho pride from its immunity to such external pressures. More worryingly, the government was finding it hard to convince even insiders. Goh Chok Tong, who was deputy prime minister at the time, revealed in an interview for the 2009 history of the PAP, *Men in White*, that his Cabinet colleague S. Dhanabalan "was not fully comfortable with the action which we took". This, Goh said, was a reason for Dhanabalan's eventual shock resignation from government.[36] Dhanabalan was no lightweight or liberal: as culture minister, he had banned *Cosmopolitan* for its permissive values. He had also been named by Lee Kuan Yew as premier-material but for the fact that Singapore's Chinese majority would not accept an Indian prime minister.

A young civil servant who was questioned as part of the Operation Spectrum investigations, Tharman Shanmugaratnam, voiced his doubts to the press when he was inducted into politics in 2001. "Although I did not have access to the same intelligence as the ISD, basically, those whom I knew had a strong social conscience and did not have a destructive political agenda," he told *The Straits Times* in 2001.[37] Tharman would go on to become deputy prime minister. Another establishment figure, legal scholar Walter Woon, who would serve as an ambassador and then briefly as attorney general, expressed his scepticism in 1991. "As far as I am concerned, the government's case is still not proven. I would not say those fellows were Red, not from the stuff they presented," he told *The Straits Times*.[38] Ironically, the ISA's obsolescence as a censorship tool was probably sealed in 2001, when it had to be used against a *bona fide* security threat. The discovery of a Jemaah Islamiyah cell plotting terrorist attacks and with links to Al Qaeda suddenly demanded a more judicious use of the ISA. At all costs, the authorities had to avoid giving Singapore's Muslims the impression that they were being targeted as a community. Its need for the support and cooperation of the wider Muslim community meant that the government had to act with precision and credibility. It could no longer apply the ISA in as loose and sweeping a fashion as in earlier decades, when anyone critical could be labelled a communist. In the past, it could be said that the government benefited from the climate of fear induced by an ill-defined ISA; post-2001, however, the authorities wanted the ISA to inspire public confidence, not paranoia. After decades of being perceived as a convenient political weapon, it would have to return to its security roots.

Cultivating a Compliant Press

David Held has suggested a useful 7-point scale indicating different reasons why people comply with authority. At one end of the continuum, there is "ideal normative agreement", where people comply with a decision because they believe it is the ideal outcome. At the other extreme, compliance is based on coercion — people have no choice but to accept it. In between are reasons such as instrumental acceptance (where people don't like it but recognise that it has some long-term benefit), pragmatic acquiescence (not ideal, but it seems like fate), apathy and tradition.[39] Every form of compliance can be found in each society, but the emphasis differs from society to society. A hegemonic regime such as the PAP can be expected to try to shift the basis of compliance for the majority of people away from coercion towards other points on the continuum. The ideological work described in Chapter 3 is one part of this process. Another is the cultivation of political apathy, through a steady depoliticisation of Singapore society. Political scientist Chan Heng Chee has studied this achievement of the PAP closely. It is not simply a matter of inducing fear or brainwashing the public — the most commonly heard explanations for Singapore's depoliticised public. Chan points instead to Lee Kuan Yew's success in turning potentially contentious politics into administrative questions, or what the PAP now likes to call "governance".[40] "The art of governance in Singapore became primarily an exercise in state management — resolving questions of how to achieve optimal utilization of scarce human and material resources," Chan said.[41]

What I suggest in this chapter is that, in addition to shifting from coercion to other forms of compliance such as pragmatic acquiescence or apathy, hegemonic regimes also choose among different modes of coercion. Coercion, represented as a single point on Held's scale, is itself a continuum. The coercive methods available to states span a wide range, varying in the actual amount of force used. Although practically all state actions, including administrative functions such as taxation, are ultimately underwritten by what Max Weber called the state's monopoly on the legitimate use of force, there are conceptually meaningful distinctions to be drawn between, say, imposing a fine on an opponent, imprisoning him, or triggering his "disappearance". Conway Henderson used a 5-point scale to rate the degree of political repression in various countries. The lowest value, 1, signified a country with a secure rule of law, in which people are not imprisoned for their views, torture is rare or exceptional, and political murders are extremely rare. At the other extreme, 5 signified a society characterised by terror: murders, disappearances and torture affect the whole population, with leaders placing no limits on how they pursue personal or ideological ends. Henderson rates Singapore as a "2", indicating that there is a limited amount of imprisonment for non-violent political activity, with few people affected; torture and beating is exceptional and political murder is rare. Henderson based these scores on the US State Department's human rights country reports for 1985.

Even Henderson's 5-point repression scale does not capture the full repertoire of coercive methods available to states. It focuses solely on violations of a range of rights associated with human dignity — the right to life, the right to the integrity of the person, prohibition of torture and inhuman or degrading treatment. These are rights that the

PAP recognises as universal. "Murder is murder whether perpetrated in America, Asia or Africa," said Singapore's foreign minister at the World Conference on Human Rights in 1993. "No one claims torture as part of their cultural heritage. Everyone has a right to be recognized as a person before the law."[42] Other types of coercion are regarded as much less heinous, though they may be no less powerful as means of censorship and control. These would include court-imposed jail sentences and fines, and publication bans and suspensions. Economic sanctions are not usually considered a form of repression and rarely figure in human rights reports, but they can be particularly effective as tools of censorship. A newspaper can be coerced into compliance by threatening non-renewal of its publishing licence, or withdrawing government advertising, or denying contracts for the publisher's other business interests. Where a government has a direct or indirect say in newsroom appointments, coercion can threaten the livelihoods and career prospects of individual reporters and editors. Threats can be multi-level, mutually-reinforcing and implicit. Journalists who know that their publisher would be powerless to resist the loss of his publishing permit might self-censor rather than put their careers at risk by acting in ways that jeopardise the publisher's relations with the government.

Censorship, whatever its mode, limits the right of listeners to receive information and ideas. Additionally, some forms of censorship — the murder or torture of media workers, for example — involve obvious violations of the sender's rights. More calibrated coercion, however, sometimes appears to have no such victims. For the censor, calibrated coercion minimises the sense of moral outrage that could be used to mobilise the public against the state. It also reduces the salience of coercion, making consensus seem like the sole basis for stability, thus strengthening hegemony. Finally, calibrated coercion preserves incentives for economic production and wealth creation, which rulers need as much as the ruled. Self-restraint in the use of coercion is a key reason for the PAP's success in winning over not just the majority of the public, but also most members of the press. The media system is kept at a dynamic equilibrium that balances the political interests of the PAP, the profit motives of publishers, the professional and pecuniary needs of journalists, and the public's demand for news and analysis. This does not mean that all these stakeholders are happy with the system, all of the time. But, neither the public nor journalists have been so provoked by PAP methods as to exercise their "power of exit" by boycotting establishment media *en masse*.

State-media relations in the early 1980s illustrate both the government's formidable power as well as its reluctance to push the press completely over the edge. In 1981, the PAP's 13-year absolute monopoly of Parliamentary seats was finally broken when J.B. Jeyaretnam of the Workers' Party won the Anson by-election. "The prime minister was furious with the *Straits Times*, in large part blaming its election coverage, including its reports of an intended rise in bus fares, for the loss of the seat," wrote Mary Turnbull, whose history of the newspaper was based on unprecedented access to company documents.[43] Lee had threatened to impose the drastic solution of dispatching government officials to take over day-to-day management of the papers. In order to avert this, chief executive Lyn Holloway and group editor Peter Lim requested an audience with the prime minister. Near the end of a series of meetings, the two newspapermen told Lee that they were planning to engage the services of S.R. Nathan as a kind of in-house expert on government. Nathan, an old acquaintance of Lim from their days working with labour unions, was about to retire from his post as permanent secretary in the foreign ministry. He had an unimpeachable record of loyal service to the state, having also served as director of military intelligence in the 1970s.

Lee saw the inch and took the yard: the trusted mandarin was to be appointed as executive chairman, no less. Nathan's memoirs, published in 2011, provide additional insights. He makes a point of stating that the decision to bring him was taken in September 1981 — suggesting that the government's unhappiness with *The Straits Times* predated the by-election defeat of that October. When he called on the prime minister before joining the company, Lee told him that Times House journalists were influenced by the "post-Watergate culture in the US" and "seeing sinister motives behind every government policy". These "little drops of venom would be disastrous for Singapore if allowed to continue". Lee did not mince words about Nathan's mission. "In his view," Nathan recalls, "the problem was essentially that some of the journalists had their own anti-government agenda. If he was right, then all that was needed was to identify them and deal with them on a disciplinary basis if they did not mend their ways. He repeated that he was willing to send in a government team to cut out the rot if necessary, and that he would give me a month to assess the situation."[44]

To Nathan, it was clear that the government and the national newspaper were on a "collision course", with a chance that *The Straits Times* would be completely revamped.[45] The evening before his move to the newspaper group, he met the prime minister again. Lee again expressed hope that his emissary would be able to manage the situation before the government found it necessary to send in its own team, acknowledging that the latter option would hurt the international credibility of the paper. "However, if it proved unavoidable he was prepared for it," Nathan writes, adding:

> As I walked to the door of his office, the prime minister called me back. I remember his words: 'Nathan — I am giving you the *Straits Times*. It has 150 years of history. It has been a good paper. It is like a bowl of china. If you can break it, I can piece it together. But it will never be the same. Try not to destroy it.'

After his first month, Nathan was supposed to recommend a remedy. Partly because he was given a wide berth by Times House staff and also because the inner workings of a newspaper turned out to be difficult to fathom, he asked the government for more time to get to the roots of the problem. However, he categorically rejected the need to remove staff arbitrarily and replace them with a government team. Eventually, he realised that the fundamental problem was not that the press had been captured by anti-government elements, but that it was sometimes genuinely difficult for journalists to answer to both government and readers. Any failure to understand government could not be addressed by simply removing editors and journalists. He also heeded S. Rajaratnam's advice not to try to become a "super-editor" and vet every controversial story. Rajaratnam, a former journalist and culture minister, pointed out that the volume of stories handled by a newspaper was simply too great. Nathan therefore opted for the more patient and painstaking approach of engaging journalists and trying to make them understand the government's point of view. He also tried to be sensitive to the editors' need to maintain their professional authority. Of course, there was no disguising the fact that his arrival represented a crossing of a line hitherto seen as sacred. Group editor Peter Lim was deeply conflicted about how to respond. He considered resigning soon after Nathan's appointment, and later actually did hand in his resignation but was persuaded to retract it. The departure of Singapore's senior-most editor would have been a strong vote of no-confidence in the government's handling of the press, possibly causing the kind of cracks in the proverbial china bowl that the prime minister preferred to avoid.

Some might say that editors should have indeed walked out, instead of allowing themselves to be co-opted. What is relevant to this chapter, though, is the political skill with which the government exercised its powers: Nathan and the political leaders he answered to calibrated their interventions in a way that would get their job done, but without forcing journalists to give up whatever shreds of professional dignity they had left. Nathan noted that he could not operate as if he were in government — his task was to "perform delicate surgery on an organisation made up of intelligent, opinionated and creative individuals".[46] Cheong Yip Seng, who took over from Peter Lim as group editor in 1986, recalled that Nathan "did not rely on clout, but reason".[47] And even Lim — who eventually had to step down when it was clear he no longer enjoyed the government's full support — would acknowledge that Nathan "knew perfectly well that that the way to get what he wanted done was by persuasion and not coercion".[48]

When Nathan arrived at the Straits Times group, opposition MP Jeyaretnam charged in Parliament that it was a case of "the censor moving into Times House".[49] But according to Turnbull, journalists' worst fears did not materialise. Nathan persuaded the government that the paper's leadership should stay, and he deliberately kept clear of the newsroom. He instead met informally with editors and reporters to help explain government thinking and to solicit feedback. He used "firm argument and quiet persuasion", acted as a buffer when there were problems with government, and gradually broke down the "barriers of suspicion" between press and state.[50] Ironically, though, Nathan's success in the mission Lee Kuan Yew had given him meant that the one-off pact that ST management had struck with the government in 1982 became a permanent arrangement. From henceforth, top corporate positions in the press were reserved for senior government figures who could give the political leadership additional peace of mind.

Singapore journalists' commitment to a fraught relationship was sustained partly by their knowledge that things could be a lot worse. The spectre of civil servants taking over the running of the newsroom would continue to haunt them. Equally crucial was their sense that aspects of the relationship were getting better. The government was gradually professionalising its media relations, acknowledging that the quality and accuracy of Singapore journalism depended partly on timely and thorough answers from officials. To keep journalists appraised of government thinking, editors and reporters are invited to background briefings and chats. At such meetings, journalists may get valuable early clues about planned government moves. (As is always the case in close relationships between news media and newsmakers — the question of who's using whom has no simple answer.)

Two similar events, 12 years apart, illustrate how coercion evolved into cooperation. Both events were fatal accidents involving the armed forces. The first was a helicopter crash in an air base in 1991, which killed all four men on board. *The New Paper* went well beyond Mindef's brief official statement to include additional information about the aircraft and speculation about the cause of the crash based on "informed sources". A furious Defence Ministry demanded that the paper reveal its sources and threatened to prosecute editor P.N. Balji under the Essential (Control of Publications and Safeguarding of Information) Regulations 1966. SPH backed Balji's decision to protect the paper's sources. The ugly stand-off ended with the government, having made its point, contenting itself with the imposition of a $12,000 fine. Mindef's own investigations found that an officer and two non-commissioned officers had been guilty of unauthorised disclosures to *The New Paper*. They were slapped with the maximum fines.[51]

Then, in 2003, the navy vessel *RSS Courageous* sank with the loss of four female sailors after a collision with a commercial vessel just after midnight. Mindef's public communication was markedly different from 1991. Reporters from *Today* and the Associated Press called Mindef, which confirmed that an accident had occurred but explained that full details were not available yet. *Today* — coincidentally edited by Balji — printed a 3 a.m. edition with a lead story that contained information from non-Mindef sources. This time, there was no question of shooting the messenger. Mindef decided to be as open and transparent about the incident as possible. Within 12 hours of the incident, Defence Minister Tony Tan was chairing the government's first press conference on the tragedy. He granted reporters a door-stop interview later the same day. Mindef issued 12 news releases over the first three days. Reporters and photographers were also given access to helicopters and a vessel involved in the search and recovery operations.

One reason why Mindef was forced to be more open about the 2003 incident is that it occurred in international waters and involved a commercial vessel, whereas the 1991 accident took place within its own air base. Nevertheless, it is probably fair to say that in between the two tragedies, Mindef's approach to bad news had also grown more sophisticated. The change was not due to any shift in power from government to press — the laws were still as strict. Rather, the government realised that it could sometimes be in its own enlightened self-interest to be more open, given a changing citizenry. Three years before the *Courageous* accident, Mindef's permanent secretary Peter Ho had said that excessive secrecy could undermine confidence in the armed forces. As a citizen's armed forces, it would have to respond to the evolving social norms in favour of greater transparency and consultation, he said.[52] Whatever the reasons for such shifts, the net effect for the press was that it became easier to report on many stories. It became easier to overlook the iron fist beneath the velvety media release.

Like all authoritarian governments, the PAP coveted the media's power as a propaganda tool. Broadcasting was seized for this purpose. Unlike most authoritarian rulers, however, Lee Kuan Yew recognised that he could only use newspapers effectively if he allowed them to retain some credibility, which would be crushed if his grip was too tight. Consumers of news in Singapore may complain about the standard of news media and voice concerns about their independence. However, the PAP has not abused its power over the press to such an extent that large numbers boycott the mainstream media and flee in droves to alternative websites, like what happened in Malaysia during the Reformasi period.[53] Indeed, Garry Rodan observes that Singapore's media policy may have been partly influenced by a conscious desire to avoid Malaysia's mistakes.[54] Admittedly, this is the kind of observation that enrages critical Singaporeans who would never concede that their press has any credibility. One hears many anecdotes of Singaporeans who have cancelled their newspaper subscriptions in disgust. A leaked 2004 diplomatic cable from the United States embassy in Singapore said, "The docile press even draws the scorn of some members of the elite. One senior MFA [Singapore Ministry of Foreign Affairs] official reportedly threatened to demote any official he found reading the *Straits Times*." However, the fact remains that audited figures show newspaper circulation trends in Singapore to be healthier than those of the free press in mature markets. Declines in newspaper sales seem to reflect changes in reading habits that are also happening in free countries, rather than any increase in political disaffection. Singapore's press, though it is stopped from championing popular issues, has been allowed just enough freedom to serve as a generally reliable source of relevant information for the public.

Unique Capacities

If indeed calibrated coercion is a rational strategy for authoritarian states that want to consolidate their power, the wonder is why it is not more common than it is. It turns out that calibrated coercion is not simple to apply, and only works in certain circumstances. First, leaders would only have the incentive to restrain themselves if they have an interest in the long term. The American economist Mancur Olson has argued that when autocratic rulers have encompassing interests, they are more likely to contain their abuses.[55] Even a Mafia family, in total control of its neighbourhood, knows better than to engage in unrestrained criminal acts within its territory, since this would diminish the community's ability to generate profits, leaving the gang less to cream off, Olson notes.[56] If they care only about the short term — like roving bandits, invading militia with no interest in holding territory, or political leaders who expect to be ousted before long — there is less reason to curb their rapacious instincts. The PAP exemplifies the paradox that a dominant party, after drawing on illiberal methods to entrench itself, can generate self-enforcing limits to its use of coercion in order to further consolidate its power. This logic may also apply to China, Vietnam and other countries with dominant or monopolistic parties.

Second, calibrated coercion in Singapore was possible only after access to the political arena was restricted to a limited number of players. Whether it was the press, trade unions or student bodies, for example, unrestricted access allowed the entry of actors who had diverse agendas and could not be easily disciplined. To render these groups amenable to subtler carrots and sticks, they had to be rationalised and streamlined. Third, such restructuring required a period of repression. Repression worked like rebooting a computer, stopping all activity in its tracks and allowing the installation of a new operating system that rendered any incompatible feature obsolete. A history of overt repression — never punished, disavowed or subject to any truth-and-reconciliation process — also makes calibrated coercion more effective because it leaves its targets in no doubt that the state would be prepared to use greater force if gentler prodding is not heeded.

Fourth, restructuring of the press and other spheres was only possible with the kind of monopoly of power that the PAP enjoyed in Parliament. The new laws that were installed were radical and far-reaching, yet enacted with little fuss. Even the highly controversial Maintenance of Religious Harmony Bill — which detoured through Select Committee hearings for greater public consultation — was passed within five months of its first reading in Parliament.

Fifth, the government needs to be able to exercise tight civilian control over the instruments of coercion, namely the military and police. Without such discipline, there would be random cases of brutality that backfire on the state — such as the black eye that Anwar Ibrahim received from the Malaysian police while in custody. In Singapore, there are close ties between the largely conscript uniformed services and the political elite. Prime Minister Lee Hsien Loong and other members of his Cabinet were inducted from high-ranking positions in the military. However, the military as such has little political clout. Armed forces chiefs are changed every few years, allowing them no chance to build an autonomous power base. Domestically, the army is viewed as a benign and professional force that helps to organise national celebrations, for example. As for the police, cases with possible political fallout are handled delicately. Activists and politicians who have been called up for police interviews generally report that they are treated politely. Even the feared Internal Security Department is reported to have refrained from any roughhouse tactics in its interrogations of suspected terrorists, to avoid losing the hearts and minds of Singapore's Muslims.

Sixth, the least visible forms of coercion are those that use instruments that the public assumes are somehow natural and outside of the ruler's control — in particular the invisible hand of the market, and the anonymous workings of technology.[57] The PAP has been adept at calibrating coercion because of its confident embrace of both market forces and new technology. It recognises that neither necessarily poses a threat to political control — contrary to naïve libertarian arguments. It has avoided frequent and visible coercive intervention in the media by structuring the newspaper market — and later the architecture of the internet — in ways that predetermine the range of possible outcomes, which are then attributed to commercial or technological realities.

Seventh, success in calibrated coercion requires a certain degree of meta-censorship: censorship of information about the exercise of censorship. Since any act of censorship, even if it uses gentle methods, can potentially backfire on the state,[58] there are advantages to hiding the act from public view. Therefore, media regulators require media organisations to keep mum about instructions they receive. Sometimes, this requirement is explicitly stated in rulings. But newspaper editors are simply expected to have the good sense to stay silent — and if necessary defend editorial decisions as having been made independently. An editor that publicises government intervention would be seen as unsuitable for the post, on account of not sharing the government's perspective and attempting to rally public opinion against the country's elected leaders. Meta-censorship would be harder to achieve in larger countries with more media players, such as China.

The PAP is unusual in its capacity to practise calibrated coercion. It may even be unique. Singapore's small geographic size greatly helps the PAP achieve tight control over armed services and other institutions that are potential opponents. Singapore's economic success also makes the PAP better placed than most authoritarian regimes to calibrate its coercion. The literature on violent dissent and repression tells us that both are tempered by rapid and equitable economic growth.[59] Singapore continues to enjoy low unemployment and a high standard of living, reducing the social cleavages around which violent discord could develop. The PAP has benefited from a virtuous circle of increased stability and material comfort, reduced repression and dissent, and strengthened hegemony. A crash course from Lee Kuan Yew is unlikely to be enough to allow the likes of China and Malaysia to replicate Singapore's success in this regard.

CHAPTER 6

The Harmony Myth: Asian Media's Radical Past

When I was working at *The Straits Times* (*ST*), it was not uncommon to hear scorn being expressed in the newsroom for the country's Chinese newspapers. In covering government news, *Lianhe Zaobao* was even more likely than *ST* to choose angles that served the government's agenda. While we English-language journalists liked to think of ourselves as trying to apply professional news judgment to the coverage of officials' speeches and press releases, our colleagues in the Chinese media seemed content to report such statements "straight". The difference extended to the papers' use of photographs. By the 1990s, *ST* photojournalists and picture editors were aspiring to the highest international standards of pictorial storytelling, with a preference for compelling, candid and creative human-interest images. We thumbed our noses at the "firing squad" photos that would appear routinely in *Lianhe Zaobao*: officials standing in a row and smiling stiffly at forgettable media events. We saw the Chinese press — as well as the Malay daily, *Berita Harian* — as less professional. (The Tamil paper, *Tamil Murasu*, was so small it barely entered our consciousness.) Signals from the government only served to support such stereotypes about the non-English press. Their coverage would be cited approvingly when officials chided *ST*. At the 150th anniversary celebrations of *The Straits Times*, then-premier Goh Chok Tong said affectionately of *Lianhe Zaobao* and *Berita Harian*, "Their headlines of important policy speeches appear to come straight from the shoulders of the Ministers." In contrast, he said, *ST* went for "human interest", slipped its own viewpoint into the presentation of stories, and revealed unnecessary "self-doubt about the Singaporean approach to problems".[1]

Explicitly or implicitly, the rhetorical question would be asked: if the Chinese and Malay press can get the angle "right", why can't you? The government's interpretation of this regrettable state of affairs was that Singapore's English press had been colonised by inappropriate Western norms, while its Asian-language media remained steeped in Asian values. "The journalists working in the English medium are particularly buffeted by ideas from the Western world," Goh said.[2] In his memoirs, Lee Kuan Yew said that the English-language press, influenced by first British and then American ideals, was "always sceptical and cynical of authority". In contrast, the Chinese and Malay newspapers reflected different principles: their "cultural practice is for constructive support of policies they agree with, and criticism in measured terms when they do not". Lee added: "Chinese-educated readers do not have the same political and social values as the English-educated. They place greater emphasis on the interests of the group than those of the individual."[3]

Essentialised notions of culture, with their sweeping generalisations, are rightly treated with suspicion by scholars. Yet, the kind of theory pushed by the People's Action Party has been echoed by many observers. Media studies have been relatively hospitable to the idea that perceived differences in journalistic practices might be explained by differences in culture. One book on normative theories of the media makes this connection in its introduction, attributing Southeast Asian democracies' "more consensual and less contestatory media policy" to "their underlying religious and cultural consensus".[4] Singapore has been described as something of an archetype of an illiberal "Asian" model of journalism.[5] The theory entertained by these Western media scholars is similar to the PAP's. It basically goes like this: Asian values (harmony and respect for authority) and Western values (confrontation and contestation) compete for influence over journalism; these values explain why Singapore journalism is tamer than Western journalism, and why, within the Singapore press, the more Westernised English-language press is bolder than Asian-language journalism.

There is one problem with this orthodox account. History. A cursory look at press and politics of the past challenges the stereotypes and disturbs the lazy consensus of conventional wisdom. History reveals that for most of the 20th century, until the PAP entrenched itself as a hegemonic regime, Singapore was replete with contentious journalism, expressing radical critiques of prevailing power centres. Journalism directed at building a harmonious consensus and supporting the *status quo* formed just one strand in a plural media environment. Nor was contentious journalism limited to — or even most apparent in — English-language newspapers, as the Asian values theory would predict. Instead, it was the Asian-language media that were most radically adversarial. When mainstream journalism became more conservative, this was not the result of journalists discovering their "Asian" values. It was partly due to a growing recognition of the PAP's competence and credibility in government. As for journalists who were too slow to appreciate the merits of the PAP, it was coercion more than culture that conservatised them.

Consider the identities of the several Singapore journalists who were detained without trial under the Internal Security Act — that most draconian of instruments, ostensibly reserved for the most serious threats to peace and harmony. Based on contemporary cultural stereotypes, one might guess that these ISA detainees were the Westernised staff of the English press. In fact, since independence, none of the detainees were from the domestic English-language media. All were Chinese or Malay media personnel. The Chinese dailies *Sin Chew Jit Poh* and *Nanyang Siang Pau* saw a string of their staff arrested under the ISA, culminating with the decapitation of *Nanyang Siang Pau*'s leadership in the early 1970s. Its publisher was detained without trial for five years. In 1976, the editor and assistant editor of *Berita Harian* were arrested. The journalist who served the longest period in detention — 17 years — was also from the Malay press. Said Zahari had been the editor of the influential Malay daily, *Utusan Melayu*, before he entered politics, and was editing the Malay newsletter of the opposition party Barisan Nasional around the time that he was arrested. This radical past of Singapore's Asian-language press has been so erased, even from memory, that its current conservative character is assumed to be timeless — the product of deep cultural traits or even genetic predispositions, rather than historical context. Why Asian journalism was once so problematic for the PAP and how it was subsequently re-oriented is an important part of the story of Singapore's media system. It is also among the least talked about. That is the gap that this chapter aims to fill.

Early Chinese-language Journalism

In keeping with the marginality of this topic, probably the best account of Singapore's early Chinese press was written by another former political detainee. Linda Chen Mong Hock was a dynamic young teacher and activist detained first by the British colonial government in 1956 (her lawyer was Lee Kuan Yew) and then again in Operation Coldstore. On her release, she entered graduate school. Her thesis on the history of Chinese newspapers was published in 1967. She would go on to run a bookshop for many years, dying in 2003.[6] Her book paints a picture of a press reflective of tumultuous times. Singapore's first Chinese-language newspaper was *Lat Pau* (1881–1932). Although seen as pro-British, it characterised itself as neutral and independent, striving for the kind of objectivity that was gaining ground in Anglo-American journalism at that time. Yeh Chi-yun, its chief writer for 40 of the paper's 51 years of existence, expressed his belief in the principle of professional detachment: "The one inside the newspaper is 'I'; the one outside the newspaper is also 'I'. However I will not bring the outside 'I' into this paper; neither will I remove the inside 'I' out. The reason is that ... the inside 'I' belongs to the community."[7] In another editorial, he stated that the newspaper is "a public institution": "It has no opinions except those of the public. It maintains no right or wrong except the rights and wrong of the public."[8]

The publication of Chinese-language newspapers with explicitly ideological aims dates back to at least 1898, with the launch of the short-lived *Thien Nan Shin Pao*. According to Chen, its publishers "consciously made the newspaper a propaganda machine for a *cause*, which in this case was Chinese nationalism and reform".[9] While the *Thien Nan Shin Pao* lasted only until 1905, its ideological brand of Chinese journalism survived for several decades more. In the early 20th century, Chinese newspapers reflected the political upheavals in China. Singapore, a distant colonial port in the southern seas, represented a safe haven from which overseas Chinese could launch campaigns in support of one side or another in the violently polarised politics of the motherland. The *Nanyang Chung Wei Pao* and the *Chong Shing Yit Pao*, both founded in 1906, backed the reformists and revolutionaries respectively in the battle to control China. In 1929, the *Sin Chew Jit Poh* was launched with the assurance that "the newspaper would regard it as its duty to attack anyone who goes against the

Kuomintang to mislead China".[10] With the rise of the Chinese Communist Party and the founding of the People's Republic, leftist newspapers surfaced in Singapore. The *Nan Chiaw Daily*, founded by philanthropist Tan Kah Kee in 1946, was banned by the British colonial authorities under Emergency regulations in 1950. Two years later, *Sin Poh* picked up the torch for communism, republishing reports from the New China News Agency. In 1957, its publisher and four reporters were arrested as part of an anti-communist swoop.[11]

The *Nanyang Siang Pau*, launched in 1923 by Tan Kah Kee, became the leading Chinese-language paper of Malaya (the region comprising the peninsular portion of what is today called Malaysia as well as the island of Singapore). Almost immediately, it was slapped with a three-month ban by the colonial authorities for getting involved in party politics.[12] While generally representing Chinese commercial interests, it allowed its editors and reporters to express diverse viewpoints.[13] One beneficiary of this latitude in the 1950s was chief reporter Lee Khoon Choy. He followed the PAP, then in opposition, with growing admiration. "I was convinced that [Labour Front leader] David Marshall's days as Chief Minister were numbered. So I played up news on the PAP and ran down Marshall and his cohorts," he wrote in his memoirs.[14] He became a PAP candidate in 1959 and left journalism for a distinguished career in politics and government.

The interests of his erstwhile employer, however, did not converge with those of the ruling party. The PAP was pragmatically wedded to British and American corporate interests, seeing them — and consequently the English language — as necessary vehicles for rapid economic development. The party's leaders were themselves largely English-educated professionals. Although most were Chinese, they had little in common culturally with Singapore's Chinese-speaking businessmen, merchants and workers or the Chinese literati — for whose interests Chinese-language newspapers were passionate champions. Before independence, such groups, together with their media, formed the single most powerful force in the anti-colonial movement. After independence, their ire was directed at government policies that were seen as shortchanging the language and culture of Singapore's numerical majority. Things boiled over in 1971, in a way that once again belied Lee Kuan Yew's later theories about Asian values and the respectful Chinese-language press. "The *Nanyang Siang Pau* openly and directly attacked the government and Lee personally," writes historian Edwin Lee. "Its game plan was, apparently, to overawe the government which it charged with killing Chinese language and culture, and to push for Mandarin to be made the language of administration and the law courts, and of official publications like the Government Gazette."[15]

Prime Minister Lee accused the Chinese-language press of stoking up chauvinism. In April 1971, a *Sin Chew Jit Poh* journalist was hauled in. Then, in the early hours of 2 May, four *Nanyang Siang Pau* executives were arrested: general manager Lee Mau Seng, chief editor Tung Tao Chang, editorial writer Ly Singko and personnel manager Quek Loong Seng.[16] Denying the charges, the paper published a blank editorial column under the headline, "Our Protest". *Nanyang Siang Pau*'s recalcitrance may have been partly due to "Asian" family values: since Lee Mau Seng was the brother of the publisher, the newspaper may have considered the arrest "a question of family honour which required public vindication", as one commentator at the time put it.[17] Lee Mau Seng would be freed only two years and five months later. The *coup de grace* came in January 1973, when the publisher himself, Lee Eu Seng, was arrested. His publishing permit was revoked and he was released only five years later. It took new legislation in the 1970s and government intervention in the ownership of the Chinese papers to tame a decades-old tradition of politicised journalism.

Early Malay-language Journalism

If activism was an organic part of Chinese-language journalism, this was even truer of its Malay-language cousin. "The cornerstone of activism in the Malay community was journalism," write Timothy Barnard and Jan van der Putten in their account of the post-war period.[18] Singapore's first non-English newspaper was the *Jawi Peranakan*, founded in 1876. Early 20th-century titles such as *Al-Imam*, *Utusan Melayu* and *Lembaga Melayu* reflected the community's strong interest in Islam.[19] Malay newspapers were a forum for important debates in the pre-war period, such as the role of Islam and the status of Chinese and Indian immigrants.[20] They were influenced by the journalism of neighbouring Indonesia, where the nationalist struggle against Dutch colonialism was more violent than Malaya's against the British. Indonesia's journalism was accordingly more radical. Singapore's journalistic community after 1945 included many followers and sympathisers of the pan-Malayan Unity movement that had arisen in Indonesia.[21] Influenced by the Angkatan 45 (Generation of 45) group, these writers believed that a new society could be created through activist-oriented literature. "Journalists saw their duty in this context as one in which they could actively fight for the independence of the nation in terms that were not only political but also in relation to issues of modernity," note Barnard and van der Putten.[22]

Utusan Melayu, revived by Yusof Ishak in 1939 after an 18-year hiatus, emerged as the leading newspaper for the Malay community in the post-war period. Its maiden issue pledged to work for religion, people and country: "These three causes are what the *Utusan Melayu* stands for and these *Utusan Melayu* will live for and will fight to the death for."[23] It was a magnet for Malay intellectuals opposed to colonial rule. Yusof Ishak, who served as editor and general manager, confidently proclaimed in a 1948 *Utusan* article that Malaya would be free of British colonial rule within ten years.[24] Another key figure, Said Zahari, wrote of the newsroom that he joined in 1951: "The editors and other journalists in *Utusan* of that time ... were anti-colonial Malay nationalists. They were simultaneously journalists and political activists, with the vision and mission of restoring the honour and independence of the Malays after decades of British colonial rule."[25] It was also a revolutionary paper with a socialist mission.[26] A colonial government report put it simply: "Nationalist. Left-Wing. Sympathetic to Indonesian cause: Critical of official policy in Federation of Malaya."[27] In 1951, *Utusan* editor A. Samad Ismail was arrested for his involvement with the radical Anti-British League Movement, after which the paper and its journalists were placed under surveillance. "All sorts of pressures were put on the leadership of the *Utusan Melayu* to support colonial government policy in Malaya and Singapore," notes Said Zahari. Nevertheless, the paper continued with its independent stand.[28] When Said Zahari took over as editor in 1959, the year Singapore won self-rule, he "resolved to hold fast the original policy of the paper, i.e. to serve religion, people and country, besides defending press freedom in general".[29]

As with Singapore's Chinese press, the anti-colonial cause made bedfellows of Malay journalists who would go separate ways after self-government was achieved. They differed on how best to serve their Malay community within the new context of post-colonial multi-ethnic national politics and an economy that was increasingly capitalist. This divergence was demonstrated in the contrasting careers of Yusof Ishak and A. Samad Ismail. They shared a common pride in *Utusan* as a symbol of the Malays, and as one of the few genuine Malay businesses in Malaya.[30] "For two decades, Samad Ismail and Yusof Ishak had symbolized the greatness and indomitable spirit of the *Utusan Melayu* as an independent national paper serving the Malays and the struggle for independence," Said Zahari observed.[31] However, their roles in self-governing Singapore could not have been more different. Upon the birth of the State of Singapore, Yusuf Ishak's part in the anti-colonial movement was amply recognised. In 1959, he was appointed Singapore's first post-colonial head of state. The visage of President Yusuf now appears on all Singapore currency notes. As for Samad Ismail, he, too, was close to the PAP: indeed, he was one of its founders. However, he fell out with Lee Kuan Yew and left Singapore for Kuala Lumpur, where he led an illustrious career as an editor. He had politics in his blood but did not leave mainstream professional journalism. This, noted one observer, was not for want of passion for politics or due to a professional desire to remain disinterested. Rather, it was because he never underestimated the influence of the press: Samad was "a case of someone sitting in the Cabinet by proxy".[32]

Of all the *Utusan*'s luminary journalists, Said Zahari's reckoning with post-colonial realities was the most painful. He was arrested during the Operation Coldstore swoop of 1963. He would spend 17 years in detention without trial, the longest period for a journalist and almost as long as any other Singapore activist. In 1976, *Berita Harian* editor Hussein Jahidin and assistant editor Nahar Azmi Mahmud were arrested for allegedly sowing discontent and propagating communist thinking among Malays. The plot was allegedly masterminded by one A. Samad Ismail.

A New Journalism for Stable Times

Adversarial, contentious journalism was thus an integral part of Singapore's nationalist awakening — not least in the Asian-language press. It was not a marginal phenomenon. Its diverse practitioners staked their claims in the centre of the public square, helping to embolden and empower Singapore's various communities. Occasionally, some were so consumed by their desire to rally their particular communities that they verged on the sectarian and chauvinistic. *Melayu Raya*, the voice of the radical Malay Nationalist Party, was one example. Its founder Dr Burhanuddin argued that the Malays were the rightful owners of the country.[33] It showed its colours in 1950, when reporting the custody tussle between a girl's natural Dutch mother and her adoptive Malay mother, who raised her as a Muslim. The case led to what came to be known as the Maria Hertogh Riots, in which seven Europeans and Eurasians and two policemen were killed by mobs incensed by the court's refusal to remove the girl from a convent and return her to her adoptive family. Newspapers had published photographs of her at the convent, surrounded by Christian symbols. During the subsequent commission of inquiry, the solicitor-general said that *Melayu Raya*, together with an Indian Muslim newspaper, *Malaya Namban*, had helped to instigate the violence. They had framed the case as a battle between Islam and Christianity, goading Muslims to defend their faith. *Melayu Raya* was banned through most of 1951.[34] The case was also mishandled by clueless colonial authorities, in ways unlikely to be repeated by a government accountable to its people. The Maria Hertogh Riots would cast a long shadow over journalism in Singapore. Its ghost would continue to be summoned through the decades to justify a policy of low tolerance for media freedom.

Putting aside extreme speech and incitement, a pluralistic media environment was simply not helpful to the PAP's hegemonic mission after independence. In the PAP's vision, there was no place for either leftist or ethnic based passions, or any kind of dissent, for that matter. Thus, groups that thought they were on the winning side in the battle against colonialism found themselves in danger of being marginalised again, this time by the PAP's hardnosed social and economic strategies. For Malay-Muslims, there was the additional trauma of Singapore's separation from Malaysia in 1965. Overnight, the community was turned into a small minority of under 15 per cent. Conveniently for the PAP, the most strident champion of Malay-Muslim rights, *Utusan Melayu*, had migrated in 1958 to Kuala Lumpur, capital of the newly-independent Federation of Malaya. From there, it would cultivate a strongly anti-PAP editorial slant, but as a foreign newspaper it had a diminishing influence in Singapore. Indeed, *Utusan*'s coverage betrayed its anti-Singapore bias so patently that its biggest impact was probably to contribute to the young republic's ideology of vulnerability and strengthen the sense of nationalism among its citizens, including Malay-Muslim Singaporeans. Although Malaysian newspapers are not allowed to circulate in Singapore and *vice versa*, *Utusan* commentaries are occasionally republished in the Singapore press to remind the public that the threat of Malay-Muslim chauvinism from across the border remains real. After *Utusan*'s exit from Singapore, the remaining

Malay-language daily, *Berita Harian*, became the *de facto* national Malay newspaper. Being part of the Straits Times group rather than an independently-owned Malay business like *Utusan*, it was never likely to project the community's interests in shrill tones.

While the minority status of ethnic Malays and Indians is obvious, many Chinese-speaking Singaporeans also felt marginalised by the PAP's linguistic and economic policies. Restive Malays and Indians might create a security threat, but only the Chinese community had the numbers to pose a potential electoral challenge to the PAP's development model. Therefore, in the early years of independence, it was Singapore's Chinese-language newspapers that were in most urgent need of re-education. The city-state was to be based on racial and religious equality with English as the working language, built on multinational investments and a disciplined workforce, and organised with bureaucratic rationality and market logic. Perhaps a free marketplace of ideas would have eventually led to the same outcome, and Singapore society would have left behind incompatible ideologies, arriving spontaneously at the consensus that the PAP was striving for. After all, PAP leaders would later claim that the choices before a small and newly independent Singapore were so constrained that any intelligent person would come to the same conclusions. Evidently, however, the PAP did not trust the press or the people enough to let them converge on those conclusions independently. It enforced compliance by using its sweeping discretionary powers — bequeathed by the British colonialists and refined over decades of monopoly control over the legislature.

After the 1971 crackdown, the Newspaper and Printing Presses Act (NPPA) of 1974 meant that Singapore would never again see the likes of the family publishers of the intractable *Nanyang Siang Pau*. "I do not subscribe to the Western practice that allows a wealthy press baron to decide what voters should read day after day," Lee Kuan Yew would later say, in keeping with his cultural narrative that portrays Asian press values as being more accommodating to power.[35] Management shares were allocated to stability-loving financial institutions and other members of the business establishment, insulating them from the values of idiosyncratic individual owners and reorienting them towards profit (Chapter 2). "They would remain politically neutral and protect stability and growth because of their business interests," Lee explained.[36] Accordingly, Lien Ying Chow, chairman of one of Singapore's Big Four banks, was in 1978 appointed chairman of Nanyang

Press, *Nanyang Siang Pau*'s publisher. As an additional check against headstrong newspapermen, trusted public servants were inserted into boards of directors. Before this practice was institutionalised in the English press, it was introduced in the Chinese media: the prime minister's press secretary, James Fu, was appointed to the five-man board of Nanyang Press in 1978. The promotion of a selective version of Asian values to further conservatise the press came much later — only after the Asian journalism's legacy of feistiness was no more. Western-style commercial structures were used to tame the radical tradition in Asian journalism.

Lee regularly expressed contempt for supposedly freedom-loving newspapers' slavish focus on the financial bottom line. But he also realised that the worst profit-seeking newspapers were those that couldn't find it. This explains his anxiety to secure a viable living for the national press. The same government that could not abide fiercely independent Chinese newspapers was equally concerned about the prospect of their decline into oblivion as the use of English spread. Multi-lingualism was a key pledge of the Singaporean social contract and newspapers in the four official languages had to be preserved. Furthermore, newspapers fighting for their survival tended to become more sensational and irresponsible, Lee believed. His government therefore sought to place the troubled Chinese press on a secure financial footing. In 1982, it engineered the merger of *Nanyang Siang Pau* and *Sin Chew Jit Poh* under a new holding company, Singapore News and Publications Limited (SNPL). The following year, the two papers were reorganised and rebranded as *Lianhe Zaobao* and *Lianhe Wanbao*.

To improve its viability, SNPL was granted a licence to publish an English newspaper, *Singapore Monitor*. Rather than build it from scratch, SNPL would take over the Straits Times group's afternoon paper, *New Nation*. "The government told the Straits Times that, since it was in the national interest for the Chinese group to publish an English paper, the Straits Times itself should help the new rival to a good start," Turnbull writes.[37] This "bombshell", as she describes it, was followed by a bigger one. In 1984, the two groups were merged into a single newspaper behemoth, Singapore Press Holdings. Journalists protested, but to no avail. Those who favoured a more diverse and competitive industry structure were up against not only an all-powerful state but also a global economic trend: increasing concentration of more and more titles in the hands of fewer and fewer owners was the norm in the newspaper industry.[38] Once again, the PAP was not working against market forces, but selectively harnessing and accentuating them.

The New Framework

Post-NPPA, the press shed a number of its old characteristics, for better and for worse. The most consequential change was to its nation-building role. If the pre-independence press believed in nation building, it did not have a clear and consistent idea of exactly what kind of nation was being built. "Only the English press transcended race, but its main interest was to safeguard British values and traditions," notes one historian. "Newspapers in the other languages expressed the views of their respective ethnic groups and helped to shape their outlooks."[39] Since most adults were immigrants, their loyalties — and those of the newspapers that served them — were divided between their new home and their motherlands. Then, in the postwar period, many newspapers assumed — along with most politicians, including in the PAP — that they were building a larger Malayan nation of which Singapore would be a part. In the course of the 1970s, the PAP focused the newspapers' nation-building energies on the Singapore project. It was an act of political leadership that with hindsight most Singaporeans would agree the PAP was duty-bound to undertake.

A second change was the quashing of the idea of the press as an independent guardian of the public interest. Up until 1971, mainstream newspaper editors believed they had a right to contest the government's interpretation of the national interest. They tried to uphold a difference between being pro-Singapore and pro-government, and insisted on the value of strong criticism of government. "The point is that no feedback is worth a damn unless it is straight from the shoulder. And straight-from-the-shoulder feedback can only be gathered honestly," said the *Herald*'s founding editor, Francis Wong, two months after the closure of his newspaper.[40] *Nanyang Siang Pau* publisher Lee Eu Seng declared around the same time that "in Singapore, the newspapers have a clear and definite duty to bring to the attention of the Government (since there is no opposition in Parliament to do so) the wishes, criticisms and legitimate grievances of the general public".[41] This was possibly the last time that a mainstream Singapore newspaper would suggest that its role was to stand in for an absent opposition. While editors continued to profess a pro-Singapore — not pro-PAP — policy, they ceased claiming any right to define being pro-Singapore in terms that conflicted with the PAP's broad agenda. By 1995, historian Mary Turnbull was able to write that the parameters within which the press operates had been settled. "The press accepts the premise that it is not the Fourth Estate and has not been elected as politicians have."[42]

Third, Singapore witnessed the delegitimisation of non-commercial motives for newspaper publication. This may seem a curious statement to those familiar with PAP politicians' frequent sermonising against the excesses of market-driven media. Rhetoric aside, however, the PAP's policies elevated the profit motive to a status never before seen in Singapore's media history. Prior to the NPPA, it was common for newspapers to be published at a loss by proprietors who craved prestige and influence more than revenue. The pioneering Chinese-language paper *Lat Pau* was more of a patriotic venture than an entrepreneurial one.[43] Linda Chen noted that "for the sake of propagating their ideas, the proprietors of these papers were prepared to pour money down the drain".[44] Looking back in time from the more capitalist 1960s, Chen found the behaviour of these publishers "astonishing". After 1974, newspaper companies had to be publicly listed, such that their directors were obliged to serve shareholders, not causes. Following the tradition of those early publishers would not be just astonishing, but also impossible.

Closely related to the delegitimisation of non-commercial motives for newspaper publication was a fourth development: the elevation of objectivity — or at least a highly instrumentalised version of it — as the gold standard for journalism. The earlier press, not just in Singapore but worldwide, included a strong partisan streak.[45] One unintended consequence of the way objectivity was ritualistically applied in newsrooms, starting in the West, was that it led reporters to pick sources that society at large considered authoritative — mainly elite newsmakers (Chapter 3).[46] This would be less of a problem in a plural democracy with multiple voices within the elite. But, in a highly centralised political system such as Singapore's, objective journalism would magnify the already-loud government voice. It is not surprising, therefore, that the PAP government has asked the press to be objective: "The local media's role is to report the news accurately, factually and objectively for Singaporeans," one information minister declared. He added that it would be "inappropriate … for the media to editorialise in its reporting of the news" — a distinction that was not observed in the past.[47] Arguably, therefore, the net effect of Westernisation on the Singapore press has been a conservative one, thanks to the twin imports of professional objectivity and commercial organisation, and the marginalisation of more cause-driven and polemical journalism.

Uses and Abuses of History

History does not just belong in the past; it can have powerful consequences for the present and future. The history of journalism is no exception. Historical analysis can help remove analytical blinkers: it can "challenge certain orthodoxies about journalism" and "redress the givens of old", as journalism scholar Barbie Zelizer notes.[48] Journalists are notorious for their lack of critical reflection on why they do what they do the way they do it. There is a tendency towards post-hoc justification: taking what happens to be the case — the professionalised, corporatised, and commercialised nature of mainstream journalism — as not just the way things are but also how things should be. It is comforting to imagine that journalism as we know it is the result of the profession's moral progress and a societal consensus over what is collectively valued. Yet, decades of sociological inquiry reveal much more prosaic forces at play, from the organisational requirements of newswork to political economy and the technological modes of production (Chapter 3).

Authoritarian governments have an interest in delegitimising journalism's more politically engaged strands. Where the state successfully extinguishes these radical forms of journalism, it next wants to erase all memory of it, privileging the professional value of disinterestedness as if that which remains is all there ever was and all there ever shall be. To ignore history is to aid and abet efforts to turn journalism into an instrument of power and to tame its more radical tendencies. This is part of the ideological purpose of Singapore's official narrative, including its loud silences. Thus, Lee Kuan Yew's account of his media management in his memoirs relishes the recollection of his battles with the Western media, but makes no mention of the 1971 crackdown against *Nanyang Siang Pau*.[49]

How the story of Singapore journalism is constructed is also relevant to the country's broader history. The sanitisation of Singapore's press history is part of a larger process of national myth-making. Since coming into power, the PAP's leaders have had to work hard to resolve a fundamental political contradiction: that their fiercest opponents were closer than they were to their own mass base. Lee and his comrades were Westernised and hyper-rational, quite different from the non-English-educated majority. "This ideological gulf had most poignantly manifest itself within the PAP and resulted in a fierce and divisive battle for political ascendancy, which characterized the first ten years before and after Singapore's independence," writes Eugene Tan, a law professor at the Singapore Management University.[50] In the 1950s and 1960s, Tan notes, demands for greater recognition of Chinese education, language and culture were demonised as antinational chauvinism and Singapore's "Chinese accent" was "deliberately downplayed".[51]

The Chinese ground would remain a major factor in the PAP's political calculus. Lee knew he could never take his eye off that ball. One sign of this was his choice of aides. He consistently picked Chinese-educated press secretaries. The first was someone who would today be labeled "foreign talent" — a former member of the Guomindang. His longest serving press secretary, James Fu, had been an Operation Coldstore detainee and a former journalist with *Nanyang Siang Pau*. Fu served Lee for 21 years. His replacement, Yeong Yoon Ying, was recruited from the national broadcaster's Chinese division. In truth, Chinese-educated Singaporeans had probably lost the capacity to seize control of the political centre in the 1960s, when their leaders were neutralised. When the government closed down Nanyang University in 1980, it marked another milestone in the marginalisation of the Chinese-educated. Nantah, as it was affectionately called, had been a community effort dating back to 1955. It was the first Chinese university outside of Greater China. It also became a hotbed of radicalism. Its closure — together with the adoption of English as the universal medium of instruction by 1987 — shut off the pipeline of graduates educated in the Chinese medium, turning its alumni overnight into a vestigial symbol of a long-lost past, heading for inevitable extinction.

Then, when Chinese language and culture had been politically defanged, the PAP embarked on a campaign to revive them. Starting from the mid-1980s, the government promoted Mandarin, Confucianism and Asian Values, and with such apparent conviction that Western analysts spoke of the "sinification" of Singapore. The government was motivated partly by a desire to keep faith with the Chinese ground. Some observers saw it as an outcome of Lee Kuan Yew's born-again Chineseness. The rise of China was another factor. But, the main goal was probably to marshal an essentialised version of traditional Asian norms — with an emphasis on family, harmony, consensus and respect for authority — as a buffer against liberal Western values. It is in this light that one needs to read Lee Kuan Yew's account of the press in his memoirs. The Chinese press in its prime may have given him a rough time, but it was now convenient to conjure up a reconstructed image of it to use against his Western critics. There were traces of this formula as far back as the 1970s, according to Singapore historians Hong Lysa and Huang Jianli. Chinese-educated PAP politicians who sided with Lee Kuan Yew helped him construct a binary framing of East versus West: Chinese-educated Singaporeans were praised as representing the best of Chinese culture while the English-educated were accused of being susceptible to the worst in Western culture. The historians stress that this "promotion of 'Chineseness' was taking place only after other challenging notions of 'Chineseness' have already been defeated".[52] By the mid-1980s, even the story of Nantah was considered ripe for selective revival. The university's luminaries had been treated as communists and chauvinists in their day, but were now considered harmless enough to qualify for rehabilitation. Nantah was essentialised into a "symbol of community spirit and perseverance".[53]

The irony of the official narrative has not escaped Singaporean scholars. Nanyang Technological University sociologist Kwok Kian Woon captures it in a set of rhetorical questions:

> Looking at the broad sweep of history, how is it that the Chinese-educated were one day regarded as subversive Communists, purveyors of a modern-day radical ideology, and the next day thought of as traditional Confucians, defenders of a heritage that has apparently remained unbroken for 5000 years? ... How is it that people now highlight the spirit of selfless dedication to a cause on the part of extraordinary individuals among the Chinese-educated when such individuals have paid very high personal costs for their — misguided? — idealism?[54]

To these paradoxes, one could add: how is it that Asian journalism, once seen as so harmful to society that it deserved the harshest of punishments, is now held up as the embodiment of social responsibility and community spirit?

The Taming of "Asian" Journalism

While it is obvious that Singapore journalism lost its contentious edge shortly after independence, what remains to be explained is why this change has been more pronounced among Asian-language newspapers — to such a degree that they have come to be seen as even more conservative than the English press. The official narrative would answer that the non-English media represent the Singapore's grassroots "heartlanders", the people most appreciative of the country's progress and grateful for the PAP's leadership. In contrast, the English media and their constituents are harder to please and overly influenced by Western liberal ideals, including the alien notion of an independent watchdog press. This cultural explanation cannot be totally discounted. Lim Jim Koon, *Lianhe Zaobao*'s chief editor from 1995 to 2011, is one of those who detects a genuine difference in perspectives along language lines. Respect for authority and putting society before self are deeply internalised values in Confucian societies, he told me. Such conservatism is not unconditional, he stressed. It depends on whether their rulers govern well. "They can be very radical if they think those in power are corrupt," he said, noting the courageous dissent of journalists during China's tumultuous past. A 1973 Nantah graduate, he grew up watching his community's leaders take personal risks in their struggle against the PAP. Since then, the PAP's good governance has allowed Chinese journalists to play a supportive role in line with their Confucian values. To Lim, this is the main reason for his newspaper's conservatism.

However, Lim acknowledged that the ideological conversion of the Chinese-educated was not always voluntary or wholehearted. Speaking to him and other knowledgeable journalists, a fuller and more complex explanation emerges for the changes in the Chinese-language press. For a start, many scholars would reject the suggestion that all members of the Chinese-speaking majority have seen themselves as winners under PAP rule. On the contrary, the fears of linguistic and economic marginalisation that stoked their activism in the early years of independence continue to be salient issues half a century later. Indeed, the quiescence of the Chinese journalists could be interpreted as a strategic accommodation, cooperating with the government on most national issues while maintaining their prerogative to speak up when their beloved language and culture are threatened.

When trying to explain the political stances of Singapore's different language media, the right question to ask is not who loves the

PAP more. Instead, we could think about who have suffered the more debilitating blows to their confidence and capabilities. The record is clear: the Chinese press has paid a disproportionately high price for Singapore's progress. The PAP's decision to push English as the main working language and the medium of instruction in schools is today credited as one key factor behind the country's economic success, but it shrank the reader base of the Chinese press. The proportion of families speaking mainly Mandarin or Chinese dialects at home has been declining steadily. The percentage of ethnic Chinese households using mainly English at home rose from under 24 in the year 2000 to more than 32 ten years later.[55] In its spoken form, the Chinese language continues to have a strong emotional hold. Thus, the national broadcaster's Chinese service, Channel 8, is far more popular than its English-language Channel 5. However, for more and more Chinese, reading the Chinese script is treated as a chore. Chinese newspapers used to outsell English ones. But by 1998, the total numbers of English and Chinese newspapers sold each day were roughly equal, accounting for 47 per cent and 46 per cent of total circulation respectively. Ten years later, Chinese newspapers' share of total circulation had fallen to 43 per cent.[56] Circulation figures by themselves do not tell the whole story. The more serious problem is that Chinese newspaper readers are not as desired by advertisers: they have less disposable income. By 2005, English was the main language spoken at home for 60 per cent of households earning $10,000 or more a month.[57] According to the 2010 Census, Mandarin and dialects remains the medium of choice in public housing estates, but among ethnic Chinese residents living in condominiums, private flats and landed homes — the most attractive demographic to advertisers — only 37 per cent use mainly their mother tongues at home.[58]

In business terms, Chinese newspapers have been on the defensive for decades, even requiring a government-engineered merger with the Straits Times group in the 1980s to guarantee their long-term viability. Such interventions suggest that the PAP would never allow the free market to kill off Singapore's Chinese as well as Malay and Tamil media, since these are important vehicles for the country's official languages. However, such guarantees of government support do little for the non-English media's self-confidence. The sense of vulnerability may extend to individual journalists. In a 2009 survey conducted by Hao Xiaoming and me, Asian-language journalists came across as less economically mobile than their English counterparts.[59]

The former were almost twice as likely as the latter to feel somewhat or very dissatisfied with their jobs (33 per cent versus 18 per cent). Yet, less than 15 per cent of Asian-language journalists said they were unsure whether they would still be working in the news media in five years, compared with the more than 26 per cent of English-language journalists who expressed such doubts. Although 68 per cent (versus 46 per cent of English journalists) said they were drawn to the profession out of interest and passion, the Asian-language journalists were also more likely to care about money when judging journalism jobs. More than four in ten said they considered pay and job security as very important considerations, compared with fewer than three in ten English journalists. The overall picture shows a corps of Asian-language journalists who may be even more committed to their vocation than their English-language counterparts, but are forced by circumstances to pay closer attention to their economic security.

Leslie Fong, one of the few bicultural editors in Singapore — he has served as editor of *Shin Min Daily News* as well as *The Straits Times* — noted that the best minds in the Chinese community had gravitated towards journalism in the first half of the 20th century. The ideological and intellectual ferment in China rubbed off on them. But the closing of China after the communist revolution would cut them off from their "intellectual Mecca". Chinese writers and intellectuals were also disciplined more harshly than the English-educated, and with more devastating long-term consequences. Operation Coldstore, which scythed Singapore's most committed and creative political minds, cut disproportionately into the ranks of the Chinese-educated intelligentsia. The detainees were just the tip of the iceberg. Many dissidents were banished to China — where, tragically, they were persecuted during the Cultural Revolution due to their foreign connections. In the late 1960s and 1970s, suspected radicals were forced to keep a low profile. Those who were blacklisted were barred from influential jobs such as journalism. Many were denied the notorious certificates of suitability required for university admission. Thus, the Chinese-educated community suffered a massive depletion of its intellectual resources. Most Chinese of ability retreated from public life and ventured into business. The individuals who entered Chinese journalism after the turbulence of the 1960s and early 1970s would have included genuine believers in the PAP, but also others who had learnt from the experiences of their predecessors the futility of challenging the *status quo*. With other avenues already proven to be dead ends, it is little wonder that Chinese journalists started taking the path of least resistance. Kwok Kian Woon has likened the Chinese community to a kite, subject to the "high winds of politics and economics". "The kite was once flying high, self-confident and able to hold its stature among all the kites. But the wind began to blow in different directions, and the kite began to lose its vigour." Now, it fears drifting aimlessly in the open sky, and "sees no choice but to have its string skillfully controlled by the kite-flier". Leslie Fong puts it more prosaically: "When you stop banging your head against the wall, it feels damned good."

CHAPTER 7

Freedom of the Press: A Cause Without Rebels

In Singapore's debates over censorship, the press is strangely silent about its own plight. One has to turn the clock back decades to find instances of professional journalists protesting collectively and publicly against their political restraints. The 1970s saw a "Save the *Herald*" campaign as government pressure mounted against the *Singapore Herald*. When *Nanyang Siang Pau* executives were arrested under the Internal Security Act, the newspaper used its own pages to protest its innocence and appeal directly to its readers.[1] In the early 1980s, the *Straits Times* responded with a page one editorial when it felt unfairly accused of unprofessionalism over a scoop about impending bus fare hikes. Then, when a former senior civil servant, S.R. Nathan, was installed as executive chairman of the Straits Times group, some journalists wore black armbands in his presence to mourn the death of independent journalism.[2] When the government engineered a merger of newspaper companies to form the Singapore Press Holdings group in the mid-1980s, more than a hundred Times House journalists protested outside the building, chanting "no merger", and displaying a big banner with the words, "Whose idea was this?"

By the 1990s, such impetuousness had evaporated. When the *Business Times* was rapped with the Official Secrets Act, journalists regarded the government's actions as grossly excessive — but they bit their tongues. The traumatic affair began with Internal Security Department officers raiding the newsroom of the *Business Times* in full view of journalists one Thursday morning in 1992. Reuters broke the news on its wires the same day, with group editor-in-chief Cheong Yip

Seng quoted as confirming that the newspaper's journalists had been questioned and speculating that it had something to do with a leak of government information. The next day, Friday, the wires carried more detailed stories, with the managing editor providing factual information, but sharing no opinion. Astonishingly, Friday's newspapers in Singapore said nothing about what had happened under their own roof the previous morning — apparently to avert any suspicion that they were using their pages to drum up sympathy. Only the next day, along with other regional papers, did the *Business Times* and *Straits Times* report the event. The delay was remarkable enough for Hong Kong's *South China Morning Post* to headline its news story, "Papers silent over government raid on Business Times".[3]

Four months later, *Business Times* editor Patrick Daniel, two economists and a civil servant were charged with breaching the Official Secrets Act. From that point, any press commentary could have been deemed to be interfering with the course of justice under Singapore's *sub judice* laws. Before charges were brought against the accused, however, there had been a window of opportunity within which the newspapers were free — at least according to the letter of the law — to criticize the authorities' actions. But political prudence resulted in the Singapore press displaying a superhuman self-restraint that most others would have found hard to muster in a similar situation. The only whimper of objection was a column written by *Straits Times* editor Leslie Fong more than a month after the raid. He pointed out the all-encompassing sweep of the OSA, asked for more clarity in the rules, and urged the government not to let fear of the OSA slow the flow of information and reduce journalists to mere postboxes. On the on-going case, Fong felt compelled to genuflect to the government's authority. "Let me hasten to stress that all this is not to say that my colleagues and I think that the authorities are wrong to have ordered the investigation," he said. "Equally, my colleagues will concede readily that if any among them has indeed broken the law, then he, or she, must face the consequences. They would not like it, but they live and learn."[4] Learn, they did.

In 2008, a rare protest event for press freedom was held outside Singapore Press Holdings' News Centre. In commemoration of World Press Freedom Day, banners were unfurled with such messages as "NEWSPAPER AND PRINTING PRESSES ACT = REPRESSION".[5] Forty years earlier, this might have been the work of rambunctious sections of Singapore's press corps. No longer. It took six political activists — none of them professional journalists — to mount this puny act of defiance. News Centre houses the newsrooms of almost all of the country's daily newspapers, but it does not appear that any of the hundreds of journalists working there that day came out to show their support — if they even knew about the protest.[6] The activists uploaded reports and photographs of the event on their own websites. Although the protest was unprecedented, it was not chronicled by the mainstream news media. Indeed, World Press Freedom Day as a whole was ignored by Singapore's newspapers.

Singapore is not alone in having a less-than-free media system: scores of other countries deny their citizens the right of free expression in ways and on grounds that human rights watchers find objectionable. However, within this category, Singapore may be unique for its virtual absence of any press reform movement. In private interactions as well as the occasional public statement, Singapore journalists may try to persuade government newsmakers to be more open with information and less sensitive about criticism. But they stop short of asking for structural changes, including to the main laws that circumscribe their work. This is despite the fact that the prevailing framework — described in Chapter 2 — is significantly out of step with international norms concerning freedom of expression.[7]

The silence is interesting because of what it reveals about media and politics in contemporary Singapore. The reason most commonly cited for the easy ride that Singaporeans give their government is that they are somehow culturally predisposed to being controlled. "Compliant Singaporeans don't have to ask or be told what to do, they just know," declares one foreign correspondent.[8] While the country's political culture is certainly one factor, it does not provide a complete explanation. The government's hand reaches into every sector of the media and culture industries, either applying direct censorship or pressuring producers to exercise self-censorship. Yet, although political control is ubiquitous, the reaction to it is not uniform. Compared with journalists, Singapore artists have been much less accepting of censorship, publicly questioning government controls and lobbying for reforms. They have even succeeded in securing some modest liberalisation, whereas press laws have never been relaxed, only stiffened, in five decades of PAP rule.

This chapter traces how different groups of content producers have responded to censorship. Comparing and contrasting them helps us to isolate more precisely those factors that account for journalists' silence. It is not that journalists and artists are cut from different cloth. Indeed, a significant number of prominent artists in drama and film have also worked for mainstream news organisations. The difference may be less about who you are and more about where you stand. The various sectors are articulated differently with political and economic power: dependencies differ, as do calculations as to the costs and benefits of speaking out for artistic and media freedom.

Other Sectors Pushing for Space

By the 1980s, the PAP's desire to control culture and to punish artists who did not toe the line was abundantly clear. Censorship was rife. The playwright Kuo Pao Kun had been detained without trial under the Internal Security Act from 1976–80. The Operation Spectrum arrests of 1987 ensnared the founders of a theatre group dedicated to socially relevant themes, Third Stage. Singaporeans working in the arts in the 1980s could have been under no illusions that the government had greater respect for artistic freedom than for press freedom. Nevertheless, the late 1980s saw members of the theatre and film communities coming out to push for more space. In later years, they would be joined by bloggers. Their methods have been tame compared with protests in other countries — involving mainly written petitions and gentle lobbying rather than demonstrations or street protests — but by Singapore standards, they have been vocal contributors to debates on civil liberties and freedom of expression.

Theatre groups made known the difficulties they were facing with the prevailing permit system, which required the vetting of scripts and licensing of performances. The backdrop to this was a growing demand for Singaporean plays. From having no professional theatre companies in 1982, Singapore had three by 1987 — Act 3, TheatreWorks and Practice Performing Theatre.[9] The Necessary Stage, which would later turn professional, also started then.[10] Over the same period, the number of ticketed, indoor performing arts events grew by more than 80 per cent, with drama productions more than doubling.[11] In 1988, a government-appointed Committee on Performing Arts highlighted the need to review censorship procedures.[12] The committee reported to a high-level advisory council, which concluded that "the private sector's efforts at organising shows are hampered by complicated licensing procedures".[13] The government eventually acknowledged that censorship should be implemented by an agency with the explicit mandate to promote, and not just regulate, the arts: in the early 1990s, the job of vetting scripts was transferred from the Public Entertainments Licensing Unit (PELU) of the Home Affairs Ministry to the new National Arts Council. Importantly, the new rules also allowed classification as an alternative to censorship.

The changes allowed Singapore theatre to emerge as a key avenue for political expression.[14] A play that had been blocked by PELU because of concerns about certain words and gestures — *Details Cannot Body Wants* by Robert Yeo — was given the go-ahead after Yeo agreed to limit the audience to over-18s under the new system. *The Lady of Soul and the Ultimate S-Machine* — a racy, satirical commentary on Singapore bureaucracy and identity penned by *Straits Times* journalist Tan Tarn How and directed by Ong Keng Sen of TheatreWorks — was also passed after earlier objections from PELU. Just before the changes, Ong had said that "the political or politicised play is a rare creature on the Singaporean theatre scene".[15] By the early 1990s, Robert Yeo observed, "Artists from many media, including writers, painters and playwrights, sensed the change and grasped the opportunity to test the new policies."[16]

Around the same period, the film industry achieved some success in lobbying for liberalisation. Censorship was identified as a serious obstacle to attracting movie-makers into Singapore.[17] A film classification scheme was introduced in 1991, allowing movies deemed unsuitable for minors to be screened uncut under a Restricted rating. The classification system was welcomed not only by cinema-goers, but also by a new breed of Singaporean filmmakers who could now venture into mature themes. Eric Khoo's feature films *Mee Pok Man* (1995) and *12 Storeys* (1997) held up a mirror to Singapore's underbelly, putting working-class poverty, prostitution, crime and dysfunctional families on the big screen. They were passed under the R(A) or Restricted (Artistic) rating. Two decades earlier, a foreign film that depicted Singapore through a similar lens, *Saint Jack*, had been banned outright.

The path of liberalisation for the performing arts and film included obstacles and u-turns. In 1994, *The Straits Times* alleged that Alvin Tan and Haresh Sharma of The Necessary Stage were smuggling Marxist ideas into the arts. The two had attended a radical workshop on forum theatre overseas. National Arts Council chairman Tommy Koh defended the artists and accused *The Straits Times* of slanted reporting. He was nonetheless powerless to prevent the imposition of a new policy: there was to be no NAC funding for unscripted genres such as forum theatre or performance art. Around the same time, a performance artist Josef Ng was arrested and convicted of an indecent act when, in his protest against the arrest of homosexuals, he exposed his buttocks and snipped his pubic hair. Most mainstream artists distanced themselves from Ng. Several were quoted in the press opining that his act was not art.[18] An exception was Kuo Pao Kun, who said that the authorities had "inflicted serious damage to their own moral credibility" by bypassing the various consultative structures they had put in place as they "arrogantly and hurriedly" responded to "an incident which did not pose any immediate danger to anyone".[19]

Film regulation was tightened in 1998, when Parliament amended the Films Act to ban "party political" films. The new Section 33 prohibited the import, production, reproduction, distribution and exhibition of any such film.[20] This move was prompted by the opposition Singapore Democratic Party's attempt two years earlier to distribute a party videotape. The effort was easily blocked under existing laws, since the Films Act empowered the government to ban any film that it believed was "contrary to the public interest". Nevertheless, the government felt that the Act should be amended to reflect explicitly the principle that political campaigns should not be waged through the sensational and emotive medium of video.[21] Although political parties were the ostensible target, the definition of "party political films" covered any film "made by any person and directed towards any political end in Singapore". A film would be deemed as such if it was "intended or likely to affect voting" in any election or referendum, or if it contained "partisan or biased references to or comments on any political matter", including on current policy or public controversy.[22]

It is impossible to tell how many potential works died in the heads of Singaporean filmmakers as a result of the ban. However, the first completed film known to have been affected was *A Vision of Persistence*, a documentary about opposition politician J.B. Jeyaretnam. It was made by lecturers at the film school of Ngee Ann Polytechnic and accepted for screening at the Singapore International Film Festival in 2002. When action was threatened against them, they withdrew the film and apologised. The next known victim of the ban on party political films was less contrite. Martyn See, an activist-filmmaker, produced *Singapore Rebel*, about opposition politician Chee Soon Juan.

When police investigated him in 2005 for a possible violation of the Films Act, he reported every step on his blog, garnering national and international attention. In response, a group of 11 filmmakers openly petitioned the government to clarify how the Films Act would be applied. "We ask because, as filmmakers, we feel that almost anything could be construed as a comment on a political matter," their letter said.[23] By Singapore standards, it was an unusually bold intervention, which explains why the story was picked up by wire agency reporters for international circulation.[24]

Time magazine raised the issue with Lee Kuan Yew in a wide-ranging interview. Lee declared that the government had overreacted to *Singapore Rebel*: "Well, if you had asked me, I would have said to hell with it. But the censor, the enforcer, he will continue until he is told the law has changed. And it will change."[25] Some eight months later, the police decided to let off Martyn See with a "stern warning".[26] In 2008, Prime Minister Lee Hsien Loong conceded that an "outright ban is no longer sensible". The following year, Parliament amended the Film Acts to relax — without removing entirely — the ban on political films. To provide some of the clarity that had been requested since the ban was introduced in 1998, a Political Films Consultative Committee of six to eight members was set up to advise the censors on whether particular films should be deemed "party political" under the law.[27]

Overall, the 21st-century censorship regime for the arts and entertainment was markedly freer than what had prevailed up to the 1980s. However, liberalisation did not keep pace with the aspirations of cutting-edge artists or an increasingly sophisticated, internationally exposed and demanding domestic audience. Artists were routinely consulted by the regulators, but increasingly felt that their feedback was being filtered and, worse, that pro-forma consultation was being used to justify what remained a fundamentally illiberal system. Occasionally, they showed their frustration. In 2003, the edgy upcoming film-maker Royston Tan was upset that censors demanded 27 cuts in his critically-acclaimed film, *15*, before they would give it even an R(A) rating. In reaction, Tan produced *Cut*, a 12-minute musical satirising censorship in Singapore and lampooning a senior bureaucrat in the regulatory authority. It featured a cast of 180 that included what *The Straits Times* called the who's who of the creative community. It was then picked to be screened at the opening of the 2004 Singapore

International Film Festival. The arts minister criticised *Cut* as an "unbecoming" attempt to undermine a public institution, but with an international media spotlight on the film festival, the authorities had little choice but to step out of the way and allow the video to be screened. Rubbing salt into the wound, a panel of judges made up of Singaporean directors then gave *Cut* the top prize in a digital film-makers award.[28]

When the government announced the next of its periodic censorship reviews, a group of artists decided that it was time to engage the policy process more pro-actively. The leading lights in this movement included theatre practitioners Alvin Tan, T. Sasitharan, Tan Tarn How and Paul Rae, and visual arts curator June Yap. Through the arts community's Yahoo! e-group, they organised Arts Engage, an anti-censorship network with the immediate goal of influencing the government-appointed Censorship Review Committee (CRC). The CRC rebuffed Arts Engage's requests for an opportunity to meet with the committee as a whole. Undeterred, the group set about preparing a position paper on censorship and managed to meet several CRC members individually. At a press conference in mid-June 2010, Arts Engage released its position paper.[29] By the end of July, its report had drawn 1,786 signatures. The Arts Engage paper rejected the idea that merely "tweaking" the system would suffice and called for systemic changes. "As citizens and residents of Singapore, we find the prevalence of censorship to be at odds both with the core values of democracy, equality and justice enshrined in the Pledge and instilled in us from young, and with Singapore's status as a dynamic, forward-looking society with a 21st century economy," it said.[30] It called for "regulation" — basically, classification — to replace censorship. It said that "except for materials which are prohibited by law and whose prohibition has been decided by a court of law, or where the producer of the work expressly requests it (in order to achieve a specific age rating, for instance) there need be no cuts to content".[31] In the past, the arts community had shied away from defending the likes of Josef Ng, who had challenged the bounds of taste. The Arts Engage statement, however, took a more principled stand in favour of free expression. "Several high profile cases of offensive speech have recently been addressed through legal avenues or by the security services," it noted. "Such measures are not the hallmark of a healthy or robust society, nor do they demonstrably contribute to the fostering of one. This is, of course, a contentious issue. However, we maintain that it is not the business of government to protect individuals from offence a priori."[32]

Arts Engage also opened an online database for artists to report "censorship and censorship-like incidents" they had encountered in recent years. The number of cases that surfaced surprised even the leaders of the group. Many incidents had been unknown to the wider artistic community, since censorship was implemented largely through confidential communication between regulators and artists, or was woven into administrative licensing processes such that applicants had not even recognised it as censorship. Some artists initially chose to keep these incidents under wraps for fear of angering the authorities, on whose funding they depended.[33] The reports also surprised members of the CRC, who had been informed by regulators that censorship of the arts had already been superseded by classification and self-regulation. Journalists covering the arts seemed equally oblivious to the extent of censorship.[34] Arts Engage called for more transparent regulatory processes that were open to public scrutiny.[35]

The group's push for fundamental changes in the government's regulation of the arts had little effect. The CRC confined itself to largely procedural recommendations. Arts Engage members were disappointed but not surprised, since their interactions with the committee had given little reason for optimism.[36] In any case, influencing the CRC had never been viewed as the sole or ultimate goal: Arts Engage was meant to be a long-term campaign against censorship. In the context of this chapter, the success or failure of Arts Engage is less relevant than the fact of its existence. It begs the question why there has been no equivalent movement among journalists. Since the late 1980s, leading practitioners in the arts have publicly expressed their unhappiness with government restrictions on their work. Journalists, no less impeded by the state, have stayed mute. They regularly take political risks by writing news reports and opinion columns that gently convey criticism of government policies — but keep clear of the media policies that most directly affect their work. Fathoming the reasons for this can help us understand the resilience of the PAP's press system.

Structural Differences Between the Arts and Journalism

Responses to censorship are partly shaped by structural factors. It is no coincidence that the enterprise of professional journalism is organised very differently from the arts. News organisations tend to be large corporations, hierarchically structured. Their content producers — those whose work is directly subject to censorship — control neither ownership nor senior management functions. In contrast, drama production is carried out mainly through small theatre companies that are controlled by their creative talent. Many of the stars of the drama world — unlike most brand-name journalists — are either free agents or are synonymous with companies that are built around them. How creative work is organised is not a trivial matter, as Vincent Mosco reminds us in his classic text, *The Political Economy of Communication*. While we tend to associate media workers with creativity and conceptual thought, their individual effort may in fact be embedded in complex production processes, making it not very different from other labour processes in the wider economy, Mosco writes.[37] Their individual talent and their professional traditions notwithstanding, they may be hired ultimately to carry out tasks within a set framework, while the most consequential decisions are taken by management. Thus, just like the media content it produces, the media workforce is itself subject to commodification. To the extent that media labour is commodified, it is less likely to protest against censorship, just as factory workers are not known to rise in revolt against corporate decisions that compromise the quality of their widgets.

The structure of a large organisation may prevent the rank and file from even knowing when censorship is applied. This is borne out by a survey of 447 SPH and MediaCorp journalists conducted by my colleague Hao Xiaoming and me. While most of the journalists understood that there were limits to their autonomy, they did not necessarily attribute those constraints to governments. When asked an open-ended question about the main limit to their freedom, editors and other newsroom supervisors were more likely to identify external political controls (41 per cent) than internal culture and policies (21.4 per cent). In contrast, among journalists who did not hold supervisory positions in the newsroom, only a quarter (27.8 per cent) cited government and political authorities as the most significant limit. More than one third (35.3 per cent) identified the newsroom culture and editorial policies of their organisations as the main obstacle.

This perception gap is probably due to the opacity of government influence on editorial decision-making in the Singapore media. Editors receiving behind-the-scenes signals from government usually keep such communication confidential. Their staff might then assume that the resulting decisions were made independently. This is different from regimes with more overt censorship, where journalists at all levels know exactly where and when censorship occurs. Such collective awareness can be a source of professional solidarity, sparking collective efforts to resist or oppose restrictions.[38] In soft-authoritarian regimes such as Singapore, however, the authorities delegate political supervision to gatekeepers within the media, who then bear the responsibility of predicting and pre-empting intervention. In such a system, as the survey shows, it is difficult for even insiders to tell where editorial judgment ends and self-censorship begins. This was precisely the intended effect of the Newspaper and Printing Presses Act of 1974, as noted in Chapter 2.

Such dynamics may not be unique to Singapore. In one survey of 1,700 journalists in 17 other countries with varying degrees of press freedom (from Australia and the United States to Egypt and China), the researchers report being surprised that respondents perceived internal influences — relating to their organisations, newsrooms and professions — to be more powerful limits on their work than external political and economic factors. This perception among journalists is contradicted by overwhelming objective evidence of political and economic constraints on journalism, the researchers note. Explaining this inconsistency, they surmise that political and economic influences are seldom experienced directly by the average journalist in the course of their everyday newswork. "The power of these influences might be absorbed by news organizations and subsequently filtered, negotiated, and redistributed to the individual journalists," they write. "News organizations may, in many cases, function as a mediator of external interests and pressures rather than as a buffer." Their impact is masked by organisational and procedural influences, which have a strong grip on everyday practices.[39] Contrast this to the arts: artists, in their small and flat organisations, are far more likely to feel the hand of government intervention.

Another outcome of organisational structure is that it influences how a group relates to power. The French cultural theorist Pierre Bourdieu has observed that all cultural producers require recognition and resources, but find them in different places. Some fields are more autonomous than others from society's centres of political and economic power — and journalism everywhere is one of the least autonomous fields.[40] On the one hand, this locates journalism closer to society's main sources of influence, prestige and wealth. On the other, it makes journalists less likely to oppose the *status quo*. No matter how passionately journalists care about their craft, the public-listed companies that they work through are less likely to take a corporate stand that is critical of the establishment than would a small arts group on the margins.

These are, of course, broad generalisations. Indeed, if structure matters as much as I claim, then we should expect to see differences within each sector. After all, not all journalism is carried out by large news corporations, and not all arts is produced by little groups on the fringe. Within any one field, the way the work is structured should predict producers' responses to censorship, if my theory holds. And, indeed, that's exactly what we find. While professional journalists in large media organisations are absent from censorship debates, amateur journalists and freelancers have been more visible. One such group was Bloggers 13, a network of socio-political bloggers led by Alex Au of Yawning Bread and Choo Zheng Xi of The Online Citizen. Bloggers 13 published a position paper and held a public seminar to press its case. "Not just specific regulations, but also the government's overall regulatory approach and processes, need urgent reform," it said.[41] The group said that freedom to use the internet to discuss political issues and promote political views should be guaranteed. It asked for community moderation to replace censorship, and added that regulation should not be based on administrative discretion. Predating Arts Engage, Bloggers 13 was at that time the only group of content producers lobbying publicly for greater freedom of expression as a right.

Another protest by amateur journalists against censorship arose from an incident involving Nanyang Technological University's student newspaper, *Nanyang Chronicle*. The president of the university ordered that the *Chronicle* spike a news story reporting the visit of opposition leader Chee Soon Juan to the campus. The president later explained that he had to exercise the NTU's "ownership rights" over the *Chronicle* in order to protect the university from the risk of being seen, presumably by the government, "as being used for the political agenda of the uninvited visitor".[42] As he acted only after the students had laid out the paper, the decision did not fall into the aforementioned category of difficult-to-discern censorship. News spread immediately to blogs and mainstream media. While faculty tried to explain the facts of publishing life to the *Chronicle* team — pointing out that the university had the right to intervene since it was paying for the paper — other students took up the cause and organised a public protest at the Speaker's Corner. The editor of the *Chronicle* made his distaste for the whole affair plain by launching an independent student-run website, Enquirer.sg. On its first anniversary, he penned a stinging rebuke of the culture of censorship and self-censorship that he claimed had routinely neutered the *Chronicle* even before the Chee Soon Juan case.[43] By then, he had graduated as valedictorian and was self-employed as a media entrepreneur. Not surprisingly, neither he nor any of the students who had organised the Speaker's Corner protest entered mainstream news media jobs.

We find a similar pattern within the arts. While the average artist is more vocal about censorship than the average journalist, artists are not a homogeneous group. Their responses differ depending on the contexts they operate in. To understand better the dynamics within the arts community, I sought out T. Sasitharan, one of the leaders of Arts Engage, and a former colleague at *The Straits Times*. A talented actor and director, he went full-time into arts administration, eventually inheriting the drama company and school of the revered, uncompromising Kuo Pao Kun — a position that came with an expectation of moral as well as aesthetic leadership. Sasi confirmed my hunches. He pointed out that the artists at the forefront of protests against censorship had come from the theatre industry. They were individuals who had built companies around them, of which they were still the "moral centres". They included Alvin Tay and Haresh Sharma, Ivan Heng, Ong Keng Sen and before them Kuo Pao Kun. Film-making is equally affected by censorship, but it is a more complex and costly enterprise, involving more parties, higher risk, and greater dependence on government patronage. While prominent film-makers have been more vocal than professional journalists, they have not been as prominent in censorship debates as theatre practitioners. Scan the 1,786 signatories of the Arts Engage position paper and you will not find the names of Jack Neo and Eric Khoo — Singapore's two most successful filmmakers and the only ones to have been awarded the Cultural Medallion. Celebrities employed by MediaCorp's entertainment arms are also absent. In contrast, makers of small independent films, such as Tan Pin Pin, Sun Koh and Boo Junfeng, readily got involved.

This is not to say that small producers are immune to government pressure. William Peterson, who helped set up the theatre studies programme at the National University of Singapore, wrote in 2001 that the liberalised licensing system had been found by many theatre practitioners to be "double-edged". Established companies had been given the freedom to check their own scripts, but there was still no freedom from fear. Thus, the system created the conditions for "overly rigorous self-censorship". Playwrights and theatre practitioners often imposed more rigid limitations on their own work than external censors might demand, Peterson said. "Established theatre companies, which have the most to lose, have generally become more politically and socially conservative in their programming than many of the smaller companies, while at the same time there has been a notable absence of new playwrights in joining the field," he added.[44]

"We are all vulnerable," Sasi says. Groups depend on the Arts Housing scheme and National Arts Council grants. This may explain why even Arts Engage presented its case in measured language and emphasised engagement with policy makers and shapers, instead of adopting more confrontational approaches. "We all knew where the lines were," Sasi says. Instead, perhaps the most important difference is in the degree of "enthrallment", he suggests, borrowing from the title of Francis Seow's book on the press, *Media Enthralled*.[45] This is a condition carefully cultivated by government by bringing individuals into the inner circle, giving them the sense of being privileged with trust that the general masses are not worthy of. His former profession, he believes, has been more successfully enthralled. "It is a state of mind. What happens when you are enthralled is that you set aside your critical faculty. You accept authority and respect its protocols on faith," he explains, likening it to what goes on in religion or celebrity worship. The pressure to conform is intensely felt by all Singaporeans, including artists. But not all question that condition, he says. "Enthrallment normalises the fact that you need to conform."

Openings for Engagement

There is an additional factor that can help account for some groups' public opposition to censorship. Theatre, film and online producers — but not journalists — were presented with openings that invited engagement with the regulators. Scholars who study social movements have noted that the ebb and flow of political opportunities is one key factor explaining why protests emerge where and when they do.[46] In Singapore, censorship has been a constant fact of life. Appeals for relaxation usually surface when a political opportunity appears. While the government has never acknowledged any need for press reform, it has periodically signalled its willingness to review regulations affecting the arts and entertainment. Theatre, film and new media practitioners have all been held up by the government as vital players in Singapore's bid to remake itself as a vibrant and creative "Renaissance City", as one iteration of the strategy was called. This has created political space for these sectors to engage the authorities on censorship.

Calls to liberalise drama and film censorship started in earnest in the late 1980s after a government rethink of cultural policy. The influential Economic Committee, set up to chart a new course for Singapore after the 1985 recession, had for the first time identified the cultural and entertainment sector as having economic potential.[47] A high-level advisory council chaired by the communications minister Ong Teng Cheong went on to stress the many benefits of culture and the arts, including their contribution to the economy. "Good facilities and activities help to attract world class performances and exhibitions, thus creating a more congenial environment for investors and professionals to stay and tourists to visit Singapore," its report said.[48]

Official recognition of the economic value of the culture industries explains why practitioners were invited to sit on various advisory panels. The government-appointed Committee on Performing Arts, which reported to the Ong Teng Cheong advisory council, comprised mainly representatives of the arts community, including arts educators and respected artists, notably the former political prisoner Kuo Pao Kun. The Censorship Review Committee constituted in 1990 included the playwright Robert Yeo, who had had a play blocked by censors, and Jacintha Abisheganadan, a co-founder of TheatreWorks, which was pushing political boundaries with gay-themed plays. Also on the committee were writers Catherine Lim and Philip Jeyaretnam. The committee was chaired not by a government minister but by National Arts Council chairman Tommy Koh. In contrast, its predecessor, the 1981 Review Committee on Censorship, was headed by the minister of state for law and home affairs, S. Jayakumar, and included no representative from the performing arts.[49]

Similarly, the assertiveness of the online content producers needs to be seen in the context of the government's love affair with information technology. In 1992, the government announced its IT2000 masterplan, positioning Singapore as an "intelligent island" where new digital technologies would touch all aspects of society, raising economic competitiveness and improving the quality of life.[50] When the public internet was launched in the mid-1990s, its early adopters in universities and private sector technology companies possessed a self-confidence that came with knowing that they were on the cutting edge of developments that the government was eager to promote. Thus, when the government announced content regulations in 1996, they were able to push back with some conviction and passion. The government duly watered down some of the rules and clarified others, promising that it would regulate the internet with a "light touch".[51] The government also appointed a National Internet Advisory Committee chaired by a scientist. As a result of the committee's recommendations and under pressure from the internet community, the regulator revised the Internet Code of Practice to make less onerous the responsibilities of licensees.[52] Around the same time, the government liberalised its content guidelines. The original list of discouraged material had included content that jeopardised public security or national defense; excited disaffection against the Government; or undermined public confidence in the administration of justice — terms borrowed from existing legislation. These items were expunged from the new code, which instead focused on sexual content and material harmful to racial and religious harmony.[53]

When Bloggers 13 came together to campaign for more internet freedom a decade later, the move was not made in a vacuum either. Their initiative was a response to the news that the government had appointed the Advisory Council on the Impact of New Media on Society (AIMS), to recommend changes to policy. Worried that the government wanted to narrow their political space and simultaneously sensing an opportunity to argue for liberalisation, the bloggers took part in consultation meetings organised by the council and raced to submit their position paper in time for AIMS' consideration. Like Bloggers 13, leaders of Arts Engage responded to positive signals from the government. If it dawned on officials in the late 1980s that the arts could add to economic growth, by the 2000s this perspective had blossomed into a belief that creativity was vital for national competitiveness. Books like Richard Florida's *The Rise of the Creative Class*[54] became essential reading for policy makers. A city that once turned away males with long hair in order to keep out hippie culture was now interested in courting and flaunting everything cool. Members of Parliament learnt hip-hop dance moves and ministers graced *avant garde* cultural events. Spotting an opening, members of the arts community came together in 2009 to put up a candidate to enter Parliament as a non-elected Member. The Nominated Member of Parliament (NMP) scheme was meant to provide for a greater diversity voices, including representatives of functional groups. The government had specifically cited the arts community as one group that could take advantage of this avenue. One of the community's candidates was duly accepted as an NMP. When the government announced a censorship review the same year and expressed interest in hearing from industry players and artists, Arts Engage was born.

The government's interest in remaking Singapore as a cosmopolitan, creative and culturally vibrant city did not just elevate the status of arts and entertainment as industries. It also raised the national profile of individual talent. Officials needed to embrace the stars of the creative sector who could help spread the message that the city state was not just the go-to place for disk drives, oil rigs and forex trading, but was also a magnet for creativity and innovation. These talented individuals could also help achieve the traditional objectives of cultural policy, lifting the quality of nation-building projects such as national events, patriotic music videos and museum exhibits. Therefore, even if officials continued to feel little genuine affinity for the artistic community, they were prepared to open their minds, if not their hearts, to its key members. Ivan Heng — whose productions regularly confronted the censors — was appointed creative director of the National Day Parade in 2009. When the National Museum of Singapore was completely overhauled in the mid-2000s to create a more compelling showcase of the country's history, it commissioned works by local artists including boundary breakers Royston Tan, Alfian Sa'at and Boo Junfeng. The government has also conceded that signature events on the country's cultural calendar, such as the Singapore International Film Festival, could grow in international credibility only if the artists organising them are given enough autonomy and support.

On the one hand, such connections can be seen as successful co-optation of artists by the government. State patronage, after all, is one of the oldest means of taming the arts. On the other hand, co-optation can be a two-way street. Once an artist reaches a certain level of national and international prominence, repressing him or her becomes a politically tricky option. In many other fields where the government is the main source of status, it can anoint, banish and rehabilitate individuals and then cast them out again, overnight and at whim. In the arts, however, those who have achieved independent critical acclaim for their work can receive additional blessings from the state — but the state cannot remove an accomplished artist's underlying stock of prestige. Indeed, as Pierre Bourdieu points out, being attacked by the orthodoxy can add positively to an artist's reputation.[55] While it would be hubris for artists to consider themselves untouchable, the government has probably had to think twice before treating them too roughly. Take the case of Royston Tan. His breakthrough film *15* caught the eye of the world's press and became the first Singapore movie to compete at the prestigious Venice Film Festival. So, when he released *Cut*, the satirical broadside at Singapore's censors was reported by the *International Herald Tribune*, *Financial Times*, Britain's *Guardian*, Hong Kong's *South China Morning Post* and *Far Eastern Economic Review*. Feature articles on the film, filed by Reuters, the Associated Press and Agence France Presse, were carried in newspapers from Texas to Australia.

Another independent film-maker who has spoken out against over-regulation is Tan Pin Pin. She was the lead author of the 2005 letter questioning the ban on political films. Barely a month earlier, she had been in the news as one of four artists selected for the President's Young Talents Exhibition 2005 at the Singapore Art Museum. The *Business Times*, in an article about the exhibition published two days after Tan's letter appeared, reminded readers that the "Oxford law graduate is famous as the only Singaporean to win an Oscar yet (a Student Academy Award for her documentary Moving House in 2002)".[56] The previous week, *The Straits Times*' film reviewer had declared Tan's latest film, *Singapore GaGa*, "the most rewarding" local production at the 18th Singapore International Film Festival.[57] Not all state-sanctioned artists have been willing to lend their voices to the campaign against censorship, but when they do, it is harder for the government to ignore them.

Press Reform: Hopeless Cause?

The history of campaigns for artistic and media freedom, as outlined above, reveals a consistent pattern. It starts when certain media or cultural fields — theatre, film, online — begin to bubble with activity. New producers emerge, stimulated by new markets or technologies or ideas from abroad. Then, a government agency spots some strategic value in developing the field. Typically, it sees the sector's potential to contribute to the economy. As the state does not possess the capacity to engage directly in the activity, it decides to cultivate private- and people-sector producers. As part of this process, it solicits feedback from leading practitioners. It creates forums for consultation, such as review committees and advisory panels. This creates the rhetorical and institutional space for producers to appeal for regulatory reforms. Regulators try to manage the consultation process, by limiting it to closed-door settings, for example. Producers may be initially satisfied with such engagement. However, as the sector develops and expectations rise, producers grow frustrated with contained consultation on the government's terms. They lobby publicly for liberalisation, appealing directly to public opinion in a more concerted and organised manner.

Looking at this pattern, it becomes clearer why professional journalists have been absent from censorship debates. None of the various government reports on developing the media and culture industries has expressed any enthusiasm for news publishers, or any concern about the conditions under which they work. Journalism has been placed outside the scope of government's periodic censorship reviews. The government seems to see the framework of news media regulation as having been settled in the 1970s and 1980s, and requiring no modification. Journalists have been invited to sit on various public committees and boards based on their interests and expertise, but none of these positions are meant to place journalism itself on the agenda for discussion. Newspapers contribute more to the country's gross domestic product than any other local content producer, but the newspaper business lacks the glamour and "cool" factor of other sectors. Edgy, independent-minded artists are sometimes consecrated by the state. Edgy, independent-minded journalists never are.

Therefore, a key reason why journalists do not protest could well be their realistic assessment that protest is futile. It is also likely to be a lonely venture, since there is little sign of an appetite among Singaporeans for First World levels of freedom of expression. In a 2007 BBC poll across 14 developed and developing countries, Singapore was near the bottom in public desire for press freedom. While 56 per cent of the 11,000-plus respondents worldwide believed that freedom of the press was very important to ensure a free society, only 43 per cent of Singaporeans surveyed held this view.[58] Therefore, any push by professional journalists to reform press regulations could backfire. Singapore editors have grounds to believe that they can gain more space to practise independent journalism only if they have the government's trust. To secure that trust, journalists have to accept the cardinal PAP principle that the press is subordinate to the government. Any campaign to push for the liberal Fourth Estate press model would be read as proof of untrustworthiness, thus eroding journalists' political capital and inviting the authorities to shorten their leash. This is the irresistible logic that counsels stoic silence. As long as gradual, incremental change on the government's terms appears to be the only achievable goal for mainstream journalists who favour more autonomy, their refusal to campaign for legal reform may be more strategic than cowardly.

Nor are journalists alone in having to accept the PAP's rules. As bold as the artists seem to be by comparison, their calculations have been equally pragmatic. This is why their anti-censorship efforts have been more instrumental and narrow rather than principled and broad-based. When artists appeal for liberalisation, they normally couch their claims in terms that the government is more comfortable with — nation building and economic progress. They avoid claiming the right to freedom of expression under, say, the Universal Declaration of Human Rights, or, for that matter, under Singapore's own Constitution. Artists are realistic about what is within reach: procedural amendments and legislative refinements that expand their space for creativity, without threatening the prevailing balance of power between state and society. For example, when the group of film-makers appealed against the ban on political films in 2005, they framed their letter as a polite plea from "sincere" filmmakers facing the practical dilemma that they might inadvertently flout the law: "We feel that the current state of the legislation poses unintended dangers for sincere filmmakers.... It would be a waste to spend resources making a work only to find that it is unlawful because it has inadvertently run afoul of the Film Act."[59] They did not challenge the legitimacy of the ban, or assert the right of citizens to use film for overtly political purposes.

When the arts community stands up to defend more overtly political work, it pays the price for it, as Arts Engage discovered. The list of 22 names that the group proposed as members of the Censorship Review Committee included Martyn See and Seelan Palay, best known for championing opposition causes through their videos (see Chapter 9). The government did not pick a single name from the list — which Arts Engage took as a slap in the face for its temerity in embracing two notorious opponents of the PAP. The community debated the issue of whether such individuals were really "artists" or just activists who happened to be using an artistic medium. Some, like Sasitharan, found this government-inspired — but ultimately self-imposed — division between art and politics to be artificial and abhorrent. "It's completely unacceptable," he told me. "It's a wedge driven in to give a semblance of rationality to what the government is doing." The divide-and-rule strategy seems to have worked — less kind observers might say that the government's job was relatively simple, what with the universal tendency for the arts to create divas. With no single, homogeneous arts community but clusters of mutually suspicious practitioners, cultural producers tend to protect their own interests rather than take a united stand against censorship. Arts Engage was unprecedented, bringing together scores of practitioners from different fields. But even this exercise was not immune to the divide-and-rule strategy.

Journalists, like artists, tend to their own turf, appealing for space in the best ways they know how. For artists, this has meant taking advantage of openings provided by the authorities to engage with them, and hoping that their celebrity will make the government more receptive to their appeals. Journalists — for whom no red carpet has been rolled out — can count only on confidence-building as the way to loosen the choke-hold on the press. In journalism, as in the arts, those with any experience know that disregarding the rules of the PAP-written game carries a cost. These calculations show no sign of changing. Therefore, the campaign for press freedom will probably continue to be a fringe activity, shunned by professional journalists and pursued by assorted amateurs and activists with a penchant for seemingly lost causes.

CHAPTER 8

Alternative Online Media: Challenging the Gatekeepers

While the People's Action Party government was able to secure its freedom from the check and balance of an adversarial press, it found it much harder to shield itself from watchdogs in cyberspace. The growth of the internet since the mid-1990s created spaces with entirely different rules, opening up unprecedented opportunities for the expression of interests and perspectives that had not been fully represented by the mainstream media. Within a decade, it was clear that the internet was transforming Singapore's political culture. The government could no longer so easily set the national agenda by silencing dissenters, who now had the ability to magnify their voices well beyond their economic or institutional heft. Nor could the government demand respect merely by virtue of rank or position. Online, more and more Singaporeans flaunted an irreverence that in the past was only betrayed in private circles and hushed tones. This steadily eroded the old culture of fear, even offline. There was also an impact on mainstream media. In the pre-web polls of 1988, the government got the news media to downplay the entire general election and treat it as almost a non-event. The keenest contest, for Eunos GRC, was practically blacked out — a crude strategy expected to favour the incumbent party. In the internet age, however, the government had to accept that doing such violence to the national media's credibility would only result in a mass migration of readers and viewers to independent online media, where it would have a harder time winning hearts and minds.

Less clear was whether such internet-induced changes to the texture of Singapore politics would have any electoral impact. The results of the 2001 election, five years after the internet's "big bang", did not suggest an impending democratic revolution. Called shortly after the September 11 terrorist attacks on the United States and in the midst of a recession, Singaporeans upped their support for the tried and true PAP. More than 75 per cent voted for the ruling party, returning only two opposition candidates to Parliament. Ten years later, though, there were heightened expectations of a new media effect on the 2011 polls. The technologies had matured and ripened. Social networking platforms, especially Facebook, were widely used, and smartphones freed netizens from their home and office computers. Like citizens elsewhere, Singaporeans had been inspired by the role of social media in Barack Obama's presidential campaign in 2008. Earlier that same year, they had seen the government in neighbouring Malaysia suffering historic election reversals, with Prime Minister Abdullah Badawi admitting that the ruling alliance had lost the internet battle. Objectively, good old fashioned economics was always going to be an important factor in Singapore's 2011 general election. Three externally triggered recessions over the previous decade, with dizzying growth spurts in between, had played havoc with government planning in key areas such as public housing and transport. Slow to admit its mistakes and address genuine grievances, the PAP entered election season with public confidence at a nadir. Such fundamentals, normally the focus of election punditry anywhere, were downplayed by the foreign press, which was instead seized by the sexier story that the medium was the message. The international media, which had been taken by surprise by the recent net-assisted ousting of dictators in Tunisia and Egypt, now wondered if a social media revolution was underway in Singapore's impending general election.

In some respects, the internet in the 2011 general election lived up to the hype.[1] Every statement by PAP politicians was nitpicked ruthlessly by anti-government netizens. Opposition parties used their own web platforms, including Facebook and YouTube, to bypass mainstream media gatekeepers. The most aggressive user of these new technologies, the Singapore Democratic Party, was the election's most improved party in terms of vote share. And, in at least one local contest, the result was hard to ascribe to anything other than a social media battle that captured the whole nation's attention. This was the election for the five seats in Marine Parade. The PAP team in this group representation constituency (GRC) was helmed by former prime minister Goh Chok Tong and included a promising high-flier, Tan Chuan-Jin. However, netizens' attention focused on their 27-year-old team mate, Tin Pei Ling. Introduced as the PAP's youngest candidate, she was meant to appeal to young voters. The strategy backfired. Asked by reporters to state her biggest regret, she flummoxed readers with her reply: she'd not had the time to take her mother to Singapore's new Universal Studios theme park. Newspaper journalists and their readers may have remarked at her shallow answer, but then moved on. Netizens, however, refused to let go. They intuited a pattern. A photograph of her from her Facebook page, showing off a new designer bag with girlish glee, went viral and sealed her reputation as an immature social climber. It did not help Tin's reputation that she was married to the prime minister's top aide, ten years her senior. To make matters worse for Tin, the opposition team contesting Marine Parade GRC included one Nicole Seah, who, though three years younger, showed a sobriety and poise beyond her years. Within days, Seah had more Facebook fans than a page put up on the social networking platform for Lee Kuan Yew.

While many of the comments about Tin were disturbingly personal, irrelevant and off-colour, she symbolised a substantive election issue: the perception that the PAP was not trying hard enough in its candidate selection. Inferior individuals were seen as getting a free pass into Parliament thanks to the GRC system, which bundled them together with heavyweight ministers. At the core of this issue, critics perceived a larger problem: the PAP didn't care what people thought. Thus, Tin's candidacy seemed to represent all that was wrong with the ruling party. The PAP won Marine Parade, but with less than 57 per cent of the vote. It even did worse there than in Tampines GRC, where the minister in charge of public housing, Mah Bow Tan, had been expected to be punished by voters. Goh Chok Tong, in contrast, had been relatively untainted before the campaign. That Tin proved as much a liability as the government's public housing policy mistakes was the single biggest harbinger of the new in Singapore's new media landscape. This, however, was no revolution. The PAP still won the 2011 election by 81 seats to 6, and with 60.1 per cent of the valid votes cast, showing that its dominance was fundamentally unshaken by media, old or new. This chapter explains these two sides of the internet in Singapore: how it developed into a genuinely alternative space for diverse views in an authoritarian society; and yet, all said and done, why PAP power remained formidable.

Regulatory Loopholes

For a country where the act of publishing, broadcasting or performing anything has always required the government's permission, the first question to ask is why access to the internet was so freely granted and even encouraged. The answer has a lot to do with the special characteristics of the internet as a multi-purpose and open-ended communication technology. Already great fans of computerisation, Singapore government planners quickly latched on to the internet as a key economic infrastructure for their "Intelligent Island" masterplan. They also recognised that they could not easily cherry-pick the purposes for which this infrastructure would be used: e-business could not be promoted without simultaneously allowing e-politics, or e-anything. Most of the internet's individual features are nothing special. Television and radio are as instantaneous, while the telephone is as interactive. What is unique is its "end-to-end" architecture. Since it is basically a set of freely shared protocols, the internet allowed users at the edges of the network to create whole new ways of using that network.[2] This is radically different from conventional communication technologies, which rely on custom-built devices with functions that are predetermined by their maker or some centralised authority. Even if you had the skill to reprogram your TV set, you could not use the device to send messages over the airwaves unless the organisations that control television broadcasting let you. In contrast, internet users could — and did — develop the means to share videos, for example, without any authority needing to unlock the network for this purpose. This makes the internet a "generative" technology, enabling an unprecedented degree of innovation.[3]

Furthermore, these new uses were harder to regulate. When dealing with older media, the government was able to discriminate easily between favoured commercial or cultural uses and unwanted political uses. The licensing system for print periodicals exploits that ability to exercise such discretion: regulators would be able to grant permits for foreign-backed competitors to lifestyle magazines such as *Her World* or *Wine & Dine*, while blocking attempts to take on *The Straits Times* in the general interest newspaper market. Similarly, regulations could discriminate meaningfully between private communication (telephone calls and letters are not censored) and public communication (films and plays are). Old media also allowed production and distribution to be regulated more strictly than consumption: you need a licence to operate a broadcast station but not to own a radio set. The internet, however, poses a dilemma for regulators because it defies such categorisation. E-mail, for example, can be used as a one-to-one medium like a phone, or as a means of disseminating newsletters to a mailing list of thousands, like a magazine or newspaper. What is more, the networked computer packed with user-friendly applications can be used for either consumption or production. To limit the political risk to the government, these digital technologies could have been banned entirely, but only at the expense of foregoing various benefits that the government was eager to tap — including through its own e-services, such as online filing of tax returns and payment of fines. In contrast, older media technologies had a one-to-one relationship with the uses they were designed for, making them easier to regulate. For example, to ban the home reception of satellite TV channels, regulators just had to ban satellite dishes; and the ban on dishes did not prevent homes from receiving government correspondence, for example.

On top of these unique technical characteristics, the internet also arrived with a symbolic and cultural status that regulators were forced to respect. From the mid-1990s, it was treated globally as virtually synonymous with the information technology revolution. The world had come to be seen as entering a new "informational mode of development", as Manuel Castells called it.[4] This revolution was seen as both a promise and a threat. Network effects meant that the benefits of being plugged in — and the costs of being disconnected — would grow exponentially. Companies and countries felt that they had no choice but to connect if they were to survive and thrive in the new global economic competition. Earlier media technologies were regarded primarily as channels for political and cultural messages, not as modes of production. In contrast, the internet's rollout was framed initially within the discourse of scientific research and the development of a new information economy.

This was reflected in the institutional framework for administering the digital revolution. The government's lead IT agency was the National Computer Board under the Ministry of Finance. Internet access was first provided to researchers and academics through Technet, set up in 1991 by the National University of Singapore and the National Science and Technology Board, which came under the Education Ministry and the Trade and Industry Ministry respectively. The first commercial internet service provider was Singnet, launched in

July 1994 by the government-owned Singapore Telecom and overseen by the telecommunication regulator, under the communications ministry.[5] Only in 2001, with the creation of the Ministry of Information, Communication and the Arts, was the internet's development overseen by the same ministry that dealt with censorship, propaganda, and press and broadcast licensing. None of this is to suggest that the government was, until then, oblivious to the potential political challenge posed by the internet. What is clear, though, is that it framed the internet first and foremost as an economic opportunity and only secondarily as a political risk. The high-tech community within and outside government set the pace in thinking about this new platform. Thus, in the critical period when internet policy was being formulated, the government decided to tolerate a lesser degree of political control online than they were accustomed to offline. Although Parliament enacted a new broadcasting law in 1994 that formally extended the government's jurisdiction to electronic communication, no specific rules were set down for online media. Speaking in 1995, George Yeo, the minister for information and the arts, explained the government's thinking. He likened the internet to a big city with both "wholesome, well-lit parts" as well as "dark alleys with dirt, sleaze and crime". But the city could not be avoided; it would eventually "envelop us, like an expanding urban conurbation absorbing small towns in its path". He added, "When books are commonplace, it is important to be able to read. In the same way, those who are not adept in information technology will be at a severe competitive disadvantage in the 21st century."[6]

The authorities introduced content regulations for the internet in July 1996. It was one of the first governments in the world to do so, and may have even inspired others to follow suit.[7] The new regulations introduced a "class licence" system, which nodded to the bedrock principle that media ownership in Singapore is not a right but is subject to government licensing. However, instead of having to apply for individual permits as with newspapers and broadcast stations, internet content providers were deemed automatically licensed as a class. They were free to launch websites without seeking government permission. Singapore sites that sought public attention and dealt with the sensitive areas of religion or politics would have to meet an additional requirement. They could be asked to register with the regulatory agency. Registration required disclosure of key personnel. The editorial team would also have to sign a declaration saying that they would take "full responsibility for the contents on the website(s) and ... all reasonable steps to ensure that such contents comply with the laws of Singapore".[8]

Registration, which ultimately affected only a handful of political sites, did not amount to a vetting or approval system. Its ostensible aim was to promote accountability, and — while it may have had a chilling effect on some — it did not require anyone to seek permission before publishing anything online. Nevertheless, the registration requirement met with deep hostility and suspicion by netizens. When asked to register as a political website in 2001, Sintercom's owners chose to close it down rather than comply. Ten years later, though, The Online Citizen received the same instruction and decided that registration was not an onerous enough obstacle to divert it from its mission — it mocked the government move by throwing a party.[9] The internet remained the only medium for mass communication that was free of prior restraints: would-be publishers faced no pre-censorship. More surprisingly, the government also refrained from blocking political content. Independent annual tests by the OpenNet Initiative have found no evidence of filtering of political sites.[10] Netizens' worst fears did not materialise, and by the late 2000s, seasoned bloggers would concede that the government had lived up its "light touch" assurance.

While willing to stomach a great deal of online criticism in ordinary times, the government was sensitive about how the internet might be used during election campaigns. Before the 2001 elections, it amended campaign advertising regulations under the Parliamentary Elections Act. Although the internet was not off-limits to parties, they were prohibited from exploiting the medium's most powerful features. Parties could not stream audio or video online, for example. They were also prohibited from doing online petitions or viral marketing. Websites that did not belong to parties or candidates but had been required by the regulators to register as political sites were banned from online electioneering. Think Centre, which fell into that category, was directed by the Elections Department during the 2001 election to remove one article that was deemed to violate the regulations.[11] Again, though, although the restrictions were highly controversial, they were not particularly debilitating. In his study of parties' use of the new media in the 2001 election, internet researcher Randolph Kluver found that they seemed to treat the medium as an afterthought, and generally underused the legal space available to them.[12] In the 2006 election, bloggers were more confused than intimidated by the rules — and largely ignored them. For the 2011 election, regulations were substantially liberalised, allowing parties and bloggers to exploit social media and multimedia features with few restrictions. One new limitation was an extension of the ban on polling day campaigning, to cover the eve of polling day as well. This so-called "cooling off" day applied to parties and candidates. News media were exempted. But this exemption applied only to licensed news media, and since independent online journalism was unlicensed, articles posted during the moratorium period could technically be declared as illegal advertising. This risk was ignored by several of Singapore's prominent independent bloggers, in a sign of their growing confidence. The Online Citizen, for example, went ahead and posted commentaries on cooling off day and polling day.

Contentious Journalism

By dramatically lowering the economic and political barriers to publishing, the internet invited a horde of individuals and groups into an arena that was previously the preserve of establishment newspapers and broadcasters. For analysts examining this trend worldwide, one of the challenges has been definitional: how to name and categorise the bewildering diversity of media practices and practitioners online. Perhaps the first thing to note is that not all the players in new media are new. Well-established news organisations have had the resources to build content-rich websites that attract heavy traffic. In most countries, Singapore included, the leading newspapers' and broadcasters' websites are among the most visited sources of news and information online. The most popular sites overall, such as Google, Yahoo! and MSN, are new players but are not major creators of original content. Their news portals depended heavily on traditional news organisations. Other than allowing more free-wheeling comments to be posted by readers than would be found in a newspaper's letters pages, these major online players do not significantly change the relationship between media and state power.

One example is STOMP, the colourful user-generated content platform launched by *The Straits Times* in 2006. STOMP marketed itself as Singapore's top "citizen journalism" site, using an in-vogue term referring to journalism that is practised from the ground up. The claim is somewhat misleading, since STOMP's professional journalists retain ultimate editorial control, with non-professionals on tap rather than on top. While STOMP relies on citizen reporting, the core of journalism — editorial judgment — is not entrusted to mere citizens, only to professional SPH staffers. (A more appropriate term for STOMP would be "participatory journalism", which covers the practice of amateurs working in collaboration with professionals.[13]) Within a liberal democratic context, the same technologies have been used to facilitate political participation. In Britain, for example, the BBC ran a portal between 2003 and 2008 — iCan, later renamed Action Network — to help citizens take part in local civic and democratic activities. In Singapore, however, STOMP's version of participatory media is depoliticised: entertainment and consumer values dominate. Postings about government tend to be of the "hyperlocal" variety, highlighting problems with municipal services, for example. Its Talkback section conducts polls, but avoids questions that cut too close to the bone. For example, after the shocking escape of alleged terrorist Mas Selamat Kastari from a detention centre, a poll went up momentarily on STOMP, asking, "Who should resign over the terrorist escape issue?" — but it was quickly taken down.[14]

The posing and probing of such politically sensitive questions has instead been the specialty of a new breed of writers and editors operating through websites that are independent of large news organisations. They fall into the broad category that scholars have called "alternative media". They are not substitutes for mainstream media, which have been too powerful to unseat. Rather, they play a complementary role, adding diversity to the media system. They are generally small and cheaply run, less formally organised than mainstream media, and less bound by professional norms and standards.[15] These attributes may seem like weaknesses, but they are precisely what enable alternative media to democratise access to the power of symbolic representation. Chris Atton notes that alternative media may deliberately resist becoming as commercial, hierarchical or professional as mainstream media organisations because these seeming strengths tend to restrict citizens' access to the modes of communication.[16] Alternative media opt instead for a more authentic discourse, reflecting the perspectives of the marginalised, including subcultural groups and social movements.

Alternative media form a very broad category. It includes the newsletters of religious groups and political parties, fanzines and the student press. One of the most long-lived and deep-pocketed in Singapore is *Catholic News*, first published in 1935. Singapore's most successful internet startup among alternative media is probably Fridae.asia, a lifestyle website for the gay and lesbian community. Other than its subcultural niche, Fridae has many of the attributes of mainstream media — including commercial success — showing that the term alternative media is elastic. For this study, the most interesting development within alternative media is what I call "contentious journalism". This subset is engaged in reporting and commenting on current events, using the methods of observation, investigation and analysis, in order to serve a public purpose — satisfying my definition of "journalism". These alternative media are "contentious" in two senses. First, in keeping with Sidney Tarrow's notion of contentious politics, they openly challenge the authority of elites in setting the national agenda and in forging consensus.[17] In Singapore, a 1991 Government White Paper on "Shared Values" proposed that the nation adopt "Consensus, Not Contention" as one of five core principles to live by.[18] Contentious journalism is instinctively suspicious of such a position. Mainstream journalism, in contrast, is more likely to value consensus. Although many journalists in liberal democracies see themselves in an adversarial relationship with the government, critical studies of the press suggest that it is really a deeply conservative institution, upholding "moderatism", mainstream values and the position of elites.[19] Even when its journalism is noisy and combative, its impact is contained: it may attack individual politicians and governments, but the regime as a whole is reproduced. Contentious journalism, on the other hand, is potentially "transgressive": it involves players who are new and who engage in actions that are either unprecedented or disallowed. Transgressive contention can produce significant short-term political and social change.[20]

There is a second sense in which such journalism is contentious: it embodies competing journalistic methods and motives. Mainstream journalism around the world has converged around a set of global professional norms: it tends to be practised through formal organisations by paid and trained professionals who try to detach themselves from social conflict when exercising their editorial judgments. Contentious journalism flouts these norms, seeing some or all of them as obstructing democratic communication. Most of such projects subscribe to a more morally-engaged and less disinterested mode of journalism than the mainstream press. Some go to the extent of weaving advocacy or partisanship into their journalism — prompting some professionals to question whether they count as journalists at all. Thus, the very claim that theirs is a form of journalism is itself contentious.

In liberal societies, contentious journalism appears in almost all media formats, including small newspapers, magazines and radio programmes. In Singapore, where the licensing system has shut it out of print and broadcast media, contentious journalism has surfaced almost exclusively on the internet. The most common form is the individual blog. Of these, the longest running and probably the most influential is Alex Au's Yawning Bread, launched in 1996. Another noteworthy blog is Singapore Rebel by media activist Martyn See, whom we will meet again in the next chapter.[21] In general, though, websites run by groups and organisations have tended to be more prominent than individual blogs. They come in various forms. Several have been run by loose networks of individuals and have no formal organisational links. These included sites that were anonymously edited, possibly by overseas-based Singaporeans, such as Singapore Window and Temasek Review. However, some are run by known individuals, many of them active in civil society. Such sites include the original online magazine, Sintercom, and the most serious contentious journalism effort to date, The Online Citizen. Another category of group websites comprises the official vehicles of political parties and non-government organisations (NGOs). For example, the pro-democracy political associations Think Centre and Singaporeans For Democracy are active online — often more than offline. Political parties were relative latecomers to cyberspace, but the Singapore Democratic Party, in particular, evolved a strong internet presence that included journalistic content.

Organisations such as Think Centre, Singaporeans For Democracy and the leading opposition parties are newsmakers as well as media practitioners. The main function of their websites has been to cover their own activities. Interestingly, The Online Citizen has also seen fit to go beyond reporting and commenting from the sidelines: it has occasionally organised its own events. In 2010, it co-organised a petition signing event at the Speakers' Corner, to supplement its online petition appealing for clemency for a young Malaysian who had been sentenced to hang, Yong Vui Kong. The same year, it held a pre-election forum. Such activities recall the concept of "public journalism", whose advocates have argued that journalists should not use "objectivity" as an excuse to wash their hands of the problem of apathy and depoliticisation. "Objectivity permits journalists to speak of 'informing the public' without worrying about how a public gets formed in the first place," notes Jay Rosen. Instead, they should act to "engage and enliven — rather than merely inform — a genuine public", he adds.[22] In the United States, a few mainstream organisations have taken such advice to heart, organising town hall meetings and other campaigns, for example. However, most professionals shun direct involvement in the news that they cover — let alone creating the news. In this and other ways, contentious journalism goes where professional media fear to tread.

Although each of these political sites in Singapore is small, their collective impact is likely to be significant because they — together with popular online forums such as Hardwarezone[23] and Sammyboy[24] — are overwhelmingly oppositional. None of the prominent independent sites feel the need to post articles in praise of the government, since mainstream media are perceived to be filling that role quite adequately. The Online Citizen, for example, does not claim to be balanced. "We *are* the balance," said one of its editors.[25] Most contributors to online forums are knee-jerk in their attacks, apparently investing as much time in thought as it takes to post a comment — which is not much. Temasek Review, cloaked in pseudonymity, was regularly libelous, rarely letting the facts get in the way of a juicy anti-PAP story. However, there are also bloggers whose criticism is backed by careful investigation. Leong Sze Hian, a financial consultant who writes regularly for The Online Citizen, delves into official statistics to unearth troubling patterns that are not apparent from government speeches and press releases. Tan Kin Lian was another critical blogger who enjoyed considerable credibility, having spent most of his career heading NTUC Income, the insurance cooperative of the government-friendly labour movement. As for Alex Au, his Yawning Bread blog frequently involves careful dissection of government positions to expose hypocrisy, inconsistency and logical fallacies. Over the years, he said, his close watching of government and politics had made him "more fair, less judgmental", and more prepared to give the government the benefit of the doubt. "Everyone is a shade of grey," he noted, adding that he prefers "thrashing out ideas rather than whacking the PAP".[26] However, when he believes that his reasoning has led him to incontrovertible conclusions, he does not pussyfoot around his prey in the trademark establishment media style of opinion writing. After the 2011 General Election, for example, he declared Prime Minister Lee Hsien Loong to be a "lousy leader" — an opinion that would never be aired in the national press.

He is indecisive and over cautious.... Worst of all, he has never demonstrated any vision. He really does not know where Singapore should go.... In any real democracy, with a fearless media, robust civil society and empowered opposition parties, he would long ago have been chased out of politics and relegated to a technocrat's job in the basement.[27]

Thus, the internet has become a lively counter-hegemonic space, where contentious journalism challenges the *status quo* in a way not seen for decades. A government not known for its tolerance of opposition showed remarkable self-restraint in its reaction to online dissent. This was certainly not because it had become liberal in outlook. Defamation suits, prosecutions for contempt of court and other actions against offline expression continued to punctuate Singapore's political calendar. In effect, the government operated a dual regulatory system for media, with stricter standards applied to print and broadcasting than to online media. The idea of differential censorship for mass media and niche media was not new: the film classification system allowed films that would have to be censored for television broadcast to be screened uncut for adult audiences in cinemas. In the early years of the web, the same logic might have applied to internet regulation: websites were niche media and did not require the same scrutiny as the national news media organisations. Quickly, though, some online media became mass media with tens of thousands of readers, as many as smaller newspapers such as the *Business Times*, *Berita Harian* or *Tamil Murasu*. In early 2012, government leaders threatened to sue Yawning Bread and TREmeritus (the new incarnation of Temasek Review) for libel, indicating its preparedness to act against prominent websites. However, wild anonymous attacks on the establishment continued unabated on various online forums and Facebook. The government appeared to reconcile itself to a new political terrain where it would no longer fully control what was said or shown publicly.

Mixed Results

In the United States in 1998, the Drudge Report website helped to push Bill Clinton's affair with Monica Lewinksy into the national spotlight, hijacking the attention of the US administration for more than a year. In Indonesia, the internet helped spread news and information under the repressive New Order regime, playing its part in the Reformasi movement that brought down President Suharto. Social media were key mobilising tools in the revolutions in Tunisia and Egypt in 2010–11. In these and many other ways, the internet seems to be fulfilling the promise of John Barlow's 1996 Declaration of the Independence of Cyberspace. "I declare the global social space we are building to be naturally independent of the tyrannies you seek to impose on us," he had told world leaders at the annual Davos summit. "You have no moral right to rule us nor do you possess any methods of enforcement we have true reason to fear."[28] But this early hyperbole soon gave way to more sober assessments. By 2003, a multi-country study published by the Carnegie Endowment for International Peace concluded that "the Internet is not inherently a threat to authoritarian rule".[29] And in a major policy speech in 2010, US Secretary of State Hillary Clinton noted that the world's information infrastructure had no natural destiny independent of what different countries made of it. "On their own, new technologies do not take sides in the struggle for freedom and progress," she said.[30]

One of the main reasons for such dampened expectations is the realisation that the internet is not immune from censorship. Lawrence Lessig has pointed out that the internet is merely a set of human-made code.[31] In the form that the internet was originally structured, it was indeed difficult for the government to regulate behaviour on the net, he notes. But he adds, "Even if it is hard to regulate behavior given the Net as it is, it is not hard for the government to take steps to alter, or supplement, the architecture of the Net. And it is those steps in turn that could make behavior on the Net more regulable."[32] China has gone down this path aggressively, effectively turning the Chinese internet into a neighbourhood separate from the global internet. It is not alone: other governments have acted in various ways to restrict freedom of expression on the internet.

Furthermore, individual dissenters are relatively unthreatening, even in large numbers. "Only when collective alternatives are available does political choice become available to isolated individuals," Adam Przeworski says.[33] Offline organisation is ultimately essential to counter hegemonic regimes. And this is the second reason why most analysts have grown circumspect about the revolutionary potential of new media. The internet can impressively magnify the power of existing networks, but can't create them where none exists. Summarising the research on the ICTs and democratisation, Clay Shirky notes that digital tools "probably do not hurt in the short run and might help in the long run — and that they have the most dramatic effects in states where a public sphere already constrains the actions of the government".[34] The internet is most democratising when it is planted in an environment where people are already dissatisfied with their economic situation and day-to-day governance, and where conversation is already buzzing, Shirky says. My own research on Singapore and its neighbours would add that the level of organisation within civil society, the strength of the opposition, and divisions within the elite are all crucial non-technological factors that explain why contentious journalism emerges more prominently in some societies than in others.[35] In the late 1990s and early 2000s, Singapore was much more advanced than Malaysia and Indonesia in terms of internet penetration and even basic literacy. If technology were a determining factor, Singapore's alternative online media should have raced ahead. Yet, its neighbours set the pace, with websites such as Harakah and Malaysiakini in Malaysia, and Tempo and Detik in Indonesia. Singapore did not have — and still does not have — any website in the same league, capable of daily original reporting by full-time staff.

Singaporean critics of the PAP want to believe that this backwardness is due to government repression. Such a claim would be an insult to media activists elsewhere — it is not as if they have it any easier than their Singapore counterparts. Malaysia's alternative media flowered in the years when Prime Minister Mahathir Mohamed was named by Reporters Without Borders as one of the world's ten greatest enemies of press freedom. President Suharto's New Order regime in Indonesia did not exactly welcome dissent, either. Indeed, if there is a relationship between repression and contentious media, these three Southeast Asian neighbours suggest that causality flows in the opposite direction: more overt repression in Malaysia and Indonesia has produced a reaction in the form of vibrant contentious politics and media, while Singapore's calibrated methods dampen the growth in demand for vigorous alternative media.

Comparing Singapore and its neighbours underlines how important it is to examine the ecosystem in which new technologies are planted. The growth of contentious journalism in Singapore has been contemporaneous with the reawakening of Singapore's civil society, with which it has a symbiotic relationship. The gay and lesbian group People Like Us outed itself in 1996, the same year that Alex Au, one of its leading lights, started Yawning Bread.[36] The migrant worker NGO Transient Workers Count Too was launched in 2003.[37] The Singapore Anti-Death Penalty Campaign,[38] the freedom of expression network Arts Engage[39] and the human rights group Maruah[40] were all born between 2005 and 2010. Over the same period, opposition parties, once dormant in between elections, have also become more active. Singapore's contentious journalism has grown in tandem, but — like the opposition and civil society — still lags behind neighbouring countries. By 2010, Singapore's most active opposition website was Singapore Democrats,[41] but it was still years behind Malaysia's leading opposition site, Harakah Daily.[42] The gap is easily explained by the difference between their parent parties: the Singapore Democratic Party still had only a fraction of the resources and power possessed by the Pan-Malaysian Islamic Party, PAS. Similarly, The Online Citizen benefits from newly emergent civil society groups, but still lacks the strong allies that Malaysiakini has been able to tap into within Malaysia's broad and deep pro-democracy movement. In the area of human rights promotion, for example, Singapore's NGO, Maruah, is fully 20 years behind Malaysia's Suaram. Singapore does not have any equivalent of its neighbour's Centre for Independent Journalism, whose full-time staff advocate for freedom of expression and conduct training for grassroots media.

Contentious journalism's reliance on an ecosystem of contentious politics explains why the Singapore government can afford to be sanguine about online dissent. Only when dissent is mobilised and organised does it become politically threatening. Then, to have significant impact, it would have to venture beyond cyberspace and enter the real world — which the PAP still regulates and dominates. Singapore's authorities do not really need to clean up cyberspace — which would be a messy, inefficient enterprise — if they can police the boundaries between the online and offline worlds. Part of this policing is delegated to mainstream media gatekeepers, who are expected to prevent the more unruly ways of cyberspace from leaking into the formal public sphere. Thus, when *Today* attempted to ride on the popularity of Lee Kin Mun's Mr Brown blog by giving him a regular column, the experiment ended badly. After the newspaper published one critical piece, the government replied that while Lee was entitled to his views, "opinions which are widely circulated in a regular column in a serious newspaper should meet higher standards".[43] It added:

> It is not the role of journalists or newspapers in Singapore to champion issues, or campaign for or against the Government. If a columnist presents himself as a non-political observer, while

exploiting his access to the mass media to undermine the Government's standing with the electorate, then he is no longer a constructive critic, but a partisan player in politics.

Today immediately terminated Lee's column, sparking the online era's equivalent of the 1990s' "Catherine Lim Affair", when the government threatened to treat the fiction writer as a political opponent after she wrote two political essays that were judged to have attacked the authority of Singapore's leaders.[44] The government maintained that Mr Brown's exit was *Today*'s own decision, raising the question of whether this was another case of unnecessary self-censorship. But, given that the government did not merely refute the offending column but virtually accused *Today* of allowing itself to be exploited by a partisan player, the editors may have correctly assessed the political risk of continuing its relationship with the blogger.

While it is easy to romanticise virtual communities, the scale and scope of their activities would be limited if they did not, at some point, accumulate or expend resources — including cash — in the real world. The internet was designed to allow information packets to flow unimpeded, but the movement of money is easier for governments to regulate. "The one thing that hasn't changed in the new media is that ultimately there is still a money trail and identity will always be unmasked," said Cabinet minister Vivian Balakrishnan. "Any political movement or political leader worth his salt will sooner or later be unmasked and, therefore, can be dealt with or can be engaged on political terms."[45] In late 2009, when Malaysiakini turned ten, I blogged that one reason why such a model would be hard to replicate in Singapore was the Political Donations Act.[46] Malaysiakini could not have started without grants and loans from the Bangkok-based Southeast Asia Press Alliance and the Soros-backed Media Development Loan Fund. Similarly, other independent media in Southeast Asia have been supported by the likes of Free Voice from the Netherlands and the US-based International Center for Journalists. In Singapore, I noted, the government could stop overseas funding simply by gazetting such a group as a political association. In early 2011, the government did exactly this, to The Online Citizen. The authorities acted a month after the site organised its much-publicised pre-election forum, which featured six opposition party representatives (the PAP declined its invitation). Although The Online Citizen had shelved plans to professionalise and had reconciled itself to continuing as an informal, volunteer-based entity, it had an on-going appeal for online donations via PayPal. It had also solicited cash donations at its pre-election forum. The government had evidently seen sufficient signs that, with enough backing, the website could morph into something more threatening.

The Political Donations Act had been passed by Parliament more than ten years earlier, with the aim of keeping the electoral contest free of money politics. In line with the PAP's zero-loophole approach to legislation, the Act was not limited to political parties; it also applied to any organisation "whose objects or activities relate wholly or mainly to politics in Singapore" and that the government chose to classify as a political association.[47] Two months earlier, Maruah was gazetted as such, despite its strictly non-partisan constitution. The Online Citizen became the first journalistic entity to be brought under the Act. The law imposes a total ban on foreign donations. Contributions from local sources are also regulated. The total amount of anonymous donations it can receive each year is capped at $5,000. Anonymous donations above the cap would have to be either returned or handed over to the Registrar of Political Donations. The law also requires the association to list in its annual donation reports the names of individuals who give sums greater than $10,000, possibly deterring any large benefactor who might wish to protect his privacy.

The Difference It Makes

The obstacles faced by alternative online media mean that they are unlikely to generate major shocks to the system. Their impact is more likely to be gradual and indirect, working in concert with other trends that are not related to media. Several such impacts can be discerned. First, it is clear that the internet has weakened the PAP's hold on the national agenda — its power to shape what people talk about and to frame how issues should be discussed. Digital technologies have accelerated the trend towards niche media, making it economically feasible to create and distribute special-interest media products serving the "long tail" of demand, instead of catering only to the mass-market peaks.[48] The internet hasn't just fragmented the consuming audience. Its more radical impact is to change who gets to produce. The public once took it for granted that their main stories and images should be generated by a small, exclusive set of media institutions. But, what seemed like a natural division labour between consumer and producer is no longer seen as legitimate.[49] With more democratic access to the modes of communication, people can surface issues that matter to them, and keep them alive for as long as they like. The Tin Pei Ling affair, mentioned at the start of this chapter, is but one example: presented by the PAP as a symbol of its rejuvenation and its ties with the young, Tin was reframed by her online critics as symptom of PAP arrogance and disconnectedness. Routinely, inconvenient issues surface online. Most are simply ignored, but some pick up momentum and reach a tipping point, after which officials and mainstream media have little choice but to address them.

Singapore's mass media remain powerful agents for the construction of social reality, but their dominance is waning. The core they occupy is shrinking, while the fringe is exploding. Alternative media have helped to publicise people, events and issues that would otherwise be pushed to the fringe by the government and downplayed by mainstream media. The death penalty, discrimination against gays, the abuse of migrant workers, recognition for former political detainees and censorship of the arts have all featured prominently in The Online Citizen, Yawning Bread and other progressive blogs. A related phenomenon is how the alternative media have elevated the profile of individual activists and politicians, lifting them rapidly from near obscurity to the national stage. One example is Gerald Giam, a former civil servant who co-founded The Online Citizen and had his own blog.[50] He quickly gained a reputation as a serious and sensible critic. In 2009, less than three years after he started blogging, he joined the Workers' Party. His GRC team was one of the top losers in the 2011 election, entitling it to one non-constituency seat in Parliament. The party's central executive committee voted to give that seat to the 34-year-old Giam, a first-time candidate who had joined the party less than two years before. The GRC team's veteran leader and party treasurer had seemed the natural choice for the seat and showed his disappointment by quitting the party. Another made-for-internet star was Tan Kin Lian, who championed the cause of small investors who had been victims of aggressively marketed mini-bonds that crashed in the aftershock of the Lehman Brothers collapse. His campaign was covered sympathetically by national newspapers. When he seemed to be getting too big for his boots — he openly contemplated running for President, more than two years before he actually did — the establishment turned its back on him. With his own blog and support from The Online Citizen, however, he could not be shut out. In 1968, Andy Warhol had predicted that pop culture would let anyone to be famous for 15 minutes. The internet's agenda-setting power allows those 15 minutes to be stretched to 15 months or more.

Second, the alternative online media have attacked the government's main ideological vehicle — the establishment media. The internet has been used to counter the influence of newspapers and broadcast news stations. The online community is constantly on the lookout for examples of pro-government bias, self-censorship and political interference. In the run-up to the 2011 General Election, online media attacked Channel NewsAsia's decision to exclude the Singapore Democratic Party from a multi-party television forum, for example.[51] Another campaign called for a boycott of *The New Paper* for an unsubstantiated story that SDP chief Chee Soon Juan was on the brink of leading an illegal march after a rally and that he had to be restrained by his party colleagues.[52] Such exposés suggest to Singaporeans that the picture of social consensus and harmony that the PAP paints is false, constructed to marginalise those who might be tempted to think differently and preserved by forcibly excluding conflicting viewpoints from the public sphere. Of course, another reason why alternative media believe in monitoring traditional media gatekeepers is that every lapse they expose strengthens their own *raison d'etre*.

One favourite tactic — dating back to Sintercom's "Not the Straits Times Forum" section in the mid-1990s — is to post the original versions of letters sent to the national newspaper, alongside the sanitised versions that appeared in print. Another method is to document cases where controversial stories are toned down when they are rebroadcast or updated. One such incident occurred in 2000–01, when Think Centre caught a radio presenter apologising on air that an item featuring opposition politician J.B. Jeyaretnam would not be re-aired as promised, due to objections from the management. Think Centre doggedly tracked the story, eventually revealing that the reporter was no longer the national broadcaster's payroll. Bloggers have also found several examples where breaking news posted on mainstream media websites was angled more pointedly than later versions. Both SPH and MediaCorp post a few paragraphs of selected stories online first, before carrying the fuller versions on their main platforms. In some cases, by the time controversial stories appeared in TV news bulletins the same evening or in print the next day, the sting had been removed. This could have been because the additional time allowed reporters and their editors to add context, introduce nuance and remove inaccuracies, as professional journalists are supposed to do. However, to eagle-eyed "gatewatchers", the changes smacked of censorship. Ironically, news organisations' ability to rush stories onto the web may have opened a window to government intervention. Singapore does not have a system of government vetting of stories before publication, but an unintended consequence of online news is to give officials early sight of stories that newsrooms are working on, allowing them to make timely phonecalls to journalists in order to spin later versions of the story to their advantage.

Overall, contentious journalism appears to have succeeded in pressuring the mainstream media to improve their performance. One of the most celebrated cases was Yawning Bread's photograph of tens of thousands of people at a Workers' Party rally during the 2006 election. For decades, zoomed-out images of rally crowds were never carried by either print or broadcast news media. Such pictures would have shown the opposition capable of pulling at least ten times more people to their rallies than the PAP. While probably an indication of people's curiosity rather than their voting intentions, the contrast was nonetheless embarrassing to the ruling party and risked influencing swing voters. While everyone already knew that opposition rallies attracted large crowds, the unofficial ban on such photos helped to prevent this fact transitioning from open secret to public truth, to borrow Shirky's useful terms. Alex Au's simple act of contentious journalism punctured this mainstream practice once and for all. *The Straits Times* decided that the policy was no longer tenable and carried similar pictures within days. In the following election in 2011, they became standard fare.

Such cases showed the limits of the government's strategy of using mainstream media gatekeepers to police the boundaries of the public sphere. The borders have turned out to be permeable to conversations that circulate in the alternative media. It is still the case that not everything that comes to journalists' attention deserves to be made public. However, whether or not to publicise something is a power that has been almost completely taken out of professional journalists' hands: increasingly, the information is already "out there" in the public realm. News organisations worldwide have been ethically challenged by this new reality, which puts pressure on them to short-circuit the practice of fact-checking before publication.[53] In the Singapore context, it has become harder for the government to justify to editors why they should hold back. Editors can argue that the choice is no longer whether or not the people should be told; but whether the people should have to rely on only alternative media accounts, when the mainstream media could offer more comprehensive, balanced and accurate versions of a story. Alternative media may be better at reflecting any negative public mood, but the professional press retains an edge when covering complex stories with multiple perspectives. Professional newsrooms have several competitive strengths: in addition to superior access to information and vastly greater man-hours to invest in reporting, writing and editing, they have the discipline of verifying information with multiple sources, the institutional memory to sense when things are more complex than they seem, and higher-order judgment honed by experience and specialised beat knowledge. These abilities are often suspended under political pressure, the factory-like routine of working under deadline, and out of complacency or sheer laziness. However, when it pushes itself, the establishment press usually surpasses the alternative media.

Singapore's mainstream journalists remain sceptical of their challengers in the blogosphere, even those that take pains to carry out original research and reporting. Take, for example, The Online Citizen's 2009–10 investigative reports on homeless Singaporeans, which its team considered a coup.[54] The website's work succeeded in eliciting news reports on the issue in the national media. Some of these mainstream follow-up stories were in the classic "objective" mode of "he-said-she-said" journalism, merely quoting The Online Citizen's claims and the government's counter-claims. However, at least one mainstream journalist attempted to get to the bottom of things — and found that The Online Citizen may have misinterpreted what it had found. Radha Basu, an experienced community beat correspondent for *The Straits Times*, had covered cases of low-income, frail and elderly Singaporeans who had been given the run-around by the government when seeking financial aid, as well as women who had lost their homes when their marriages failed. She knew that there were indeed cases of genuine hardship who were neglected by Singapore's hardline attitude to welfare. However, she found that the trend that The Online Citizen had highlighted seemed to be something different. Her interviews with homeless families on Changi Beach, checks with the authorities and input from NGOs all pointed to a problem of younger households that had taken unnecessary risks by selling their subsidised flats for a quick profit or for reinvesting in property they could not afford.[55]

The Online Citizen had framed their stories to highlight the authorities' apparent heartlessness. But Basu felt she had to take into account the reality that Singapore taxpayers would not tolerate housing policies that liberally bailed out households who squandered their subsidised housing. Looking back, she felt that the case was symptomatic of different reporting methods. When she reached out to The Online Citizen offering to interview their contacts, they were unable to provide her any that panned out. Her own experience had taught her to get identity card numbers of such interviewees, in case their accounts were contradicted by agencies and caseworkers. "I have an informal checklist of things to look out for to suss out genuine victims," she told me. "Over the years, I have seen that genuine victims seldom hesitate in handing over IC numbers and relevant documents, where available." Like most mainstream journalists whose reports contradict bloggers' accounts, Basu had to endure abuse from the rabidly anti-government sections of TOC's readership. Overall, however, she is glad that The Online Citizen exists, as it often has its finger on the pulse of issues on the ground, she says. Many professional journalists seem to share such sentiments. Even if the alternative media are not seen as always reliable, the mainstream media have learnt to monitor them closely for tip-offs and leads. Bloggers, meanwhile, remain dependent on establishment media for most of their raw material. There is thus a love-hate relationship between the two sectors, simultaneously competitive and symbiotic.

The third major impact of alternative online media has been on Singapore's political culture, particularly citizens' attitude to authority. Up to the 1990s, PAP leaders were claiming that they should be treated with deference, in keeping with Singapore's supposed "Asian" or "Confucian" values. The vision of a nation predisposed to kowtowing to authority was never more than a work in progress — there had always been a streak of rebelliousness in Singaporean society. James Scott's description of Southeast Asian peoples who have quietly conspired to resist the totalising embrace of the modern state could easily apply to sections of the Singapore population.[56] Scott notes that most people throughout history have been compelled to engage in a public performance designed to appeal to the expectations of the powerful. Offstage, in relatively unmonitored spaces, people would produce a "hidden transcript" at odds with the official culture.[57] In Singapore, these spaces included coffeeshops and taxi cabs. There, people were free to contradict and ridicule government officials and bemoan their lot in life. The internet brought this hidden transcript out into the open and enabled the crowd-sourcing of jokes and insults. Even if such exchanges revealed no high-level scandals or skeletons in the PAP closet, they had a powerful demonstration effect. Singaporeans showed one another a different way of relating to their government, not as obedient children, but as citizens who deserved to be treated with respect.

By the time of the 2011 elections, the public had been exposed to the ambient noise of online criticism for some 15 years. Public space became less of an echo chamber and more of a cacophony — still dominated by the government's voice, but often accompanied by the hissing and heckling of disaffected Singaporeans. Much more troubling for the PAP than the election result was the open contempt that citizens were showing, online and offline, for a government who they felt had not done enough to earn their respect. Not even Lee Kuan Yew was spared. When he warned Aljunied voters that they would "repent" if they elected the opposition, the reaction was furious and could not be contained: only sinners needed to repent, and voting opposition was a right, not a sin, people retorted. The continuous barrage of comebacks stunned the PAP and kept it off-balance throughout the campaign. As Scott points out, ruling elites are often taken by surprise by how quickly an apparently deferential subordinate group rises up in defiance. They would be less surprised if they had paid attention to the hidden transcript. "When the first declaration of the hidden transcript succeeds, its mobilizing capacity as a symbolic act is potentially awesome," he says. "That first declaration speaks for countless others, it shouts what has historically had to be whispered, controlled, choked back, stifled, and suppressed."[58]

True, Singapore still had no equivalent of Malaysiakini or South Korea's OhmyNews, generating large volumes of original reporting every day. Professional journalists might regard the alternative media as somewhat parasitical, since they mostly feed off mainstream media output. Internet scholar Axel Bruns, however, suggests that we should not be too quick to dismiss such tactics, which may be solidifying into a creative and distinct form of journalism in its own right. While bloggers may draw on mainstream news reports and official publications, they "frequently use journalists', politicians', and corporate actors' own words against them by creatively (but, ideally, truthfully) reappropriating, repurposing, recombining, recontextualizing, and reinterpreting such content to show a very different conception of reality".[59] It remains to be seen whether these internet-assisted developments will permanently damage PAP dominance. Conventional wisdom is that they will. However, many predictions wrongly assume that the PAP is a static organisation, remaining passive when faced with changes that are beyond its control. The PAP's goal has not been to resist change entirely but to manage it such that the state can adapt to it and remain on top of it. Several of the government's internet policies seem designed as temporary holding positions, buying time for the government to adjust to the new environment. It helps to remember that the internet is not, in itself, a political challenger: it is not a case of PAP vs The Internet. Instead, the internet is radically transforming the terrain on which the combatants must do battle. This new environment has certainly favoured insurgents. But, the outcome is not determined. In theory, the state can adapt itself to internet politics, a prospect I shall say more about in the concluding chapter.

CHAPTER 9

Rise of the Unruly: Media Activism and Civil Disobedience

In 2008, a dissident lawyer by the name of Gopalan Nair let fly an online tirade against Singapore leaders Lee Kuan Yew and Lee Hsien Loong, accusing them of being, among other things, "nothing more than tin pot tyrants who remain in power by abusing the courts to eliminate your political opponents".[1] By the standards of the wild wild web, the content of Nair's diatribe was not earth shattering. Singaporeans had grown accustomed to reading unbridled and even unlawful criticism of their leaders on online forums and blogs. However, there was something about his blog posts that made Nair stand out from the crowd: he was, quite literally, asking for trouble. "There is no doubt in the Singaporean sense, I have defamed [Lee Kuan Yew] and his Prime Minister son, not only in my last blog post but in almost all my blog posts since my blog's inception in December 2006," he wrote.[2] This was not the false bravado of a critic cloaked in anonymity or relishing freedom in exile. Although he lived in the San Francisco Bay Area, he was now visiting the country of his birth to observe a trial involving opposition leader Chee Soon Juan. He was within reach of the authorities — and he wanted them to know it. "Mr. Lee Kuan Yew, look here. I am now within your jurisdiction and that of your corrupt police and your corrupt judiciary who will do anything you want of them, however criminal and illegal. What are you going to do about it?" He even volunteered his hotel address — "Broadway Hotel, Room 708, 195 Serangoon Road" — and local mobile number.³ His blog carried a photograph of him — middle-aged, portly, bespectacled — in the top right hand corner. Leaving a trail as clear as a Changi airport runway, Nair was eventually arrested and jailed for two months for insulting a judge.⁴ (As he was not sued for defamation, he was not given the satisfaction of facing the Lees in court.)

The curious case of Gopalan Nair, like so much of Singapore's media and politics, turns conventional wisdom on its head. For decades, those studying the internet's role in political dissent and insurgency have focused on guerrilla-style campaigns. In this mode, the opponents of authoritarian governments use information technology to transcend geography and evade censorship and capture. During the internet's pre-web era, the Zapatista insurgency in Mexico was a favourite example of this emerging trend.⁵ The Zapatistas achieved considerable success in getting their messages out to the world's media while remaining in their jungle hideouts. Gradually, though, analysts realised that governments could master the same technologies and engage in online surveillance and censorship. States could also use their offline dominance to mute the impact of their online challengers. Bloggers were put behind bars. But, even if observers were no longer so certain about who would win, at least the rules of the game seemed straightforward enough. Watching the cat-and-mouse game being played in China, Myanmar, Iran and other authoritarian societies, the strategy for insurgents was clear. They had to stay one step ahead of the authorities, bypassing government filters and firewalls, and using the anonymity and separation of cyberspace to avoid the knock on one's door at midnight. Apparently, though, nobody told Gopalan Nair.

Was his come-and-get-me stunt just an idiosyncrasy? Politics attracts more than a fair share of crazies and not all observed political behaviour deserves deeper analysis. However, the Nair case could in fact tell us something significant about media and power. While the internet is commonly harnessed in authoritarian societies as a vehicle for guerrilla-like hit-and-run communication, his action is an example of a radically different use: as a medium for civil disobedience, with activists deliberately remaining within physical reach of the police. This was a template already used by Chee Soon Juan and his followers in the Singapore Democratic Party. Instead of seeking anonymity or extra-territoriality, they use the internet to magnify their presence and even to invite repression. If such behaviour does not fit into the old conceptual boxes, it could be time to develop new ones. This would entail refining our understanding of the nature of power, how authoritarian systems operate, and the role of media within them.

The guerrilla model is implicitly based on the commonplace view of power that equates it with the exercise of violence; from this perspective, countering power is about evading violence or meeting force with force. This view ignores at least a century's worth of political theory, centred on the idea of hegemony. Hegemonic domination, as Antonio Gramsci observed, involves the gradual replacement of overt coercion with seeming consent.[6] Violence may emerge from centralised power, but it also depreciates power, as Hannah Arendt noted.[7] For this reason, every act of censorship — an act of violence against ideas — poses risks for the state. "Attempts to repress 'dangerous ideas' sometimes have the opposite effect: that is, they serve as catalysts for expanding the reach, resonance and receptivity of those ideas," write Sue Curry Jansen and Brian Martin.[8] Political struggle through non-violent action can exploit what Gene Sharp called "political jiu-jitsu", using the attacker's strength to his disadvantage: "The non-violent resisters can use the asymmetry of non-violent means versus violent action in order to apply to their opponents a political operation analogous to the Japanese martial art of jiu-jitsu. The contrast in types of action throws the opponents off balance politically, causing their repression to rebound against their position and weaken their power."[9]

Strains on "Light Touch" Regulation

Singapore's leaders may not be steeped in political science theory, but they are sufficiently schooled in the art of maintaining power to possess an intuitive grasp of the disadvantages of state violence. In Chapter 5, I argued that "calibrated coercion" was a key factor behind the PAP's consolidation of power.[10] In line with this philosophy, internet regulators promised a "light touch" approach. The Media Development Authority (MDA) has said that it tries "to ensure that minimum standards are set for the responsible use of the Internet while giving maximum flexibility to industry players to operate".[11] Content regulations were introduced in 1996, requiring internet service providers (ISPs) to channel all traffic through proxy servers to facilitate the filtering of content. ISPs have to accede to any instruction from the regulator to block content.[12] In practice, however, the Singapore government never attempted the futile — yet internationally widespread — exercise of trying to censor all objectionable material.

It chose to ban only a "symbolic" list of 100 "high impact" sites, to signpost Singapore's societal values. The blocked sites purvey pornography and racial or religious extremism, not political content.

Although Singaporeans greeted the 1996 "light touch" promise with scepticism, the government indeed refrained from placing any political website on its banned list. While it pioneered the installation of national gateways to enable internet censorship, other jurisdictions raced ahead in actually applying such methods. The OpenNet Initiative, which carries out the world's most thorough analysis of internet filtering practices, has exposed the proliferation of such censorship around the world, but never found evidence of political sites being blocked by Singapore.[13] Malaysia had declared a "no internet censorship" policy in 1997 — partly to cock a snook at Singapore after the latter introduced its internet content regulations — but finally appeared to abandon it in 2007 when faced with the extreme provocation of political blogger Raja Petra Kamarudin.

But by not engaging in prior censorship, the Singapore authorities created a new paradox. In the past, only establishment media had been allowed into the public square. Their editors could be trusted to practise self-censorship behind the scenes. The commercial footing of the mainstream media makes them susceptible to subtle commercial pressures and aligns them with a pro-business, pro-stability government (Chapter 2). The government has not had to wield a big stick in order to secure their cooperation. The gatekeepers are essentially members of the establishment who, while not seeing eye to eye with the government on every issue, value their insider status in what they regard as a common national project. In the internet age, however, the barbarians were allowed to enter the gates. These internet insurgents have been harder to co-opt. Since most are voluntary, non-profit ventures, they are immune to financial pressures. Threatening to suspend a newspaper or fine a broadcaster is a threat to jobs and shareholders, so much so that the threat need not even be uttered. In contrast, independent bloggers and radical filmmakers have relatively little to lose. They already see themselves as marginalised. Disqualified from the PAP's patronage, there is little disincentive against crossing the political out-of-bounds markers. The government has faced fairly sustained and irreverent assaults on its painstakingly constructed aura of authority by publishers who did not try to hide their identities, such as Colin Goh of Talking Cock, Lee Kin Mun of Mr Brown and Alex Au of Yawning Bread.

At least, such individuals were savvy enough to stay on the right side of the law. For some others, online freedom included the latitude to step on legal landmines. Paradoxically, therefore, the "light touch" regulatory regime for the internet produced a situation in which the government found itself having to reach for rarely used legislative weapons to deploy against the unruly newcomers. The reputational cost of government action may have been high in the mid-1990s, but it soon fell. Researchers with the OpenNet Initiative have noted a "sea change", even in more democratic countries:

> States no longer fear pariah status by openly declaring their intent to regulate and control cyberspace. The convenient rubric of terrorism, child pornography, and cyber security has contributed to a growing expectation that states should enforce order in cyberspace, including policing unwanted content.[14]

It is probably more than coincidence that Singapore's first prosecutions for internet communication occurred in late 2001, soon after the 9/11 Al Qaeda attacks increased the West's appetite for order at the expense of liberty. A government critic, Robert Ho, was charged for attempting to incite disobedience to the law in a way likely to lead to a breach of peace — an offence punishable by up to three years imprisonment. The authorities later dropped the charges, saying that the man was mentally ill.[15] In 2002, Ho was again a government target, this time for criminal defamation, but the case was not pursued. Another criminal defamation case involved Fateha.com, which had positioned itself as the true voice of Singapore's Muslim minority. The authorities threatened to charge its editor, Zulfikar Mohamad Shariff, over articles critical of senior establishment figures. Zulfikar fled to Australia before investigations were completed.[16] Note that while defamation is globally recognised as one of the legitimate grounds for limiting freedom of expression, the norm is to treat it as a civil matter. Criminalising defamation is widely regarded as an excessive and disproportionate encroachment on free speech.[17] Even in Singapore, which had earned a reputation for using defamation to discipline political debate, previous cases involving the media or opposition politicians had all been pursued as civil actions. It was never explained why the authorities broke with precedent and resorted to the Penal Code against Ho and Zulfikar in 2002. However, it illustrated how the internet had opened the door to new challenges that were seen as meriting the attention of the police.

In the regulation of film, there was a similar pattern. New, low-cost technologies — starting with the videotape — provided a public platform to a breed of producers who lacked the self-censoring instincts of the commercial and state sectors of the local film and broadcast industry. The Films Act, which had been used mainly to tackle obscenity, was wielded in 1996 to ban a videotape by the opposition Singapore Democratic Party on the grounds that it was "contrary to the public interest". In 1998, the Act was amended to ban any film "directed towards any political end in Singapore" (Chapter 7). In 2001, action was threatened against a documentary about the opposition veteran J.B. Jeyaretnam, *A Vision of Persistence*. It was produced by lecturers and students of Ngee Ann Polytechnic, who obediently withdrew it rather than risk provoking the government's wrath against them and their institution. When the internet emerged as the main platform for independent video, filmmakers were less easy to tame. Media activist Martyn See was threatened with prosecution under the Films Act when his work was distributed online. The widely publicised case was eventually dropped. See's activism will be discussed in greater detail below.

The strongest penalties for online speech were meted out against individuals found guilty of threatening Singapore's ethnic relations by offending racial or religious groups. One such case in 2005–06 was sparked by the publication in *The Straits Times* of a letter querying taxi companies' policy on transporting uncaged dogs, noting that any drool left on seats would bother Muslim passengers. In reaction, two 20-something Singaporean men posted offensive remarks against Muslims on an online forum for dog lovers and a personal blog. A third person, aged 17, made unrelated racist comments on his blog. Another Singaporean blogger made a police report, leading to the three young men being charged and convicted under the Sedition Act — the first use of this colonial inheritance since independence. The two older bloggers were sent to jail — one for a month in prison and another for a day. The 17-year-old, on account of his youth and evidence of childhood trauma, was sent for counselling and made to do community service.

The Sedition Act was also wielded in 2006 against "Char", a Singaporean blogger who, describing himself as a free-thinker, posted a cartoon that depicted Jesus as a zombie biting into a boy's head. The following month, he received an online message from a forum member asking him to remove the image. Char responded by trawling the internet for other unflattering images of Jesus, publishing three of them on his blog. Responding to a complaint, the police called Char in for questioning and later arrested him under the Sedition Act. He was eventually let off with a "stern warning". In 2010, a YouTube video emerged of a Christian evangelical priest, Rony Tan, mocking other faiths during a service. He was called up by the Internal Security Department for questioning. A government statement said that his comments were "unacceptable as they trivialised and insulted the beliefs of Buddhists and Taoists" and risked causing "tension and conflict between the Buddhist/Taoist and Christian communities". The ISD told the pastor that "in preaching or proselytising his faith, he must not run down other religions, and must be mindful of the sensitivities of other religions". The statement said that the pastor expressed deep remorse and extended his apologies. No further action was taken.

Unlike political dissent, these cases of racial and religious offence saw the government acting with considerable public support. While many Singaporeans are in favour of greater freedom of speech with regard to political debate, there is a broad and strong consensus that race and religion should remain off-limits. Indeed, in all the above-mentioned cases as well as others, police interventions were triggered by complaints from members of the public. In two cases involving intolerance expressed by evangelical preachers, their messages did not surface on popular social media sites by accident. They were uploaded by individuals who wanted to alert the public to their controversial content. Netizens commenting on Rony Tan's speech openly suggested that he should be reported to the authorities, with one saying that the Internal Security Department might wish to investigate Tan's ministry. Another posted a link to the Singapore Police Force's crime reporting website. In such instances, therefore, government action carried little risk of backfire. Even so, there was little evidence that the government was trigger-happy. After sending a clear message by imprisoning the so-called "racist bloggers" in 2006, it found it unnecessary to mete out such harsh punishments in subsequent cases, preferring instead to issue warnings. Asked in Parliament to give "a stronger and clearer signal for every breach", the Home Affairs Minister said that disagreements should ideally be "mediated or resolved on the ground through common sense, and moral suasion using the collective efforts of the community, grassroots and religious leaders".[18]

In one case involving reservist soldiers who unwittingly violated the Singapore Armed Forces Act in 2005 by posting images from their overseas training stints, the authorities took pains to emphasise that, while some images had to be taken down, they were not trying to dampen self-expression. The bloggers were even encouraged to carry on their good work. In this and several other instances, investigations did not lead to charges being filed.[19] Thus, in policing freedom of expression, the government tried to avoid criminalising those who did not match its description of trying to bring down the system. Harder to ignore, however, was a small group of media activists who began using the internet in a more directly confrontational campaign. Clearly comprehending that their underdog status could be used to their advantage, these activists experimented with a style of politics new to independent Singapore. It involved openly nudging or even crossing legal boundaries. Intervention by the authorities would not end the game. Instead, being on the receiving end of government force — especially when it was unwarranted, disproportionate and unfair — could win points for the activists.

Turning the Tables

In Singapore, the first to use the internet as a means of "political jiu-jitsu" was probably James Gomez, a political activist who founded Think Centre.[20] Think Centre embarked on a number of activities that put it on a collision course with the authorities. Gomez recognised that there were advantages to be gained regardless of the outcomes of these encounters: even if a project were obstructed by the authorities, that fact could be exploited to embarrass the government. So, when Think Centre organised public events, it chronicled on its website the convoluted process of obtaining the necessary permits. Police investigations into Think Centre activities were also quickly reported in detail on the internet. The tone of these reports was sometimes morally indignant, but often humorously irreverent. The police probe into one Think Centre forum, for example, was referred to as a "comedy-drama" and "festivities". The group even wrapped up the final interview at a police station with a photo session, the result of which was posted on the web, along with a written account. "The group's request to take a picture of this 'warning' session, which took place in [the investigating officer's] room, was predictably declined," the online report said. "Determined to have a group picture to commemorate this session at Tanglin, the group thus enlisted the help of a gangster-type loitering at the station. He was very obliging and helped the group out with a few photographs."[21]

Think Centre also turned the tables on government surveillance. Gomez called this tactic "watching the watchers". Plainclothes agents are widely assumed to be present at any political event in Singapore. At large public events such as election rallies, they make no attempt to conceal their presence, pointing video cameras at the crowd or opening briefcases full of recording equipment. The mainstream news media do not report their presence, perhaps because they are no longer deemed newsworthy. The targets of surveillance also tend to shrug it off, "failing to acknowledge that they feel in some ways intimidated and violated," Gomez noted.[22] He launched his first "internet counter-surveillance offensive" in mid-1999, before Think Centre was formed. He posted on the web what he observed outside the venue of a meeting organised by two opposition politicians. He counted 8 to 12 individuals whom he believed to be agents, including women carrying boxy handbags that appeared to conceal cameras — "the camera lens was the size of a five-cent coin and was merged in the middle of an elaborate gold ornament in the front of the handbag".[23]

When Think Centre began organising its own activities, "watching the watchers" became standard operating procedure. Members would approach suspected agents of the government, on one occasion posting a photograph of their uninvited guest. "The Internet has made surveillance interactive," Gomez said.[24] He noted that the agents, when confronted, tended to leave and not be seen again. Of course, it is hardly likely that the authorities would have then aborted or scaled back their surveillance activities. At most, realising that the target was not intimidated by overt surveillance, officials would have switched to covert methods. However, the activists' deeper objective was served: to make censorship and surveillance backfire through the logic of non-violent action.

Continuing in this tradition was political filmmaker and blogger Martyn See. His 2005 documentary about Chee Soon Juan, *Singapore Rebel*, was banned. So was his 2006 film, *Zahari's 17 Years*, an interview with former political detainee and journalist Said Zahari. With these films making their way onto the world wide web, the bans did not prevent interested viewers from watching See's creations. More importantly, he used his blog to publish a blow-by-blow account of his encounters with the authorities, including a 15-month police investigation before he was let off with a stern warning. "Under this climate of fear and self-censorship, the only tool available to me by way of publicising my story was the internet," he said. "So I posted updates of the police investigation on my blog, and immediately it was picked up by news wire agencies based in Singapore."[25] The case thus attracted the attention of international human rights organisations. Statements were issued by Amnesty International, Reporters Without Borders, Committee to Protect Journalists and Southeast Asian Press Alliance.[26]

Assessing the net effect of the *Singapore Rebel* ban, Kenneth Paul Tan noted,[27] "Censorship has seriously backfired, having turned a mediocre film into an icon of freedom, a relatively unknown filmmaker into a martyr, and the perception of inconsistencies in the application of law into a sign of political hypocrisy." In hindsight, See himself recognised that the authorities had done him a favour: "If the censors had cleared the film, it would have been screened to an audience of no more than 80 people, and not all of them would be interested or much less impressed with its content. It would have died a natural death not long afterwards."[28] By 2008, he was openly challenging the authorities to clamp down on the uploading of political films onto the internet.

Think Centre and Martyn See were willing to turn the spotlight on themselves in order to make a public point about censorship and surveillance in Singapore. For them, the internet was not a hiding place but a stage on which to perform their acts of impertinence against the *status quo*. They ventured into uncharted political territory, probing shadowy areas in regulations and reporting the results to the public. However, they stopped short of deliberate law-breaking. For example, when Think Centre was ordered to take down material from its website that allegedly contravened a ban on online electioneering, it complied immediately.[29] Martyn See, similarly, was careful to stress that, while his banned films were easily found online, they had not been uploaded by him, which would have made him "culpable of distributing a prohibited film which does carry a jail term".[30]

Non-violent Resistance

Another small group of committed activists decided to take political jiu-jitsu to its logical extreme. They were willing to break what they considered unjust laws, forcing the government to reveal its repressive self. Their campaign of civil disobedience was publicised primarily through the internet. It was led by Chee Soon Juan, secretary-general of the Singapore Democratic Party (SDP). In 1999, he was convicted for twice breaching the Public Entertainment Act by speaking in public without a permit. Instead of paying fines totalling $3,800, he chose to go to jail — showing his willingness to martyr himself. These initial acts of civil disobedience evolved into a series of protest events in which handfuls of activists confronted the power of the state. Most of such incidents are what Daniel Boorstin would have called "pseudo-events" — too small to have any impact by themselves, and with a significance that is entirely dependent on magnification by media.[31]

A 2007 protest in support of democracy in Myanmar was typical of the SDP's *modus operandi*. The event was a response to the Myanmese junta's infamous crackdown on anti-government demonstrators that year. The Singapore government had joined the chorus of concern, but stuck with its policy of engagement with the regime. To the SDP, Singapore was yet again allowing its economic interests to run roughshod over human rights. On its website, the party announced that Chee and party chairman Gandhi Ambalam would be stationed outside Myanmar's embassy with petitions for members of the public to sign. This would be followed in the evening with a candlelight vigil.[32] The day's events were subsequently reported in detail on the website. One photograph showed the half-dozen protest leaders, outside the embassy walls in front of a table and a poster of Aung San Suu Kyi. Two other pictures were of plainclothes policemen videographing and approaching the protesters. The written report said that the police warned the activists that the gathering constituted an illegal assembly and would be investigated. It also referred to Burmese supporters arriving to sign the petition, while others "waved, smiled and showed the thumb-up sign" as they drove past.[33] A more detailed report said that at one point, there were more than 200 people present in front of the embassy to sign the petition. Their behaviour — "polite but defiant"; "many were deep in prayer"; "others sat stoically"; "no shouts, no cussing. Just dignified anger" — was contrasted with what was seen as unreasonable police interference and "the pig-headedness of a government" that would "not allow any peaceful gathering as long as it didn't adorn the PAP badge".[34]

The SDP's next step was to organise a protest march. Its website announced that its application for a permit had been rejected by the police: "While citizens in other countries all over the world conduct protests against the Burmese regime, the PAP Government continues its clampdown in Singapore."[35] Two days later, the SDP website announced that it was proceeding with the protest the following day. The organisers advertised their itinerary: they planned to hand a petition to the Myanmese ambassador at 11 a.m. and then proceed to the Istana to deliver a letter to the Prime Minister, after which they would commence a 24-hour protest to ask the Singapore government to cease the "nefarious nexus" with the Myanmar regime. The protesters' petition was not accepted by the Myanmar embassy, and they did not have better luck at the Istana. Soon after Chee and three others lined up in front of the Istana, they were escorted one by one to a police van waiting nearby. The bystander public was conspicuous by its absence; the only people interested seemed to be the police and the media. Brief news reports filed by the Associated Press and the German press agency, DPA, were reproduced on the SDP website.[36] The SDP also reproduced a report by the local tabloid, *The New Paper*, as an example of the government's "propaganda wing" in action: the newspaper said that the protest became a "farce" and labelled previous SDP activities as "antics".[37]

While the SDP's actions over this period were ostensibly in aid of Myanmar, they were also directed toward a second objective — drawing attention to Singapore's lack of civil liberties. This was a thread that ran through virtually all of the party's activism under Chee's leadership. It may be unfairly cynical to say, as one online comment did, that the SDP was "capitalising on the plight of the Myanmese" to score political points in Singapore.[38] But it was certainly true that their framing of the protests focused on Singapore's political environment at least as much as on Myanmar's. For example, the videos uploaded onto YouTube were almost entirely devoted to the battle of wills between the protestors and the police — they did not address the substantive issues raised in the petition. Ironically, this observation mirrors the criticism frequently levelled at mainstream media reports of protest movements: news media coverage tends to be distracted by the sensational methods employed by the unruly protestors, at the expense of reporting the substance of their grievances. The SDP seemed to be doing the same — except that, in its script, the role of irrational goons was to be played by the authorities. Unreasonable police action would, the SDP hoped, chip away at the state's hegemony. The strategy could work if the provocation was visible, and the police reaction equally so. This in turn required an accessible mass medium, which the internet provided. The internet offered its users other possibilities, like anonymity and distance, but these were irrelevant to activists whose game plan required that they remain in harm's way.

Counter-moves

The relationship between social movements and dominant interests is nothing if not dynamic. Each responds to the other's moves, locked in a dance that is potentially endless. Therefore, it should not be surprising to learn that the Singapore government did not follow the SDP's civil disobedience script. In the classic version of non-violent resistance, protest leaders gain the moral high ground when their targets take the low by resorting to excessive force. It is the asymmetry of their behaviour — peaceful citizens versus violent state — that turns the coercive might of the government from a strength into a public relations liability. A government can resist the trap by responding with restraint, or not at all. The authorities in Singapore chose the latter strategy — simply looking away — when confronted with most online dissent. However, they could not ignore the provocations of the SDP. If they had, Chee and his band of activists would surely have upped the ante, with ever bolder stunts. Therefore, the government took legal action against their slightest infringements. It demonstrated restraint not in its decisions of whether or not to prosecute the law-breakers — it invariably did — but in the manner in which police handled the situations on the ground.

Instead of deploying baton-wielding riot police, the protesters were handled by small numbers of policemen — and policewomen — many in plain clothes and with no visible weapons. They spoke firmly but did not raise their voices or use megaphones. The SDP YouTube video of the gathering outside the Myanmar embassy showed an avuncular looking inspector walking amidst the protestors informing them in measured tones that it was an offence to assemble without a permit and that the police would be investigating the case. "We advise you all to leave," he told them. Other men tried to control access to the area. Off-camera, an activist is heard telling visitors, "Don't let the police scare you; this is not Burma, although this is the Singapore police trying to act as if they belong to the Burmese junta."[39] However, the comparison with Myanmar only serves to highlight Singapore's conspicuous lack of physical brutality in dealing with anti-government protests. The police at the Myanmar embassy did not forcibly disperse the crowd. Indeed, the SDP's own report characterised the police response as "half-hearted and confused".[40] It is probably more accurate to say that the authorities were biding their time, confident that the protest leaders could be dealt with in the courts rather than on the streets. Again and again, videos of SDP's civil disobedience campaigns show police refusing to take the bait. Activists' cameras hovering literally at arm's length from law enforcers' faces provoke no instinctive retaliation. Compared with countless videos of similar encounters from around the world — including crackdowns on campus protests in the United States in 2011 — the Singapore footage reveals an extraordinarily disciplined gritting of teeth on the part of state security forces. Even when arrests were made, coercion was carefully calibrated. At the SDP's four-person protest outside the Istana, the video shows them being escorted to a police van one at a time, by a plainclothes male officer and a dimunitive policewoman in uniform.[41]

The Singapore authorities have thus denied activists the publicity coup that more ham-fisted regimes have gifted to their opponents. At worst, the online videos are embarrassing to the authorities: many viewers would be mystified by the sight of police bothering to expend their resources on protests so puny that only the paranoid would consider them a threat to public order. For opposition sympathisers, the reports would be greeted with some glee, as they portray the mighty PAP unable to break the will of the protestors. That, however, would have been as far as the effect went. The videos do not provoke the kind of universal moral outrage that follows images of more brutal, grossly one-sided encounters between peaceful protestors and men with guns, water canons, tear gas and tanks.

Civil disobedience as a form of non-violent political struggle is most effective when it is mounted on behalf of a popular cause, and when the government's response is obviously and disproportionately violent. In such situations, members of the public have been known to throw caution to the wind and join the struggle. If the authorities escalate their use of violence, the state itself can fracture, as the rulers' loss of legitimacy prompts non-cooperation within the bureaucracy and even mutinies within the police and army.[42] Most of Singapore's neighbours have experienced such convulsions. Such dynamics were also witnessed in the Arab Spring of 2010–11. That Singapore's non-violence practitioners have not achieved similar results is an understatement. There are a number of interconnected reasons: their causes have not caught the popular imagination, their protests have been small enough to be managed by minimal deployments of police, and the police have calibrated its responses on the ground, leaving the courts to punish offenders. Nevertheless, SDP's civil disobedience campaign evidently discomfited the government enough for it to amend the Films Act in 2009. The filming of illegal events such as unlicensed demonstrations was outlawed, except by licensed broadcast news media. Henceforth, police would be able to arrest videocam-wielding activists as they attempt to document the SDP's lawbreaking events. Of course, given the logic of non-violent protest, such action could itself backfire.

The exemption for *bona fide* news organisations is noteworthy: it would not be illegal for CNN, the BBC or the national broadcaster MediaCorp to film illegal demonstrations. At first glance, this appears to be a generous concession to media freedom. More likely, it is an astutely calculated risk on the part of the authorities. To try to prevent TV news cameras from recording activities on the street would contradict the government's stand that it has no quarrel with factual news coverage. It would also relegate Singapore from the category of the benignly authoritarian to that of pariah state. Besides, major broadcast media have shown no great interest in the SDP's campaigns. By international standards — compared with, say, the Bersih rallies in neighbouring Malaysia — they are too miniscule for the likes of BBC or CNN to pay attention to. As for the domestic media, the government does not need to rely on the Films Act in order to discourage editors from giving sympathetic coverage to radical causes.

In Singapore's mainstream media, direct censorship has been replaced by self-censorship. It is difficult for even insiders to detect where independent editorial judgment ends and government intervention begins. As a result, censorship rarely backfires. Therefore, one radical application of the internet in Singapore has been to circumvent the gatekeepers of the establishment media and engage in public acts of defiance. If coercion is the response, this does not necessarily represent a failure of the medium but a potentially rewarding tactic in a strategy of counter-hegemony. Gopalan Nair's stunt has to be seen in that light. His arrest drew the condemnation of Amnesty International and Reporters Without Borders. The United States government also took an interest, its diplomats meeting with Singapore government officials and the country's ambassador to Washington, DC, to register their belief in freedom of expression. Domestically, these interventions appeared to have no effect. The government has argued that the SDP's illegal activities are just a stunt, since it could — like more moderate groups — have used legal channels to get its message across. Other opposition parties, notably the Workers' Party and the National Solidarity Party, have stuck scrupulously to the letter of the law. So far, the government's strategy of isolating and demonising Chee and his followers appears to have worked. His SDP appeals to many of the Singaporeans who are already anti-PAP but — unlike opposition parties that use more conventional methods — seems to have failed to win over swing voters. Its vote share has been 10–20 percentage points behind the Workers' Party in the three elections since 2001.

It may be a mistake to look only at the movement's immediate and direct electoral impact — which has certainly been unimpressive. What the civil disobedience campaign has succeeded in doing is to place freedom of expression on the national agenda, to the benefit of more moderate pro-democracy forces. Chee Soon Juan's protests embarrassed the government sufficiently into designating Hong Lim Park as a "Speakers' Corner" in 2000. It remains the one outdoor venue where events can be held without a permit. Although critics derided it as a fig leaf, the Speakers' Corner was occasionally used to good effect by activists. For example, financial consultant and blogger Tan Kin Lian organised a series of well-attended meetings there as part of his campaign to lobby for the rights of Singaporeans who lost their savings through questionable mini-bond instruments in the wake of the 2008 Lehman Brothers collapse. Think Centre, The Online Citizen and Singaporeans For Democracy have all taken advantage of the venue, while continuing to call for greater freedom of expression and assembly.

It remains doubtful whether the idea of freedom of expression as a basic human right, being sown by Chee and his followers, is taking root in Singapore. This is a question explored in the 2011 play, *Fear of Writing*, by Tan Tarn How. The production, which includes the screening of SDP videos of its encounters with police, describes a playwright's struggle as he tries to pen a political play about Chee. He must contend with a director who would rather he picked a safer topic, and ultimately with his own fears. In the end, the writer fails, admitting that he does not have the moral courage for the task. Ironically, however, Tan manages to achieve in *Fear of Writing* what his fictional character does not — a sympathetic rendering of Chee's struggle to reawaken the PAP's Singapore — suggesting that Singaporeans are not uniformly insensitive to the need for greater civil and political rights. Singapore is a place that is "almost perfect", his character says, but its imperfection is intolerable, because it is an imperfection of the spiritual: "That is, we would be less human if we see these imperfections and do nothing about them." Some people could detect it, like the lingering odour of rotting flesh, but most seemed oblivious — and perhaps they were the lucky ones, Tan muses. Like Chee and other political activists pushing for radical liberalisation, writers and artists must face the prospect that "all the keys have been thrown away", Tan writes. Not the keys to the physical jails where some who have crossed the line have been imprisoned, but to "the rooms in our minds and hearts that could have been opened, should have been opened".[43] It remains to be seen what, if anything, can recover those keys.

CHAPTER 10

Networked Hegemony: Consolidating the Political System

Dictatorships don't last. In the long run, the divergence of interests between leaders and led rips regimes apart. Of course, history tells us that the long term can be extremely long: civilisations have lasted millennia without conceding anything to democracy. Today, however, it is much harder for autocrats to protect their monopoly of unaccountable power. In the short time since Singapore became a sovereign state, more and more nations have transitioned to democracy, or at least away from autocracy and towards more or less democratic forms of government, watched over by a public assisted by a vigilant press. "The world has gone from dictatorship to democracy as the modal system — from democracy limited to one part of the world to democracy widespread in most parts of the world," writes Larry Diamond.[1] While there is still no shortage of rapacious and repressive regimes, the indefinite suppression of free expression and rejection of the popular will is no longer seen as a viable formula. Instead, the most robust political systems are consolidated democracies — those where rule-bound electoral competition is seen as "the only game in town" by all sides, allowing peaceful changes of government.[2]

What is less clear are the prospects for states such as Singapore, that are not fully democratic but hardly tyrannical either. These hybrid regimes may hold regular elections and refrain from the grossest human rights abuses. But, weak civil liberties and poorly institutionalised checks and balances allow the state to dominate over society, and partially insulate leaders from public criticism and scrutiny.[3] Singapore's soft authoritarianism is largely benign, but also has its victims. Simultaneously responsive and reactionary, the People's Action Party is difficult to place on the continuum between consolidated democracies and fragile dictatorships. Most believers in democracy want and need to believe that Singapore is closer to the unstable end of the spectrum. They find too disconcerting the idea that a modern state may have found a way to consolidate authoritarianism — possibly serving as a model for other societies in transition that are not enamoured of liberal democracy as a final destination. This book has taken seriously the possibility that the PAP may have indeed found ways to buck the global democratic trend. In preceding chapters of this book, I have tried to analyse these strategies in detail. First, the PAP has not made the mistake of opposing global capitalist forces that — as much as the hunger for liberty or democracy — have shaped the destiny of nations in the modern era. Its media controls have not denied, and have often exploited, the media's need for profits. Second, even if it has never used the term, the PAP has mastered the concept of hegemony: while coercion underwrites PAP domination, consent is the main medium of political transaction. To achieve this, it has systematically shifted towards more calibrated forms of coercion to minimise the risk of backfire. It has also engaged in unrelenting ideological work, as well as striving to ensure that most of its policies please most of the people over the long term.

This concluding chapter contemplates the PAP's longevity from a third angle. The key question it explores is how the PAP avoids what could be called a dictator's dilemma. Even if a leader has no respect for the intrinsic value of democracy, he cannot deny that this system of government offers two practical benefits to rulers. First, democracy generates information about the level of genuine popular support for rulers and their policies. An army of spies and informants operating in an environment of fear is not as reliable, opening dictators to the risk of sudden and surprising revolution and reprisal, as the likes of East Germany's Erich Honecker and Egypt's Hosni Mubarak learnt the hard way. Second, democracy provides strong incentives for ruling elites to pay heed to signals from the people. No mechanism has proven better at focusing officials' minds on the public interest than democracy's assurance that they will lose their jobs if they don't.

Therefore, dictators who want to monopolise power must deal with the fact that doing so can be self-defeating. This chapter analyses both how the PAP limits political competition, as well as how it overcomes resulting gaps in information and incentives, thus avoiding the fate that befalls run-of-the-mill authoritarian regimes. I argue that in order to mitigate the informational vulnerability of authoritarianism, the PAP has embedded itself in dense networks that keep it connected with its mass base, local elites, and global economic actors. To compensate for the lack of political competition for power as an incentive for performance, the PAP has tried to institutionalise an ethic of internal discipline and self-motivation. The party does not let itself forget that Singapore faces remorseless international economic competition as well as regional political hostility, requiring the state to dedicate itself to perpetual self-improvement and vigilance. The PAP formula for defying the dictator's dilemma thus entails staying open to information and to change, even as it insulates itself from competition for power.

The results of the 2011 general election suggest that this strategy, which I call networked hegemony, has limits. The PAP was taken aback by the strength of feeling against it from a sizeable minority of voters. Government leaders were forced to acknowledge a disconnect between the party and the population. It was precisely the kind of symptom one expects to see in a society where those in power have for too long shielded themselves from democratic accountability. Perhaps, therefore, the strategy that has helped entrench PAP dominance thus far cannot do so indefinitely. This chapter considers two weaknesses inherent in networked hegemony. One is its inability to tap the full potential of open networks, which are emerging as a major source of innovation globally. The PAP's model of centralised control by an elite class of technocrats — even if they try to consult widely — may result in a steady erosion of the country's policy-making capacity. A second vulnerability is the PAP's reliance on internal watchdogs to preserve its integrity. These are necessary but not sufficient. They appear to work best when reinforced by external checks such as independent media. The conundrum for the PAP in the coming years is how to open itself more to the benefits of media scrutiny without suffering the cost of conceding power. Either holding on or giving up too much of its freedom from the press could have the same effect — an erosion of PAP dominance.

Political Protectionism

That dominance is profound and undeniable. The political structure is designed to protect those in power from being thwarted by other groups. The PAP government is insulated not just from the full impact of the press and public opinion, but also from all other institutions that democracies ordinarily count on to limit the power of the executive. Raj Vasil, a scholar relatively sympathetic to the PAP, writes plainly of its leaders: "They have always considered it essential that Singapore's government remains all-powerful and controls all instruments and centres of power. There are to be no limitations on government action, intervention and regulation."[4] With so much power concentrated in the hands of the Prime Minister and Cabinet, constitutional law scholar Kevin Tan wonders if they should be called an elected dictatorship.[5] While the supremacy of Parliament is formally recognised, the legislature has not provided an effective check. From 1968 to 1981, there were no opposition members in the House. In the following 30 years, the number voted into Parliament grew from one to six. The 2011 election result was viewed as a great leap forward for the opposition cause, but it is premature to conclude that it heralded the beginning of the end of PAP dominance. Even if the Parliamentary opposition doubles in size in every election, it would still not capture by the early 2020s even the minimum one-third of seats required to block Constitutional amendments.

The reasons for the PAP's Parliamentary dominance deserve some exploration here, since it is the single most important feature of Singapore's political system. To give the PAP its due, it needs to be said that it has consolidated its position partly by governing so well that the opposition has found it difficult to compete. The American State Department's annual human rights reports have taken election results to be generally indicative of "broad public support" for PAP government.[6] Elections are "generally fair and free of tampering", it says.[7] In a confidential cable published by Wikileaks, US diplomats said:

> The biggest challenge to the development of the opposition in Singapore is the PAP's highly successful track record. It has consistently delivered peace, stability, and rapid economic growth for four decades, while avoiding corruption and mainly avoiding cronyism.... Furthermore, in a small city state susceptible to external shocks and surrounded by much larger neighbors, few people are willing to

trade the able and experienced hands of the PAP for the untested opposition.[8]

Enjoying such electoral advantages, the PAP has never needed — even if they were that way inclined — to suspend elections, ban opposition parties or indulge in any of the more flagrant abuses of voting procedures found in larger and less developed countries. However, if elections are the goalmouth of democracy — where the final skirmishes take place before one or the other side scores for victory — it is not there or in the penalty box where the unfairness of the Singapore game is most apparent. Instead, it is elsewhere on the playing field that the contest is tilted decisively in one side's favour, to the extent that there is never any doubt which end of the pitch the goals will be scored. It is when democracy is defined as a broad and continual set of processes that Singapore falls short. Robert Dahl has identified five necessary processes. Two of them — voting equality and inclusion of all adults — have been largely respected in Singapore. Singapore's record is less healthy with regard to Dahl's three other criteria. All deal with public deliberation: there must be effective participation, enlightened understanding arising from learning about policy alternatives, and citizen control of the agenda.[9] Observing how most countries by the late 20th century had adopted elections as a minimum requirement for global respectability, Andreas Schedler notes that many such regimes found less-than-democratic ways to minimise their chances of defeat. In common with Dahl and others, Schedler sees democratic choice as a chain with several links that must all be intact. Regimes can respect the sanctity of elections but still sever other links of the chain if they want to "reap the fruits of electoral legitimacy without running the risks of democratic uncertainty".[10]

This has been precisely the PAP's approach to democracy. Participation in opposition politics is discouraged in Singapore by a long history of harassment and lawsuits against opposition politicians. Historically, the 1963 round-up of some 150 opposition politicians, activists and journalists in Operation Coldstore was the most decisive of these moves, removing some of the brightest political stars from what had been and could have continued to be a vibrant political stage.[11] Actions against the opposition have not been — and have not needed to be — as repressive since then. However, Singapore continues to be inhospitable to opposition politics. The opposition is hindered by strict rules on outdoor talks, marches and other common tools for communication and mobilisation. While many of these restrictions theoretically apply to the ruling party as well, they disproportionately disadvantage the opposition, which needs these avenues more than the incumbents do. Similarly, restrictions on free speech, even if applied equally to everyone, will always constrain political challengers more than those who hold power. Incumbents can rely on actions alone but their opponents cannot succeed without the freedom to speak. Singapore's defamation laws are particularly problematic for the opposition. While there is a well established legal principle globally that people, including politicians, must be able to defend their reputations against unfounded attacks, the PAP has successfully sought from the courts an uncommonly low threshold, such that statements that would be considered part of the cut and thrust of heated political debate elsewhere are judged deserving of legal redress in Singapore. The size of the awards has been sufficient to bankrupt prominent opposition leaders, disqualifying them from contesting in elections.

In the 1980s, the PAP introduced a severe impediment for smaller political parties. Most electoral divisions have been grouped into so-called Group Representation Constituencies or GRCs. Each GRC must be contested by a team that includes an ethnic minority. The stated purpose is to guarantee minority representation in Parliament, but as a side effect (whether intended or unintended is a matter of heated dispute) the GRC system has helped to consolidate PAP rule by raising the hurdle for smaller parties. In 2011, 87 Parliamentary seats were decided by just 27 constituency contests — 12 single-member wards and 15 GRCs. While the largest single-member constituency (SMC) had around 33,000 voters, GRCs had between 87,000 to almost 180,000 voters. For small opposition parties, GRCs are practically impossible to contest meaningfully, particularly as door-to-door campaigning remains an important method of raising candidates' visibility in the absence of mass media endorsements. While the opposition's 2011 victory in one five-seat GRC proved that these aggregated seats are not invulnerable, it remains the case that, overall, the system works to the PAP's electoral advantage. Large GRCs are unlikely to be affected by local factors that, in a single seat, might tip the battle in the opposition's favour. Demographic pockets with concentrations of a particular ethnic group or class — which could be exploited by smaller parties — are already rare because of the integrative public housing programme. Any remaining anomalies are then wiped out by the GRCs, which are so large that they become microcosms of the national profile, unlikely to deviate much from the overall voting pattern. Thus, in 2011, the PAP share of the valid votes in single-seat constituencies ranged from 35.2 to 70.6 per cent — a spread of 35.4 points — but the spread in GRCs was just 24 points. Even for larger parties, the electoral terrain has been tough to contest because boundaries tend to be redrawn less than three months before the polls — and by a committee reporting to the Prime Minister's Office rather than an independent commission. Closely-fought districts in one election have tended to be reconfigured before the next.

The marginalisation of opposition parties is only one part of the government's formula for executive dominance. Almost as significant is the extremely hierarchical structure of the ruling party itself, such that backbenchers and the PAP's rank and file have little power to challenge their leadership. Within Parliament, the whip is only rarely lifted to allow backbenchers to vote according to personal conscience. Any MP who defects would lose his seat, under a Constitutional amendment introduced in the wake of a major defection in the 1960s, when 13 Assemblymen elected on the PAP ticket formed the Barisan Sosialis party. Considering its hegemonic status in Singapore, the party as such is surprisingly small and weak.[12] Party membership is not a prerequisite for admission into the nomenklatura: there is no tradition of politicians rising through the party ranks to reach senior government positions. Instead, it is by shining in their respective professions that Singaporeans get noticed by the PAP's talent scouts. It is not uncommon for political high-fliers to be inducted into the party just months before being fielded in elections. On the one hand, this system demonstrates the government's admirable ability to co-opt individuals based on merit. It also reflects the leadership's realistic assessment that party work is different from running a government.[13] On the other hand, it is part of a strategy to limit the executive's dependence on its party base.

This intent is shown most clearly in the party's cadre system. Cadres are appointed by the central executive committee (CEC) and in turn elect the CEC at biannual party elections. The list of CEC nominees does not surface from the branches but is provided by the outgoing CEC. The CEC essentially renominates itself, with some changes to keep up with the rejuvenation of Cabinet, which the CEC basically mirrors.[14] This highly centralised, Leninist-inspired system was born out of what political scientist Chan Heng Chee has called a "deep-seated distrust of a democratic election process for the party".[15]

Lee Kuan Yew's moderate faction was voted out of the CEC in 1957, while the PAP was in the opposition. Lee was able to reclaim the party leadership only because the radical leftists were detained by the government of the day. He swiftly installed the new cadre-based election system, such that when the leftists were released, they could not recapture the party leadership despite their popularity among the rank and file. In structure and spirit, the PAP remains a top-down organisation, with the party base relied on for grassroots work and election campaigns but never allowed to dictate terms to the top leadership.

Unsurprisingly, the PAP government has not created many state institutions powerful enough to stand up the executive. A notable exception is the Corrupt Practices Investigation Bureau, whose fearless actions against public sector graft have rightly won international kudos. In contrast, there are no independent public commissions to oversee elections, human rights or anti-trust. When the Singapore state introduced broadcasting, it did not opt for the BBC model of its former colonial masters — an independent public service broadcaster operating under a public charter — but instead put it directly under the minister for culture. Organised labour was disciplined and prevented from becoming an independent centre of power. Unions were shepherded under the umbrella of the National Trades Union Congress, whose secretary general is traditionally a Cabinet minister.[16] The two public universities, although technically corporatised, remain supervised by the education ministry, which is known to intervene in academic appointments. Thus, power flows to the leaders of state institutions directly from the executive. "One unique feature of these state institutions is the low degree to which they respond to political demand and claims from below and outside them," writes political scientist Ho Khai Leong. This insulates them from populist pressures and challenges. "Such an arrangement provides systemic stability that the leaders believe they need to operate efficiently," Ho adds.[17]

The position of the judiciary merits special attention. Occasionally, the courts have nudged Singapore towards greater respect for civil liberties. In 2011, for example, the Court of Appeal decided on a stricter test for contempt cases. Up till then, Singapore had applied the less liberal "inherent tendency" test, under which someone could be ruled in contempt even when there was only a remote possibility that his words would undermine confidence in the administration of justice. Adjudicating the case of author Alan Shadrake, however, the

Court of Appeal opted for the "real risk" test, requiring the court concerned to make a call as to the likely effect of a statement on the average reasonable person.[18] On the whole, though, while the courts in other Commonwealth countries such as Canada and India have been able to assert themselves to enlarge people's freedoms significantly, the Singapore judiciary's power to do so has been reduced. "Even in instances when the courts have attempted to check the discretionary power of the executive, Parliament has moved swiftly to reverse the trend," notes Kevin Tan.[19] In one landmark case, the Court of Appeal's declared that the judiciary would in future review detention orders on the substantive ground of irrationality — but this was countered with a Constitutional amendment apparently restricting judicial review to procedural grounds only.[20] Key media legislation has been written to exclude judicial review, through clauses that state that the minister's decision is final. Many media rules are written into subsidiary regulations under administrative control, effectively moving them a step away from Parliamentary as well as judicial scrutiny.

The Singapore bench's more limited scope, compared with its cousins in the Commonwealth or the United States Supreme Court, is crucial for understanding the PAP's power over media. In most countries that are today categorised as having free media, freedoms were neither guaranteed at birth nor won by the press fighting on its own. Invariably, the courts played a major role. Judges in these countries found within their constitutions justifications for strengthening protections for the press. Even in the US, press freedom did not arrive fully formed with the First Amendment in 1791. It took a series of groundbreaking Constitutional reinterpretations by the Supreme Court in the 20th century to evolve the principles that are today recognised as the First Amendment model.[21] Conversely, the lack of such progress in Singapore is very much due to the absence of the kind of judicial activism seen in the US, India and elsewhere. Singapore's judges are sometimes accused of a lack of impartiality in political cases — a charge that is vigorously denied and results in swift prosecution for contempt of court. The problem is more accurately expressed in terms of the bench's adherence to the Parliamentary intent behind the law and a reluctance to construe the spirit of the Constitution in more pro-liberty terms.[22] This attitude is in line with Singapore's political culture. Chief Justice Chan Sek Keong has accordingly stated that more cynical interpretations of Singapore's defamation laws are missing the point, as "criticizing the Singapore courts is really criticising them for recognising the political, social and cultural values of Singapore society as expressed in its laws".[23] That attitude is not accidental or a matter of personal preference, but conditioned by a government that has moved decisively to restrict judges' room for discretion when this might result in challenges to the authority of the executive branch.

The Power of Networks

Clearly, the Singapore regime's defences against political competition are formidable. It believes that the ballot box provides adequate accountability, retaining the democratic core of Singapore's political system. "The greatest attraction is, you can change governments without violence," Lee Kuan Yew has said of the merits of electoral democracy.[24] "We have created a system whereby if Singaporeans believe we're unfit to govern, they vote us out."[25] Recognising that free and fair elections confer legitimacy on the government, Lee Hsien Loong has emphasised that the system must remain "contestable". Hence, his decision to tweak the proportion and size of GRCs in time for the 2011 election. In previous elections, the GRC system had resulted in a large number of walkovers, which effectively disenfranchised a high proportion of voters. The inability to vote became a common complaint, compromising the very legitimacy of elections in Singapore. In response, the government shrank the average size of GRCs and increased the number of SMCs, making the 2011 election more hotly contested than ever before. This reflected the PAP's recognition of political limits to how much it can get away with tilting the playing field in its favour. Still, it continues to reject the idea that the system should facilitate the development of multi-party democracy. The Cabinet's view is this: "If voters elect more opposition MPs, so be it. But we do not believe that helping to build an opposition, to buy insurance in case the PAP fails, will work. Instead it will lead to more party politicking and distraction from long-term issues."[26]

The degree to which the Singapore system protects the executive from competition and accountability would appear to make it ripe for creeping corruption and unresponsiveness to the needs of the people. However, the state appears to have compensated for the lack of electoral competition to some extent (how much and whether enough, we'll examine later) by embedding itself in networks of information. The idea of "networked politics" has stimulated some scholarly discussion in recent years. Networked actors are contrasted with traditional, hierarchical institutions. They connect with other nodes in order to benefit from resources within the network. The networked actors that are most familiar to scholars are flat and loosely structured groups such as transnational civil society movements and terrorist groups. However, more hierarchical organisations could also plug into networks successfully. "In effect, they can become more or less 'networked' as political demands shift or their environments change," says Miles Kahler, editor of a recent volume, *Networked Politics*. "As part of their organizational repertoires, successful network actors have developed an ability to hybridize their hierarchical forms."[27] The PAP has attempted exactly that. Former civil service chief Peter Ho has spoken of "networked government". "Certainly the world we operate in is too complex and mutable for the people at the top to have the full expertise and all the answers to call all the shots," he says. "For us to survive and thrive, we must have horizontal reach in a networked government, and the readiness to discover and experiment, in order to gain insight, decision and action."[28] These efforts, which go back decades, have resulted in a networked hegemony: a regime that cultivates voluntary connections while continuing to dominate state and society.

The PAP's networks operate at three key levels. The first connects the leadership with its mass base. The executive comprises a technocratic, administrative elite most of whom have neither the charisma nor the background to connect with the ground. To make up for this, it has diligently maintained a grassroots network of party branches, residents' committees and other organisations. PAP MPs, including ministers, conduct weekly Meet the People Sessions in their wards. Constituents make use of these sessions to ask their representatives to intercede in problems such as financial distress and school admissions. The clinics provide intelligence on how policies are working on the ground. The PAP also maintains a close relationship with workers through the National Trades Union Congress. The party rose to power on the back of organised labour and has not allowed itself to forget the potential political power of disaffected workers. While it has crushed any independent union activity that could threaten its business-friendly economic model, the political leadership has not neglected networking directly with workers on the ground. "You've to talk to them in small groups — and one to one — they tell you their problems before these become big," Lee Kuan Yew has said. Their support cannot be taken for granted, he adds. Their trust is conditional on delivering the goods. "Do not believe for one moment that we'll always carry the workers. We only carry them if they feel they've had a fair deal whether in a downturn or an upturn.... This relationship needs to be nurtured and they must actually get benefits."[29]

A second level of networking aims to connect the PAP with segments of the population who want to be consulted in the making of public policy, and who are relied on to lead and manage various organisations. This group would include professionals and other better-educated, middle-class citizens. The PAP acknowledged the need to reach out to them in the 1980s, after its stinging defeat in the 1981 by-election to Workers' Party leader J.B. Jeyaretnam. Initially furious that Singaporeans could be so ungrateful and irrational, the PAP gradually came round to accepting that they needed to feel consulted. Citizen consultation is institutionalised in the government's Feedback Unit, established in 1985 to "feel the pulse of the ground and keep the government apprised of key issues of concern amongst Singaporeans".[30] Renamed REACH in 2006, it organises closed-door discussions on controversial policy issues as well as managing the government's main online consultation platform. The 1980s also witnessed party self-renewal, with a second generation of leaders taking over key Cabinet positions. A series of major national consultation exercises was engineered as a way for the new leaders to get closer to Singaporeans. Starting with the Action Committees of the 1980s, the process continued with the Next Lap document in the early 1990s, followed by Singapore 21 in 1997 and Remaking Singapore in 2002. Singaporeans who were socially and politically engaged were included in these exercises through various sub-committees. Although the final reports and actual policy outcomes were never likely to reflect the more radical positions expressed in these meetings, such processes helped to extend the state's network, co-opting elites who had no desire to join the party but would be willing to contribute some time to the national cause.

The idea of omnibus national consultations may have fallen out of fashion, but the principle of including non-government views in policy formulation has been firmly entrenched. Most agencies conduct *ad hoc* feedback exercises for major policies, with the internet emerging as a key platform. Representatives of the private and public sectors are also included on government boards and consultative committees. One of the most established of these is the National Wages Council, formed in 1972 to formulate annual wage guidelines. The Council comprises representatives from government, employers and unions. The government's numerous statutory bodies, which perform a wide range of important functions, have several board members and even chairmen drawn from the private sector. In certain domains, the government has partnered civil society organisations with recognised competence. In the past, such links were almost entirely with voluntary welfare organisations such as church groups, which were relied on to pick up the slack in the government's services for the disabled, the poor and the otherwise disadvantaged. But, more recently, government agencies have also worked with groups representing new social movements. These include Action For Aids, the animal rights group ACRES and various environmental groups. Underlying this trend is the government's recognition of the public sector's limitations in an increasingly complex policymaking environment.

In addition to connecting with its mass base and more active citizens, the government has plugged itself into a third kind of network, comprising drivers of the global economy. With an open economy dominated by foreign direct investments, export industries and international services, Singapore's policymakers are more exposed to global market signals than the authoritarian governments of more insular countries. Officials do not just sit back and wait for the economic data to speak. They cultivate connections with the global economy's movers and shakers, in order to be among the first to respond to emerging threats and opportunities. These links have been institutionalised through the boards of key economic agencies. The Economic Development Board (EDB), the government's powerhouse investment promoter, was overseen in 2011 by a 15-member board that included senior executives of multinationals Dell, DHL, PriceWaterhouseCoopers, Procter & Gamble, Tata, Shell Chemicals and Siemens. The Government of Singapore Investment Corporation (GIC) and Temasek Holdings are among the world's largest sovereign wealth funds. As a byproduct of scouring the world for investment opportunities, they keep the government attuned to global economic trends. At the individual level, Lee Kuan Yew, in particular, has traded his highly regarded assessments of geopolitics for access to some of the world's best minds and top corporate leaders. He was on the international councils of JP Morgan Chase and the French oil giant, Total, for example.

Asymmetry of Linkages

Through such networks, the PAP keeps itself open to information, allowing it to be more responsive to the changing needs of the country than most authoritarian governments. The links within these networks are not symmetrical. Relations are conducted on the government's terms. Thus, while the non-government actors may reap some benefits from access to policymakers, the government is able to protect its core from competition and contention. One way it does this is through selectivity in access. Individuals and groups who can be counted on to play by the rules of the game are most likely to be granted high-level, long-term access. On the other hand, those seen to represent a higher political risk are kept at arm's length or consulted only on a case-by-case basis, regardless of the expertise they have to offer. Links also differ depending on the policy area. As noted above, economic policy is highly welcoming of external inputs through such institutions as EDB and GIC. Security and cultural policy are relatively closed and hierarchical. The Media Development Authority's board had only two industry representatives in 2010–11: one from the local book retailer and publisher, Popular; and the other from FreemantleMedia, the entertainment production company behind the *Idol* franchise and *The Price is Right*. The news media sector was not represented on the MDA board.

Similarly, the National Arts Council is striking for the lack of professional artists or arts administrators on its board of directors — it had only one such member in 2011, compared with four government officials. Artists, who have had a fraught relationship with government, tend to be consulted through *ad hoc* dialogues instead of institutionalised mechanisms. In 2009, when the arts lobby group Arts Engage proposed 22 names for inclusion in the government's Censorship Review Committee, not a single one was picked (Chapter 7). The snub was seen as a reaction to the group's temerity in including on its list two prominent dissident filmmakers, Martyn See and Seelan Palay, who have been at the forefront of the fight against political censorship. The underlying message was clear: access is not a right and is subject to demonstrating one's trustworthy intentions; each group would be judged by its membership as well as its role and competence. Such implicit rules of the game are well understood by those at the fringes of Singapore's governance networks. Civil society activists tend to give opposition politicians a wide berth and are also wary of forging links with foreign organisations. The Working Committee, a milestone project among prominent civil society groups, had its biggest internal debates over whether to invite opposition leader Chee Soon Juan to a public event and accept a grant from a foreign foundation. In the end, the majority decided that it would be politically unwise to do either.[31] Similarly, Maruah, a human rights group, felt that opposition involvement would further complicate its already intricate challenge of opening a dialogue on human rights with the government. For a group that needs government cooperation — whether to change policies or for something as simple as a permit to organise an event — there is therefore tremendous pressure to self-police. To raise the government's comfort level, the group needs to bend over backwards to show that it is not a proxy for opposition parties or foreign pressure groups, and that it will not use its influence to mobilise the public towards any broader political end. Its activity must be narrow, contained and respectful of the government's ultimate authority. It must not give the impression that it is engaging in what PAP leaders, based on their experience fighting the communists, see as "united front" tactics. Or, to use network terminology, it needs to show that it would be nothing but an endpoint node in the governance network, with no links to potentially destabilising nodes.

The government employs similar containment strategies when managing the flow of critical opinion. As noted in Chapter 8, it has grown increasingly tolerant towards individual self-expression, but continues to police organised dissent much more rigorously. It is the mass producers of dissent, not its retail consumers, that are the focus of government attention. Adam Przeworski has noted that "as long as no collective alternatives are available, individual attitudes toward the regime matter little for its stability". He explains: "What is threatening to authoritarian regimes is not the breakdown of legitimacy but the organization of counter-hegemony: collective projects for an alternative future. Only when collective alternatives are available does political choice become available to isolated individuals."[32] The PAP has understood, with Przeworski and others, that if it discourages and disrupts collective action, it need not silence individual-level criticism, which can provide important feedback to the system. "Mobilization of certain forms of 'active citizenship' or 'empowered participation' entails a state political strategy shaping, so as to contain, the permissible extent and nature of conflict and means for addressing it," note political scientists Garry Rodan and Kanishka Jayasuriya. "This strategy is intended to undermine independent collective action, including through state-sponsored and state-defined groups, and through the fostering of atomized, individual political engagement."[33]

Accordingly, the government is vigilant at the border between individual expression and more organised dissent. This line of separation is policed using Singapore's strict regulations on forming societies and organising public gatherings. In the arena of sexual politics, a vibrant underground gay culture has been permitted to flourish, and one of the region's most successful gay community websites, Fridae.asia, operates openly out of Singapore. A gay rights lobby group, People Like Us (PLU), operates as an informal network with more than 2,300 people on its email discussion list. However, attempts to register it formally have been blocked by the Registrar of Societies.[34] Individuals in the network, together with sympathetic companies, have been able to organise IndigNation, an annual season of "LGBT Pride" activities for the lesbian, gay, bisexual and transgender communities. However, the organisers note that government departments responsible for issuing various permits are of "anything that is gay-themed". "Outdoor events such as parades, a common feature of pride festivals in other countries, are virtually impossible since the authorities have a habit of refusing to issue licences," they add.[35]

Falling Behind in the Network Race

Thus far, the asymmetry of linkages has allowed the PAP to have its cake and eat it too. But it could emerge as a key limitation of PAP-style networked government. While it may receive sufficient information to avoid the dictators' dilemma, its model may hamper Singapore's international economic competitiveness. Although founded on its strategic location and deep natural harbour, Singapore's economy is reliant on innovation, especially in the public sector. Singapore's developmental state — perhaps irreversibly, if the theory of path dependence applies — plays a major role in the economy. To a greater extent than *laissez-faire* economies that are able to thrive despite governmental under-performance, Singapore depends on timely and creative policy-making. This is why the PAP government believes strongly in inducting individual talent into its close-knit team. However, mounting evidence suggests that the PAP model for developing policy-making capacity is outdated. In recent years, several writers have pointed to a fundamental shift in the sources of innovation, away from closed, centralised organisations and towards open networks — with the stress on open. Their book titles celebrate this paradigm shift: *The Wisdom of the Crowds* (by James Surowiecki); *We-Think: Mass Innovation, Not Mass*

Production (Charles Leadbeater); and *Wikinomics: How Mass Collaboration Changes Everything* (Don Tapscott and Anthony D. Williams).[36] All are inspired by the astounding development of the internet. They note that the internet's genius lies in its "open source" architecture. Its underlying codes and protocols were given away freely, allowing anyone who plugged into any part of the network not only to use pre-existing applications, but also to develop and share their own. Features we now take for granted — from the world wide web to free Skype calls and social networking — did not require approval from the internet's inventors or those who owned the physical infrastructure, and in most cases were not even foreseen by them.

The internet is thus a "generative" technology.[37] Its architecture recognises every node as a potential collaborator and co-creator, and not just as a user. Of course, the vast majority of people are happy to remain relatively passive and have no ability or desire to write programs or create content. There are also rules to ensure requisite order. But, enough individuals and groups have seized the opportunity to dream up and develop new ways to use the network, making it easily the most powerful platform for innovation in the history of human civilisation. Contrast this with centralised online services rolled out in the 1980s and early 1990s, such as France's Minitel and Singapore's Teleview. These were based on a centralised architecture modelled on telephone services: the ones who controlled the core of the network controlled its innovation. The organisations in charge may have hired the best engineers, programmers, designers and content creators they could find, yet they were still no match for the internet's diverse, distributed army of innovators. The internet's big bang in the mid-1990s turned the likes of Teleview into white elephants and relegated what were grand national projects to mere footnotes in the history of the online revolution.

Advocates of the open source movement argue that its lessons apply to realms beyond information technology. Not all important tasks can be handled this way, but many can. In particular, mass collaboration is worth tapping when faced with a high degree of uncertainty and complexity, and where creative solutions are required. Decentralised decision-making introduces different ways to look at a situation and to approach challenges and opportunities. Groups with diverse skills and outlooks tend to come up with smart solutions more often than homogeneous groups, no matter how individually brilliant its members. "Innovation often involves trying out many vantage points before finding the one that makes the problem look simple," notes Charles Leadbeater.[38] The approach does not negate the value of expertise or of leadership: a collaborative network still needs a core. "Everything has to start somewhere," Leadbeater says. "Somebody has to be willing to work harder than everyone else or nothing ends up getting done."[39] However, a good core invites outsiders to join a creative conversation. The "crowd" may be less intensely engaged in the project but their aggregate contribution can be powerful. The authors of *Wikinomics* write that while hierarchies are not disappearing, we are seeing the rise of "powerful new models of production based on community, collaboration, and self-organization rather than on hierarchy or control".[40]

Some may wonder whether these ideas apply to governments or only to companies. No doubt, states are bound to remain fundamentally hierarchical. Yet, there is growing recognition globally that greater citizen participation improves public sector governance. The most striking evidence of this has been the spread of open government initiatives and freedom of information (FOI) laws since the 1990s.[41] Also called access to information or right to information, the principle basically turns traditional official secrets legislation on its head: disclosure becomes the norm and secrecy the exception, justified in specific circumstances when sanctioned by independent courts or ombudsmen. At their most ambitious, open government schemes provide data in formats that allow users to create new products and services. FOI empowers citizens to check on official corruption, prompting even China to adopt elements of it at the local level. The demand worldwide has come not just from citizens who are increasingly intolerant of secretive decision making, but also from the World Bank, International Monetary Fund and other intergovernmental bodies that see disclosure as essential for good governance. "It is a key component of public policy effectiveness and efficiency," notes Ann Florini, a leading authority on transparency based at the Lee Kuan Yew School of Public Policy. "Even the most competent and honest decision makers need feedback on how the policies they have set are working out in practice, feedback that is only possible when information flows freely in both directions."[42]

The open government trend is separate from the open source movement, but the underlying principles are the same. First, hierarchical organisations produce better results when they open up their decision making to people outside their core. Second, people can add value to the process only to the extent that they are empowered to do so. Third, this requires giving away the organisation's information, leaving it up to the users to decide what to use and how, instead of pre-judging what would or would not be constructive. Fourth, access should be as broad as possible, including — and especially — to people who think differently, to counter the group-think and vested interests that are inevitable within an organisation. Singapore's public sector leaders claim to acknowledge the risk of group-think. Hence, their efforts to embed the administration in networks from which they can extract information and ideas. However, these efforts fall short of the radically collaborative networking that open source proponents say is required for 21st-century innovation. The PAP is networked but it remains stolidly hegemonic. It encourages citizen participation, but places illiberal limits on the diversity that it is prepared to tolerate. This constrains the wisdom that it is able to tap. As Leadbeater observes, "Crowds are intelligent only when their members have a range of views and enough self-confidence and independence to voice their opinions."[43]

If these principles indeed turn out to be key drivers of innovation and improvement, Singapore's fundamentally incompatible political system may increasingly lag behind. There are already signs of this. September 2011 saw the formal launch of the Open Government Partnership, which describes itself as "a new multilateral initiative that aims to secure concrete commitments from governments to promote transparency, empower citizens, fight corruption, and harness new technologies to strengthen governance".[44] To qualify as a partner, a government must exhibit a demonstrated commitment to open government in four key areas: fiscal transparency, access to information, disclosures related to elected or senior public officials, and citizen engagement. In August 2011, 79 governments were said to have met the minimum criteria for membership. Singapore was not one of them.

In the 2011 elections, the PAP's networked hegemony showed signs of strain. It lost an unprecedented six seats, including the GRC helmed by foreign minister George Yeo, and secured a record low 60.1 per cent of the valid votes. For the ruling party, more worrying than the numbers was the palpable intensity of feeling against it, expressed on the internet as well as offline.[45] "We hear all your voices," the prime minister assured the public in his election night press conference.[46] To demonstrate that the past was past, his two predecessors, Lee Kuan Yew and Goh Chok Tong, stepped down from

Cabinet. The government at last embarked on a review of the hugely unpopular policy of high ministerial salaries and promised to address unhappiness over public transport and housing. But what was striking about these and other substantive issues that dominated the elections is that none of them should have come as a surprise to the PAP. All of them had been aired, especially online but also — albeit more politely and less often — in the mainstream media and even in Parliament. The PAP's grassroots network must also have surfaced most of these issues. Thus, well before the election, the PAP horse had been led to the water of public discontent — but turned its back on it. Only when the public's message was backed by the power of the ballot box did the government take it seriously.

This suggests that no matter how efficiently information flows within a dense but asymmetrical network, there is a tendency for the hub to ignore inconvenient data. Knowledge matters — but so do incentives. And human society has found no better incentive system than open societies with democratic elections for ensuring that rulers remain responsive to the ruled. Of course, it is not foolproof: many democratically accountable leaders preside with seeming impunity over gross inefficiency, social injustice and corruption. To the PAP, such cases justify its own model of performance incentives. It has argued that, no matter what the institutional set-up, governments can inflict terrible damage. Singapore's political system is therefore based on choosing and empowering leaders of high integrity and ability, and keeping rogues out. There is a better chance of attracting good people into public service if public life is not overly political and cynical, the PAP adds. A system of internal discipline — inspired by the Catholic Church and Leninist communist parties — is thought to be as effective as, or even superior to, external watchdogs. The PAP government's track record in resisting graft suggests that these are not merely idle or self-serving claims.

However, the 2011 election suggests that the party's deeply held values are unable to protect it from — and may actively contribute to — groupthink and hubris. According to Donald Low, this explains why the PAP lost touch with the people. Low, a former administrative service officer who had studied government policy-making closely, penned a series of essays in the wake of election going to the heart of what went wrong. He argued that the government had not taken seriously enough the unintended consequences of its growth-promoting policies. This was mainly due to "cognitive failures and blinkers" resulting from PAP ideologies. The PAP government may not be as filled with "bad intentions, ignorance or incompetence" as its critics allege — but it is also "not as rational or pragmatic as it claims", he notes. "Instead of subjecting new arguments or evidence to critical analysis, it often reverts to a few unspoken but deeply held ideological biases," he added.[47] These include the ideology of elite governance and "our *leadership delusion* — the naive belief that smart and competent leaders can do marvellous things". The PAP also suffers the effects of its ideology of performance legitimacy: its past successes justify sticking with the *status quo* and brushing aside new ideas and fair political processes. "Over time, these ideologies bred hubris and created the illusions of invulnerability and indispensability. Invulnerability is the belief that we can't be wrong; indispensability is the belief that only we know how to govern Singapore well," Low said.[48] One indicator of Lee Hsien Loong's seriousness about reform would be whether his agenda included measures such as freeing up the media, he added.[49]

Prospects for Reform

I first started studying Singapore's state-media dynamics in earnest more than 20 years ago, when I chose this as my undergraduate thesis topic. Wanting more insights into the PAP's perspective, I secured an interview with S. Rajaratnam, one of the party's founding fathers. Before entering politics, he had been a journalist of repute, known for his fiery editorials and columns against British colonialism. As a former culture minister, he had helped the PAP articulate its stand on the press. He was a headline writer's dream. Once, speaking to the Foreign Correspondents' Association, he launched a diatribe against what he called "JBJ". This was what opposition leader Joshua Benjamin Jeyaretnam was affectionately known as, but Rajaratnam clarified that he was instead talking about "James Bond journalism" — "a form of Western journalism now on the prowl in Asia and whose devotees believe they have a journalistic 007 licence to destroy the reputation of leaders and governments in South-east Asia with impunity".[50]

Now it was 1988, and Rajaratnam had just retired from government and joined the Institute of Southeast Asian Studies as a fellow. Interviewing him there, I asked him if the press system would ever change. He did not discount the possibility — indeed, he supported it:

Once upon a time we said opposition was unnecessary. At that time our purpose was so urgent: what we called a battle for survival was a real thing.... A lot of unpleasant things had to be done. And because a newspaper thrives best when it gives vent to feelings against government, we had to curb it.... That phase is over; not completely over, but there's no sign of any imminent threat from Malaysia or Indonesia, or internal disaffection to the point of rebellion.... That being the case, open up.... I think there will be a different approach to the press, provided the press also understands that the model is not the western press, [but] constructive journalism, that you want to build a secure, prosperous, peaceful Singapore.... This is the way I think that if Singapore is to survive it must move.[51]

Pondering the significance of his words as a 23-year-old Singaporean, I noted in the conclusion of my dissertation that the PAP was not a reactionary party: its hegemonic strength gave it the confidence to tackle problems before they manifested themselves in a severe form. "Rajaratnam is no longer a member of the leadership and can afford to be more liberal now, but it is not inconceivable that the new leaders are reconsidering, or will reconsider, their news media policies," I wrote. I added a dollop of realism: "But, as is the habit with governments, the outcome of any reform is likely to be determined as much by bureaucratic expediency as by the national interest."

Now, in 2011, the record shows that Singapore's framework for media management has been one of the most unchanging parts of the entire edifice. Over the past two decades, major reforms have been undertaken in various other sectors, from banking to healthcare and education. Yet, over the same period, no law governing newspapers has been liberalised. As for television, foreign cable news channels were allowed in from the 1990s and the state broadcaster was progressively commercialised, but the government did not budge on its fundamental position on the role of the media. This does not necessarily mean that Rajaratnam's pragmatic acceptance of the need for change was unrepresentative of PAP thinking. His main concern had been a potentially explosive build-up of steam if the government continued to bottle up people's desire for freedom. One could argue that the PAP has indeed moved to address this problem by opening up multiple avenues for feedback and allowing virtually free play online.

The 2011 election lengthened one of the world's longest winning streaks in the history of electoral politics. But it also opened the door to self-doubt, forcing the PAP to promise changes. The government resolved to engage with new media, which it believed played a major role in the election. A government-appointed advisory committee had recommended in 2008 that the state needed to speed up e-engagement or "risk being disconnected from this generation of digital citizens".[52] By the second half of 2011, most ministers had Facebook accounts. The establishment also began to rethink its stand of not recognising alternative media as *bona fide* journalism: Presidential hopeful Tony Tan courted Singapore's most prominent socio-political bloggers, inviting them along with the national media to his press conference and meeting them for lunch.

"The Government cannot stand still. It must evolve in tandem with our society and our people," Lee Hsien Loong said in his swearing-in speech after the general election. "Our political system can and must accommodate more views, more debate and more participation."[53] The PAP Government had made similar pledges in the past, notably in the early 1980s when its absolute monopoly of Parliament was broken, and in the early 1990s when the baton was handed to Goh Chok Tong's team of second-generation leaders. Each time, steps were indeed taken to institutionalise more openness and consultation. Always, however, reforms left the media system untouched. Would the post-2011 changes be any different? Probably never before has there been a greater need for structural reform of the media — including for the PAP's own sake. One of the major problems it faces is its rapidly eroding ability to engage the public in national conversations. When it came to power in the 1950s and 1960s, the media were at the heights of what could be termed their modernist or industrial era: symbolic power was concentrated in a few centralised institutions, namely national radio and television stations and a few strong newspapers. Through these national media, leaders could command the attention of most of the people, most of the time. Today, the audience is fragmented, thanks to niche publishing, cable television and the internet. In 1989, before cable TV and the world wide web, half of Singapore's adult population tuned in to watch the National Day Parade on channels 5 and 8. By 2007, less than one-third was doing so. Facebook and various online forums accelerated the trend of dissipating attention, prising Singaporeans out of the ideological grip of the government.

The problem for the PAP is compounded by the appeal of anti-government online media — an appeal enhanced by their contrast to the mainstream media. While some bloggers are as competent as the best mainstream columnists and deserve respectful attention, many online commentaries enjoy an influence that is not in proportion with their quality of analysis or their respect for facts. They benefit from a marketplace where professional journalists must compete with hands tied behind their backs by a government that is hypersensitive to criticism. Alternative online media can and must continue to play an important complementary role, but only an independent mainstream press would be able to provide the kind of accountability that Singaporeans increasingly expect, and the forum for the exercise of public reason that a diverse city requires. When it is allowed to live up to its full potential, professional journalism can serve as a credible clearing house for rumours and as a shared platform for discussing complex and controversial issues. Singapore's national media could produce such journalism regularly, but they are thwarted by political restraints.

The PAP may actually have more to gain than its opponents from a vibrant press. In public relations circles, there is growing recognition that "earned media" is more powerful than media attention that is bought, owned or controlled. The PAP government should be capable of earning positive publicity on a fair playing field. The 2011 election did establish that it no longer monopolises talent: a handful of opposition politicians were superior to the PAP's new candidates. However, the PAP — especially while it is in government and can tap an able civil service — remains well ahead of the opposition in its ability to run the country. This superiority should be manifest in more open debate. Having the most strength in depth, it can improve instead of wither under public scrutiny. Just as in sports, in which the best teams have the most to gain from fair rules and strict refereeing, the PAP should be more committed than most other groups — including less able governments elsewhere — to a media system that is directed by autonomous professional journalistic judgment. Thus, a rational long-term strategy for the PAP's self-preservation would seem to require investment in independent and credible mainstream media. It can do this by demanding media accountability through self-regulation without constantly threatening retribution; pushing facts, not pulling rank; encouraging social responsibility in the national interest, not politically-motivated self-censorship; and allowing meritocracy in newsroom and corporate appointments in the media.

Unfortunately, such a prescription seems to be too much of a mental leap for those in power. Thus far, the reverse argument has prevailed: precisely because unregulated online media are predominantly anti-PAP, the government feels it needs to count even more on mainstream media to reflect the truth as the PAP sees it. The ideology of elite governance includes a fundamental distrust of the masses and of the marketplace of ideas. Singapore's leaders are convinced that they have the best answers to most questions — and equally convinced that, in the short term, most people would not recognise better answers from worse ones. International best practices do not count, because Singapore is held up as exceptional — in the vulnerability of its circumstances and the superiority of its leaders. Furthermore, since the PAP has sanctified its approach to media management as a fundamental necessity for good governance, any questioning of that approach is treated as an irresponsible or ignorant assault on everything that works in Singapore. The debate ends before it starts. Thus, the PAP's pragmatic focus on what works has, over the decades, been transformed through the lens of exceptionalism into dogmatic resistance against any liberalisation. This was not lost on a young journalist who interviewed Lee Kuan Yew for more than 30 hours for the aptly titled *Hard Truths to Keep Singapore Going*. She wrote that she felt overwhelmed by the constant message that "this country was so fragile that ... it was his way or the highway". Singapore began to sound to her "like a castle under siege defended by dogmatic, extremely irritable knights".[54]

Even the 2011 election setback did not seem enough to penetrate these ideological walls. Just as with its past promises of more open and responsive government, the PAP's press policy was not up for negotiation. It acknowledged that it would need to communicate better and use more channels, but placing the stewardship of newspapers fully in the hands of professional publishers and journalists remained unthinkable. The much-touted "new normal" in government-people relations was no match for the urge to preserve the press as a deeply conservative establishment institution. Thus, less than six months after the general election, Singapore Press Holdings named Lee Boon Yang as a board member and chairman-designate. Lee was minister for information before his retirement in 2009. A veterinarian by training, he worked for the government's primary production department before taking up political office in 1984. Other than a brief post-retirement stint as non-executive chairman of the government-linked Keppel Corp, he arrived at the blue-chip SPH with no private-sector credentials of any sort, let alone any background in media management.

The anomaly was barely even remarked on, since he was not the first but the third former Cabinet minister to be asked to helm the country's largest media group — as part of the company's long established policy to "suck up to the government of the day", as one small-investor blog put it.[55]

Opposition politicians and their followers are counting on the PAP's inertia to be its undoing, causing Singapore to succumb eventually to the tide of freedom and democracy. However, one should not be surprised if the critics have to wait longer than they expect to see such predictions materialise. As this book has tried to show, the PAP's form of authoritarianism is intelligent enough to avert catastrophic collapse. The system, while illiberal, is still sufficiently democratic to provide an outlet for grievances and to bestow legitimacy on the elected government. Even at its heights, public discontent has not come close to the street protests and open defiance that are increasingly common sights around the world. The media system reflects these broader realities. Freedom from the press is part of a political system designed to dampen the impact of public opinion and political competition on governance, thus preserving PAP dominance. But as long as the PAP does not completely insulate itself from the ground — and there is no evidence that it will — it can avoid the kind of sustained and extreme maladministration that inevitably results in regime collapse. Singapore may continue to confound its critics by remaining a stable and wealthy city-state — and still a curious outlier on the press freedom charts. Ironically, though, the PAP's skill in managing crises and its bias for the *status quo* may deny Singapore the opportunity for necessary radical reforms. Overall, the most likely prospect for Singapore is an ambiguous patchiness in the country's development. There may be vibrant dynamism in some areas, but also signs of stagnation, provincialism and decline in others, where the PAP's instincts for elite control suppress the creative energies that would normally surface in a cosmopolitan city of five million. The press will mirror this unevenness. It may continue to be sufficiently professional to remain relevant and highly profitable, but it will not be allowed to lift itself out of the mediocrity in which it is often mired. This is the price of the PAP's single-minded focus on the risk of total failure. While avoiding thunderous collapse, Singapore may continue to echo with the sighs of a society that, deep in its heart, knows it is less than what it could be.

Notes

Singapore Politics and Media: A Primer

1. Department of Statistics Singapore, "Key Annual Indicators", <http://www.singstat.gov.sg/stats/keyind.html> [accessed 1 Aug. 2011].
2. Parliament of Singapore, "Historical Development of Parliament", <http://www.parliament.gov.sg/timeline> [accessed 1 Aug. 2011].
3. People's Action Party, "Party Milestones", <http://www.pap.org.sg/partyhistory.php> [accessed 1 Aug. 2011].
4. Elections Department Singapore, <http://www.elections.gov.sg/> [accessed 1 Aug. 2011].
5. Department of Statistics Singapore, "Singapore in Figures 2011", <http://www.singstat.gov.sg/pubn/reference/sif2011.pdf> [accessed 1 Aug. 2011].
6. SPH Mediapedia, <http://sph.com.sg/pdf/Mediapedia/2nd/SPHMediapedia(13May).pdf> [accessed 1 Aug. 2011].
7. Today Rate Card, <http://www.mediacorp.sg/en/foradvertisers/mediaratecards> [accessed 1 Aug. 2011].

Chapter 1

1. "Home", Freedom House, <http://www.freedomhouse.org> [accessed 19 Feb. 2011].
2. "Reporters san frontieres", Reporters Without Borders (English website), <http://en.rsf.org> [accessed 19 Feb. 2011].
3. "Why RSF's press freedom index is flawed — and why it works", Journalism.SG, <http://journalism.sg/2009/10/28/why-rsfs-press-freedom-index-is-flawed---and-why-it-works/> [accessed 28 Oct. 2009].
4. "Singapore ranked No. 140? Why SM isn't worried", *The Straits Times*, 1 Nov. 2005.
5. William Case, *Politics in Southeast Asia: Democracy or Less* (Richmond, Surrey: Curzon, 2002).
6. Fareed Zakaria, *The Future of Freedom: Illiberal Democracy at Home and Abroad* (London and New York: W.W. Norton & Company, 2003).
7. Larry Diamond, "Thinking About Hybrid Regimes", *Journal of Democracy* 13, no. 2 (2002): 322–38.

8. Carl A. Trocki, *Singapore: Wealth, Power, and the Culture of Control, Asia's Transformations* (New York: Routledge, 2005).
9. Goh Chok Tong, "Government as Trustee: The Role of Government in the East Asian Miracle", *Straits Times*, 24 Sept. 1995, pp. 1, 4–5.
10. Martin Jacques, *When China Rules the World: The Rise of the Middle Kingdom and the End of the Western World* (New York: Penguin Press, 2009).
11. George Soros, *The Soros Lectures: At the Central European University* (New York, N.Y.: Public Affairs, 2010).
12. David Harvey, *A Brief History of Neoliberalism* (Oxford: Oxford University Press, 2005).
13. Ibid., pp. 71–2.
14. Ibid., p. 83.
15. See, for example, Harold Evans, *Good Times, Bad Times* (London: Weidenfeld & Nicolson, 1983).
16. Perry Anderson, "The Antinomies of Antonio Gramsci", *New Left Review* 100 (Nov.–Dec. 1976): 5–80.
17. Kor Kian Beng, "Pritam Singh calls for Freedom of Information Act", *The Straits Times*, 21 Oct. 2011.
18. Daniel C. Hallin and Paolo Mancini, *Comparing Media Systems: Three Models of Media and Politics* (Cambridge, UK: Cambridge University Press, 2004).
19. Fred S. Siebert, Theodore Peterson and Wilbur Schramm, *Four Theories of the Press: The Authoritarian, Libertarian, Social Responsibility and Soviet Communist Concepts of what the Press should be and do* (Urbana: University of Illinois Press, 1956).
20. John C. Nerone (ed.), *Last Rights: Revisiting Four Theories of the Press* (Urbana: University of Illinois Press, 1995).
21. See, for example, David Hugh Weaver and Wei Wu, *The Global journalist: news people around the world* (Hampton Press, 1998); and "The Worlds of Journalism Study", <http://www.worldsofjournalism.org> [accessed 1 Sept. 2011].
22. Amartya Kumar Sen, "Democracy as a Universal Value", *Journal of Democracy* 10, no. 3 (1999): 3–17.
23. Georgette Wang and Eddie C.Y. Kuo, "The Asian communication debate: culture-specificity, culture-generality, and beyond", *Asian Journal of Communication* 20, no. 2 (2010): 152–65.
24. Ibid., p. 161.
25. Clifford Geertz, "Thick Description: Toward an Interpretive Theory of Culture", in *The Interpretation of Cultures* (New York: Basic Books, 1973), p. 15.
26. Pierre Bourdieu, *The field of cultural production: essays on art and literature*, ed. Randal Johnson (New York: Columbia University Press, 1993).

228 *Notes to pp. 16–28*

27. David Bandurski and Martin Hala, *Investigative Journalism in China: Eight Cases in Chinese Watchdog Journalism* (Hong Kong: Hong Kong University Press, 2010); Jingrong Tong, *Investigative Journalism in China: Journalism, Power, and Society* (London and New York: Continuum International Publishing Group, 2011).
28. Hallin and Mancini, *Comparing Media Systems*.
29. Worlds of Journalism Study, <http://www.worldsofjournalism.org> [accessed 1 Sept. 2011].
30. Lee Kuan Yew, "Exciting Times Ahead" (speech given at the Tanjong Pagar GRC National Day Dinner, World Trade Centre, Hall 1, Singapore, 12 August 1995), <http://stars.nhb.gov.sg> [accessed 19 Feb. 2011].
31. Nick Davies, *Flat Earth News* (London: Vintage Book, 2009).
32. Human Development Report Office, *Human Development Report 2010, The Real Wealth of Nations: Pathways to Development*, <http://hdr.undp.org/en/reports/global/hdr2010/> [accessed 19 Feb. 2011].
33. Human Development Report Office, "A Human Movement: Snapshots and Trends", in *Human Development Report 2009*, Human Development Reports (New York: United Nations Development Programme, 2009), <http://hdrstats.undp.org/en/indicators/10.html> [accessed 19 Feb. 2011].
34. "Migration Could Triple Populations in Some Wealthy Nations", Gallup, <http://www.gallup.com/poll/142364/migration-triple-populations-wealthy-nations.aspx> [accessed 19 Feb. 2011].
35. "Juris Articles: Interview with Criminal Lawyer, Mr. Subhas Anandan", Singapore Law Review, <http://www.singaporelawreview.org/2008/04/interview-with-criminal-lawyer-mr-subhas-anandan/> [accessed 19 Feb. 2011].

Chapter 2

1. "Letter from Singapore", PranayGupte, <http://www.pranaygupte.com/article.php?index=199> [accessed 16 Jan. 2011].
2. Han Fook Kwang, "The Lee way at the ST", in *150 Years of The Straits Times*, ed. Cherian George (Singapore: Singapore Press Holdings, n.d.), p. 100.
3. Quoted in Martin Indyk, "For Once, Hope in the Middle East", *New York Times*, 26 Aug. 2010, <http://www.nytimes.com/2010/08/27/opinion/27indyk.html> [accessed 1 Aug. 2011].
4. *Newspaper and Printing Press Act* (Chapter 206), Section 21.
5. "Black Ops: Tussle is over S'pore's freedom, says Raja", *The Straits Times*, 16 May 1971, p. 1.
6. C. Mary Turnbull, *Dateline Singapore: 150 years of The Straits Times* (Singapore: Singapore Press Holdings, 1995), p. 291.

7. Ibid., p. 293.
8. Ibid.
9. Francis T. Seow, *The Media Enthralled: Singapore Revisited* (Boulder, Colorado: Lynne Rienner Publishers, 1998), pp. 39–40.
10. *Internal Security Act* (Chapter 143).
11. Ibid., Section 8(1).
12. Ministry of Information, Communication and the Arts, "Prohibition on the film 'Dr Lim Hock Siew'", news release, 12 July 2010, <http://app.mica.gov.sg/Default.aspx?tabid=79&ctl=Details&mid=540&ItemID=1167> [accessed 1 Oct. 2010].
13. Leslie Fong, "A time to cheer, a time to dissent", *The Straits Times, 150 Years anniversary supplement*, 15 July 1995, p. 30.
14. Jothie Rajah, *Authoritarian Rule of Law: Legislation, Discourse and Legitimacy in Singapore* (New York: Cambridge University Press, 2012).
15. *Newspaper and Printing Press Act*.
16. Ibid., Section 8(1).
17. "Main shareholders", Singapore Press Holdings, <http://sph.listedcompany.com/main-shareholder.html> [accessed 16 Jan. 2011].
18. *Newspaper and Printing Press Act*, Section 10(11).
19. Ibid., Section 10(2).
20. Main shareholders.
21. Edmund Terence Gomez and Jomo K.S., *Malaysia's Political Economy: Politics, Patronage and Profits*, 2nd ed. (Cambridge: Cambridge University Press, 1999).
22. Attributed to Canadian media owner Roy Thomson, describing his commercial television franchise in 1957.
23. Turnbull, *Dateline Singapore*, p. 294.
24. Ibid., pp. 338–9.
25. Singapore Press Holdings, "Lim Kim San to step down as SPH Executive Chairman, remains as Senior Advisor", media release, 11 Nov. 2002, <http://www.sph.com.sg/article.display.php?id=27> [accessed 1 Oct. 2010].
26. "Board of Directors", Singapore Press Holdings, <http://sph.listedcompany.com/directors.html> [accessed 16 Jan. 2011].
27. Peter Lim, "No monopoly on wisdom", in *150 Years of The Straits Times*, ed. Cherian George (Singapore: Singapore Press Holdings, 1995), p. 97.
28. Lee Kuan Yew (election rally at Fullerton Square, Singapore, 29 Aug. 1972).
29. See, for example, Robert W. McChesney, *The Political Economy of Media: Enduring Issues, Emerging Dilemmas* (New York: Monthly Review Press, 2008), p. 60.
30. Lim, "No monopoly on wisdom", p. 98.
31. Goh Chok Tong, "The Singapore Press" (speech given at the *Straits Times* 150th Anniversary Gala Dinner, Singapore International Convention

and Exhibition Centre, Singapore, 15 July 1995), National Archives of Singapore <http://stars.nhb.gov.sg> [accessed 16 Jan. 2011].
32. Goh Chok Tong (speech given at the 5th Anniversary Dinner of *Today* Newspaper, Shangri-La Hotel, Singapore, 31 Oct. 2005), <http://www.stars.nhb.gov.sg> [accessed 16 Jan. 2011].
33. Goh, "The Singapore Press".
34. "My Reports Slanted to Champion the Overall Red Cause: Ho", *The Straits Times*, 18 April 1977.
35. "Davies told of impending law two years ahead", *The Straits Times*, 27 Sept. 1989, p. 23.
36. "You must have a deterrent that matches the situation", *The Straits Times*, 22 Aug. 1986, p. 14.
37. "Davies told of impending law two years ahead."
38. *Newspaper and Printing Press Act*, Section 24.
39. "Time magazine's circulation to be cut", *The Straits Times*, 16 Oct. 1986, p. 1.
40. Ibid.
41. *The Right to be Heard: Singapore's Dispute with TIME magazine & the Asian Wall Street Journal: The Facts*.
42. Ibid.
43. *The Right to be Heard: Singapore's Dispute with TIME magazine & the Asian Wall Street Journal: The Facts* (Singapore: Ministry of Communications & Information, May 1987).
44. "You must have a deterrent that matches the situation."
45. Garry Rodan, *Transparency and Authoritarian Rule in Southeast Asia: Singapore and Malaysia* (London: RoutledgeCurzon, 2004), p. 27.
46. Ibid., p. 35.
47. Ibid., p. 37.
48. Manmohan, Singh, *A critical analysis of the Straits Times' reporting on the Singapore Armed Forces: the RSS courageous and dunking incidents in 2003* (Singapore: Nanyang Technological University Master of Mass Communication Thesis, 2008).
49. "ST columnist ticked off", *The Straits Times*, 12 March 1994, p. 26; "Leader of House accepts ST columnist's apology and declares matter closed", *The Straits Times*, 16 March 1994, p. 21.
50. "All five men found guilty and fined for breaching Act", *The Straits Times*, 1 April 1994, p. 1.
51. Tey Tsun Hang, "Confining the Freedom of the Press in Singapore: A 'Pragmatic' Press For 'Nation-Building'?", *Human Rights Quarterly* 30, 4 (2008): 876–905.
52. *Supreme Court of Judicature Act* (Chapter 322), Section 7.
53. Clark Hoyt, "The Public Editor: Censored in Singapore," *New York Times*, 3 April 2010, <http://www.nytimes.com/2010/04/04/opinion/04pubed.html> [accessed 16 Jan. 2011].

54. Ibid.
55. Rodan, *Transparency and Authoritarian Rule*, p. 88.
56. Ibid., p. 37.
57. David Plott and Michael Vatikiotis, "The Life and Times of the Far Eastern Economic Review", in *Free Markets Free Media? Reflections on the Political Economy of the Press in Asia*, ed. Cherian George (Singapore: Asian Media Information and Communication Centre, 2008), p. 145.
58. Ibid.
59. McChesney, *Political Economy of Media*, pp. 39 and 58.
60. Ibid., p. 179.
61. Rodan, *Transparency and Authoritarian Rule*, p. 6.
62. David Harvey, *A Brief History of Neoliberalism* (Oxford: Oxford University Press, 2005), p. 2.
63. Han, "The Lee Way", p. 100.

Chapter 3

1. AWARE is the Association of Women for Action and Research.
2. See, for example, "Sniffing Out The Straits Times Agenda in the Aware Saga", Gimme Some Truth, <http://givemesometruth.wordpress.com/2009/05/08/sniffing-out-the-straits-times-agenda-in-the-aware-saga> [accessed 10 July 2011]; and comments by "Checkpoint" and "ilovetocomment" in "Why We Covered Aware Saga the Way We Did", *Straits Times* website, <http://comment.straitstimes.com/showthread.php?t=20647> [accessed 1 June 2009].
3. Jeremy Au Yong, "That Poses the Biggest Threat to S'pore, Says Prof Koo in Apparent Reference to Aware Saga", *The Straits Times*, 28 May 2009.
4. Comment by "ilovetocomment", in "Don't Mix Religion and Politics", *Straits Times* website <http://comment.straitstimes.com/showthread.php?t=20010&page=23> [accessed 1 June 2009].
5. "Exercise Restraint, Mutual Respect, Tolerance", *The Straits Times*, 15 May 2009.
6. Comment on "Aware Coverage — Straits Times Defends Itself", *The Online Citizen*, 30 May 2009, <http://theonlinecitizen.com/2009/05/aware-coverage-straits-times-defends-itself/comment-page-1/#comments> [accessed 1 Aug. 2010].
7. Pamela J. Shoemaker and Stephen D. Reese, *Mediating the Message: Theories of Influences on Mass Media Content*, 2nd ed. (New York: Longman, 1996).
8. Herbert J. Gans, *Deciding What's News: A Study of CBS Evening News, NBC Nightly News, Newsweek, and Time* (New York: Pantheon Books, 1979).
9. "Racial harmony is not a given", *The Straits Times*, 24 July 2006.
10. Attributed to British press baron Lord Northcliffe (1865–1922).

11. Peter Lim, "No monopoly on wisdom", in *150 Years of The Straits Times*, ed. Cherian George (Singapore: Singapore Press Holdings, 1995), p. 96.
12. Mary C. Turnbull, *Dateline Singapore: 150 Years of The Straits Times* (Singapore: Singapore Press Holdings, 1995).
13. Mark Cenite, *et al.*, "Perpetual development journalism? Balance and framing in the 2006 Singapore election coverage", *Asian Journal of Communication* 18, no. 3 (2008): 280–95.
14. Turnbull, *Dateline Singapore*.
15. Cherian George, "'Asian' Journalism: More Preached than Prized?" (paper presented at the Association for Education in Journalism and Mass Communication Western Conference, Stanford, California, 2002).
16. I analysed citations for winners of the annual awards for the years 1999–2004 and monthly awards for the year 2001: a total of 34 citations in the News Story and Feature categories. In addition, I examined the citations for the annual Special Awards categories of excellence or consistently good work, and the Young Journalist of the Year award. My findings for the study of 2001 monthly awards were presented in the paper, "'Asian' Journalism: More Preached than Prized?"
17. United States Embassy in Singapore, "Singapore's Opposition", 18 Oct. 2004, released by Wikileaks, 30 Aug. 2011, <http://wikileaks.org/cable/2004/10/04SINGAPORE3001.html> [accessed 1 Oct. 2011].
18. Mitchell Stephens, *A History of News* (New York: Viking, 1988).
19. Jack Lule, *Daily News, Eternal Stories: The Mythological Role of Journalism* (New York: The Guilford Press, 2001).
20. Wolfgang Donsbach, "Factors Behind Journalists' Professional Behavior: A Psychological Approach to Journalism Research", in *Global Journalism Research: Theories, Methods, Findings, Future*, ed. Martin Loffelholz and David Weaver (Malden, Maine: Blackwell, 2008), pp. 65–78.
21. David Mindich, *Just the Facts: How "Objectivity" Came to Define American Journalism* (New York: NYU Press, 2000); Michael Schudson, *Discovering the News: A Social History of American Newspapers* (New York: Basic Books, 1978).
22. Gaye Tuchman, "Objectivity as Strategic Ritual: An Examination of Newsmen's Notions of Objectivity", *The American Journal of Sociology* 77, no. 4 (1972): 660–79.
23. Edward S. Herman and Noam Chomsky, *Manufacturing Consent: The Political Economy of the Mass Media* (New York: Pantheon, 1988).
24. Leon V. Sigal, "Who? Sources Make the News", in *Reading the News: A Pantheon Guide to Popular Culture*, ed. Robert K. Manoff and Michael Schudson (New York: Pantheon Books, 1986), pp. 9–37.
25. William A. Dorman, "Press Theory and Journalistic Practice: The Case of the Gulf War", in *Do the Media Govern?: Politicians, Voters, and Reporters*

in America, ed. Shanto Iyengar and Richard Reeves (Thousand Oaks, California: Sage Publications, 1997), pp. 118–25.
26. "The Times and Iraq", *New York Times*, 26 May 2004, <http://www.nytimes.com/2004/05/26/international/middleeast/26FTE-NOTE.html> [accessed 10 July 2011].
27. In this survey by Hao Xiaoming and me, we received a total of 447 completed responses representing around one-third of journalists at the two organisations.
28. Itai Himelboim and Yehiel Limor, "Media Institutions, News Organizations, and the Journalistic Social Role Worldwide: A Cross-National and Cross-Organizational Study of Codes of Ethics", *Mass Communication and Society* 14, no. 1 (2011): 71–92.
29. "Home", The Worlds of Journalism Study, accessed July 10, 2011, <http://www.worldsofjournalism.org> [accessed 10 July 2011].
30. "David Marshall: Praise as Well as Criticise Govt", *The Straits Times*, 18 Jan. 1994.
31. Peter Lim, "No monopoly on wisdom", in *150 Years of The Straits Times*, ed. Cherian George (Singapore: Singapore Press Holdings, 1995), pp. 96–9.
32. Beate Josephi, "On The Cusp Between Global And Local: Young Journalists At The Straits Times", *Asia Pacific Media Educator*, no. 12/13 (2002): 123–38.
33. James S. Ettema and Theodore L. Glasser, *Custodians of Conscience: Investigative Journalism and Public Virtue* (New York: Columbia University Press, 1998).
34. "David Marshall: Praise".

Chapter 4

1. "SM takes SCMP reporter to task", *The Straits Times*, 3 Nov. 2001, p. 2.
2. Lee Kuan Yew, "Exciting Times Ahead" (speech given at the Tanjong Pagar GRC National Day Dinner, World Trade Centre, Hall 1, Singapore, 12 Aug. 1995), <http://stars.nhb.gov.sg> [accessed 16 Jan. 2011].
3. "Lee will attend IPI meeting in Helsinki", *The Straits Times*, 28 May 1971, p. 1; "I'm sure Lee knows what he's doing: IPI chief", *The Straits Times*, 19 May 1971, p. 1.
4. Lee Kuan Yew, "The Mass Media and New Countries" (speech given at the General Assembly of the International Press Institute, Helsinki, 9 June 1971), <http://journalism.sg/lee-kuan-yews-1971-speech-on-the-press> [accessed 23 Jan. 2011].
5. Bilahari Kausikan. "The 'Asian Values' Debate: A View from Singapore", in *Democracy in East Asia*, ed. Larry Diamond and Marc F. Plattner (Baltimore, Maryland: John Hopkins University Press, 1998), pp. 17–27.
6. Lee, "Exciting Times Ahead".

7. "Press 'jail' warning an election issue, says Mr. Lee", *The Straits Times*, 21 May 1950, p. 1.
8. Lee Kuan Yew, "Mr. Lee Kuan Yew replies to the Straits Times", *The Straits Times*, 22 May 1959, p. 8.
9. "SM takes SCMP reporter", p. 2.
10. "EL1 may lead us to become a pseudo-Western society", *The Straits Times*, 15 Aug. 1988, p. 14.
11. Lee, "Exciting Times Ahead".
12. Han Fook Kwang, Warren Fernandez and Sumiko Tan, "What People Want is Good Government", in *Lee Kuan Yew: The Man and his Ideas* (Singapore: Times Edition, 1998), p. 381.
13. Ibid., p. 380.
14. Kausikan, "The 'Asian Values' Debate", p. 21.
15. Lee Kuan Yew, "Singapore can survive if two preconditions are met", *The Straits Times*, 8 June 1996, p. 34.
16. K. Shanmugam (speech given at the "A Free Press for a Global Society" Forum, Columbia University, New York, 4 Nov. 2010), <http://app2.mlaw.gov.sg/News/tabid/204/Default.aspx?ItemId=515> [accessed 23 Jan. 2011].
17. Goh Chok Tong, "The Singapore Press" (speech given at the Straits Times 150th Anniversary Gala Dinner, Singapore International Convention and Exhibition Centre, Singapore, 15 July 1995), <http://stars.nhb.gov.sg> [accessed 16 Jan. 2011].
18. Lee, "The Mass Media".
19. Goh, "The Singapore Press".
20. Lee Kuan Yew (speech given at the PAP Paya Lebar Branch 15th Anniversary Dinner, Singapore, 13 May 1971), <http://stars.nhb.gov.sg> [accessed 23 Jan. 2011].
21. Commission on Freedom of the Press, *A Free and Responsible Press. A general report on mass communication: newspapers, radio, motion pictures, magazines, and books* (Chicago, Ill.: University of Chicago Press, 1947).
22. K.S. Rajah, "Negotiating Boundaries: Ob Markers and the Law", in *Impressions of the Goh Chok Tong Years in Singapore*, ed. Bridget Welsh, et al. (Singapore: NUS Press, 2010), p. 77.
23. Lee, "Singapore can survive".
24. "The Global Competitiveness Economic Report", World Economic Forum, <http://www.weforum.org/reports/global-competitiveness-report-2010-2011-0> [accessed 14 Jan. 2011].
25. "IMD 2010 World Competitiveness Yearbook rankings", IMD, <http://www.imd.org/news/IMD-World-Competitiveness-Yearbook-2010-Rankings.cfm> [accessed 14 Jan. 2011].
26. Li Xueying, "Unstable Myanmar a 'time-bomb' for S-E Asia", *The Straits Times*, 5 Oct. 2007, Factiva [accessed 3 Aug. 2009].

27. "Methodology, Results & Findings", GPI, <http://www.visionofhumanity.org/wp-content/uploads/PDF/2007/2007%20%20%20%20Results%20Report.pdf> [accessed 14 Jan. 2011].
28. "International Covenant on Civil and Political Rights", Article 20, OHCHR, <http://www2.ohchr.org/english/law/ccpr.htm> [accessed 14 Jan. 2011].
29. Frank La Rue, "Report of the Special Rapporteur on the Promotion and Protection of the Right to Freedom of Opinion and Expression" (United Nations: Human Rights Council, 11th Session, 30 April 2009).
30. "Singapore Shared Values", Singapore Infopedia, Singapore: National Library Board, <http://infopedia.nl.sg/articles/SIP-542-2004-12-18.html> [accessed 15 Jan. 2011].
31. Goh, "The Singapore Press".
32. Géraldine Muhlmann, *Journalism for Democracy* (Cambridge: Polity, 2010).
33. Rajah, "Negotiating Boundaries", pp. 107–16.
34. Theodore L. Glasser, "The Idea of Public Journalism", in *The Idea of Public Journalism*, ed. Theodore L. Glasser (New York: Guilford Press, 1999).
35. "Commission on Freedom of the Press", in *A Free and Responsible Press. A General Report on Mass Communication: Newspapers, Radio, Motion Pictures, Magazines, and Books*, ed. Robert D. Leigh (Chicago: University of Chicago Press, 1947), pp. xii, 138.
36. "Statement of Shared Purpose", Committee of Concerned Journalists, <http://ccj.p2technology.com/node/380> [accessed 15 Jan. 2010].
37. Goh Chok Tong, "Government as Trustee: The Role of Government in the East Asian Miracle", *The Straits Times*, 24 Sept. 1995, pp. 1, 4–5.
38. Goh, "The Singapore Press".
39. "Part IV: The Theory of Democratic Elitism", in *Democracy*, ed. Philip Green (New Jersey: Humanities Press, 1993), pp. 67–118.
40. Walter Lippmann, *The Phantom Public* (New York: Harcourt, Brace and Company, 1925), p. 21.
41. Ibid., p. 39. Across the Atlantic, French cultural theorist Pierre Bourdieu has been equally convinced that specialists have a greater right to the public sphere than non-specialists, including journalists. See Geraldine Muhlmann, *Journalism for Democracy* (Cambridge: Polity Press, 2010), pp. 19–32.
42. Joseph A. Schumpeter, *Capitalism, Socialism and Democracy* (New York: Harper & Row, 1950), p. 269.
43. Samuel P. Huntington, Joji Watanuki and Michael Crozier, "Chapter III — The United States", in *The Crisis of Democracy: Report on the Governability of Democracies to the Trilateral Commission* (New York: New York University Press, 1975), pp. 53–119.

44. Ibid., p. 115.
45. Ibid., p. 114.
46. Simone Chambers and Anne Costaine, eds., *Deliberation, Democracy and the Media* (Lanham, Maryland: Rowman & Littlefield Publishers, 2000).
47. Jurgen Habermas, *The Structural Transformation of the Public Sphere* (Cambridge, Mass.: MIT Press, 1991), p. 27.
48. James W. Carey, "The Press and Public Discourse", *The Center Magazine*, March 1987, p. 14.
49. Huntington, Watanuki and Crozier, *The Crisis of Democracy: Report on the Governability of Democracies to the Trilateral Commission*, p. 114.
50. Ibid., p. 115.
51. Lee, "The Mass Media".
52. Ibid.
53. "Constitution of the Republic of Singapore (Amendment) Bill, Second Reading", *Parliamentary Reports* (Singapore: Parliament, 25 July 1984) 1823.
54. Lee, "The Mass Media".
55. Lee Kuan Yew (speech given to the American Society of Newspaper Editors, Washington DC, 14 April 1988), <http://stars.nhb.gov.sg> [accessed 16 Jan. 2011].
56. Lee Kuan Yew (speech given at the Asian Media Conference, Los Angeles, 29 Oct. 1998), <http://stars.nhb.gov.sg> [accessed 23 Jan. 2011].
57. See for example, "An Open Letter from the Chairman: The PSC Interview", Public Service Commission Singapore, <http://www.pscscholarships.gov.sg/An+Open+Letter+from+the+Chairman.htm> [accessed 15 Jan. 2011].
58. Shanmugam.
59. Lee Kuan Yew, *The Singapore Story: Memoirs of Lee Kuan Yew* (Singapore: Times Editions, 1998), p. 16.
60. Lee, "Singapore can survive", p. 34.
61. Chan Heng Chee, "Political Developments, 1965–1979", in *A History of Singapore*, ed. Ernest C.T. Chew and Edwin Lee (Singapore: Oxford University Press, 1991), p. 179.
62. Frank La Rue, "Statement by the Special Rapporteur on the Promotion and Protection of the Right to Freedom of Opinion and Expression" (14th Session of the Human Rights Council, Geneva, 3 June 2010); for a concise review of Commonwealth law, see Rajah, "Negotiating Boundaries", p. 114.
63. "Commission on Freedom", pp. xii, 138.
64. For an overview of media accountability systems, see Claude-Jean Bertrand, "Media Accountability", *Pacific Journalism Review* 11, no. 2 (September 2005): 5–16.

Chapter 5

1. "The Man Who Saw It All", Time Asia, <http://www.time.com/time/asia/covers/501051212/story.html> [accessed 19 Feb. 2011].
2. Brendan Pereira, "Anwar Affair: Some Errors in Judgement Were Made", *The Straits Times*, 18 Aug. 2000, p. 43.
3. Francis Fukuyama, *The End of History and the Last Man* (New York: Avon Books, 1993).
4. Juan J. Linz, "Opposition In and Under an Authoritarian Regime: The Case of Spain", in *Regimes and Oppositions*, ed. Robert A. Dahl (New Haven, CT, and London: Yale University Press, 1973), pp. 171–259.
5. James Ron, "Varying Methods of State Violence", *International Organization* 51, no. 2 (1997): 275–300.
6. Edward Aspinall, *Opposing Suharto: Compromise, Resistance, and Regime Change in Indonesia* (Stanford, California: Stanford University Press, 2005), p. 2.
7. Ibid., pp. 6–7.
8. Ibid., p. 47.
9. Sam Whimster, ed., *The Essential Weber: A Reader* (London: Routledge, 2004).
10. Perry Anderson, "The Antinomies of Antonio Gramsci", *New Left Review* 100 (Nov./Dec. 1976): 5–80.
11. Hannah Arendt, *On Violence* (Orlando, Florida: Harcourt Brace Jovanovich, 1970), pp. 50–1.
12. Ibid., p. 54.
13. Chen Hwai Liang, "Govt Doesn't Depend on 'Calibrated Coercion'", *The Straits Times*, 12 Oct. 2005, p. H7.
14. Ahmad Osman, Leslie Koh and Jason Leow, "6 Held for Espionage", *The Straits Times*, 22 Jan. 1999, p. 53.
15. Soh Lung Teo, *Beyond the Blue Gate: Recollections of a Political Prisoner* (Kuala Lumpur, Malaysia: Strategic Information and Research Development Centre, 2010); Francis T. Seow, *To Catch a Tartar: A Dissident in Lee Kuan Yew's Prison* (New Haven, Connecticut: Yale Center for International and Area Studies, 1994); Zahari Said, *The Long Nightmare: My 17 Years as a Political Prisoner* (Cheras, Kuala Lumpur: Utusan Publications & Distributors, 2007).
16. Quoted in Seow, *The Media Enthralled*, p. 83.
17. Anthony Polsky, "Premier Lee Kuan Yew and the Singapore Press Controversy" (speech given at the Hong Kong Foreign Correspondents Club, 20 July 1971).
18. Raj Vasil, "Trade Unions", in *Management of Success: The Moulding of Modern Singapore*, ed. Kernial Singh Sandhu and Paul Wheatley (Singapore: Institute of Southeast Asian Studies, 1989), pp. 144–70.

19. Chan Heng Chee, "Political Developments, 1965–1979", in *A History of Singapore*, ed. Ernest C.T. Chew and Edwin Lee (Singapore: Oxford University Press, 1991), pp. 157–81.
20. Chan Heng Chee, *Singapore: The Politics of Survival, 1965–1967* (Singapore: Oxford University Press, 1971), p. 25.
21. Vasil, "Trade Unions", pp. 144–70.
22. Michael Fernandez and Kah Seng Loh, "The Left-Wing Trade Unions in Singapore, 1945–1970", in *Paths Not Taken: Political Pluralism in Post-war Singapore*, ed. Michael Barr and Carl A. Trocki (Singapore: NUS Press, 2008), pp. 206–26.
23. Chan, *Singapore: The Politics*.
24. Huang Jianli, "Positioning the Student Political Activism of Singapore: Articulation, Contestation and Omission", *Inter-Asia Cultural Studies* 7, no. 3 (2006): 403–30.
25. Chan, "Political Developments", pp. 157–81.
26. Huang, "Positioning the student", p. 405.
27. Michael Barr, "Singapore's Catholic Social Activists: Alleged Marxist Conspirators", in *Paths Not Taken*, ed. Barr and Trocki p. 234.
28. Ibid., p. 242.
29. Sonny Yap, Richard Lim and Weng Kam Leong, "Puppets in a Dangerous Game", in *Men in White: The Untold Story of Singapore's Ruling Political Party* (Singapore: Marshall Cavendish, 2010), pp. 435–49.
30. Seow, *The Media Enthralled*, p. 148.
31. Legal Profession Act (Chapter 161).
32. Teo Chee Hean, Parliamentary Speech on the Internal Security Act, 19 Oct. 2011, <http://www.mha.gov.sg/news–details.aspx?nid=MjEzMg%3d%3d-as%2b9gJeLXQ0%3d> [accessed 24 Oct. 2011].
33. United States Department of State, 1979, 1981 Country Reports on Human Rights Practices. Report submitted to the Committee on International Relations, US House of Representatives and Committee on Foreign Relations, US Senate.
34. United States Department of State Country Reports on Human Rights Practices. Report submitted to the Committee on International Relations, US House of Representatives and Committee on Foreign Relations, US Senate, 3 Feb. 1978, p. 269.
35. Stan Sesser, *Lands of Charm and Cruelty: Travels in Southeast Asia* (New York, N.Y.: Vintage, 1994).
36. Yap, Lim and Weng, *Men in White*, p. 468.
37. Leong Ching, "Politics Not New to Former Student Activist", *The Straits Times*, 29 Oct. 2001, p. H8.
38. Sumiko Tan, "Stand Up and Be Quoted", *The Straits Times*, 6 July 1991.
39. David Held, *Political Theory and the Modern State* (Stanford, California: Stanford University Press, 1989).

40. Chan, "Political Developments", pp. 178–9.
41. Ibid., p. 177.
42. Wong Kan Seng, "The Real World of Human Rights" (speech given at the World Conference on Human Rights, Vienna, 14 June 1993).
43. Ibid., p. 334.
44. S.R. Nathan, *An Unexpected Journey: Path to the Presidency* (Singapore: Editions Didier Millet, 2011), p. 453.
45. Ibid., p. 453.
46. Ibid., p. 459.
47. Ibid., p. 493.
48. Ibid., p. 494.
49. Parliament of Singapore, "Budget Debate, Ministry of Culture", *Singapore Parliament Reports*, 25 March 1982, <http://www.parliament.gov.sg/publications-singapore-parliament-reports> [accessed 1 Oct. 2011].
50. Ibid., p. 338.
51. Manmohan Singh, *A critical analysis of the Straits Times' reporting on the Singapore Armed Forces: the RSS courageous and dunking incidents in 2003* (Singapore: Nanyang Technological University Master of Mass Communication Thesis, 2008).
52. Ibid.
53. Cherian George, *Contentious Journalism and the Internet: Toward Democratic Discourse in Malaysia and Singapore* (Singapore and Seattle: Singapore University Press and University of Washington Press, 2006).
54. Garry Rodan, *Transparency and Authoritarian Rule in Southeast Asia: Singapore and Malaysia* (London: RoutledgeCurzon, 2004).
55. Mancur Olson, *Power and Prosperity: Outgrowing Communist and Capitalist Dictatorships* (New York: Basic Books, 2000).
56. See also Charles Tilly, "War Making and State Making as Organized Crime", in *Bringing the State Back In*, ed. Peter Evans, Dietrich Rueschemeyer and Theda Skocpol (Cambridge, UK: Cambridge University Press, 1985), pp. 169–91.
57. Jean K. Chalaby, "New Media, New Freedoms, New Threats", *Gazette* 62, no. 1 (2000): 19–29.
58. Sue Curry Jansen and Brian Martin, "Making Censorship Backfire", *Counterpoise* 7, no. 3 (2003): 5–15.
59. Christian Davenport, "Multi-Dimensional Threat Perception and State Repression: An Inquiry into Why States Apply Negative Sanctions", *American Journal of Political Science* 39, no. 3 (1995): 683–713; Scott Sigmund Gartner and Patrick M. Regan, "Threat and Repression: The Non-Linear Relationship between Government and Opposition Violence", *Journal of Peace Research* 33, no. 3 (1996): 273–87; Dipak K. Gupta, Harinder Singh and Tom Sprague, "Government Coercion of Dissidents: Deterrence or Provocation", *The Journal of Conflict Resolution* 37, no.

2 (1993): 301–39; Conway W. Henderson, "Conditions Affecting the Use of Political Repression", *The Journal of Conflict Resolution* 35, no. 1 (1991): 120–42; Will H. Moore, "The Repression of Dissent: A Substitution Model of Government Coercion", *The Journal of Conflict Resolution* 44, no. 1 (2000): 107–27.

Chapter 6

1. Goh Chok Tong, "The Singapore Press: Part of the Virtuous Cycle of Good Government and Good Society" (speech at the Straits Times 150th Anniversary Gala Dinner, 15 July 1995).
2. Ibid.
3. Lee Kuan Yew, *From Third World to First: The Singapore Story: 1965–2000: Memoirs of Lee Kuan Yew* (Singapore: Times Editions and Singapore Press Holdings, 2000), p. 212.
4. Clifford G. Christians, *et al.*, *Normative Theories of the Media: Journalism in Democratic Societies* (Urbana and Chicago, Ill.: University of Illinois Press, 2009), p. 22.
5. See, for example, John C. Merrill, Peter J. Gade and Frederick R. Blevens, *Twilight of Press Freedom: The Rise of People's Journalism* (Mahwah, New Jersey: Lawrence Erlbaum, 2001); and Christians, *et al.*, *Normative Theories*, p. 22.
6. Jackie Sam, "A Top Woman Detainee Is Freed", *The Straits Times*, 21 June 1964.
7. Quoted in Chen Mong Hock, *The Early Chinese Newspapers of Singapore 1881–1912* (Singapore: University of Malaya Press, 1967).
8. Ibid.
9. Ibid., p. 74.
10. Lim Jim Koon (ed.), *Our 70 Years 1923–1993: History of Leading Chinese Newspapers in Singapore* (Singapore: Chinese Newspaper Division, Singapore Press Holdings, 1993), p. 86.
11. "Sin Pao Office Deserted", *The Straits Times*, 24 Aug. 1957.
12. Lim Jim Koon (ed.), *Our 70 Years 1923–1993*, p. 42.
13. "Survey of All Newspapers in Singapore".
14. Lee Khoon Choy, *On the Beat to the Hustings: An Autobiography* (Singapore: Times Books International, 1988), p. 44.
15. Edwin Lee, *Singapore: The Unexpected Nation* (Singapore: Institute of Southeast Asian Studies, 2008), p. 305.
16. Lim Jim Koon (ed.), *Our 70 Years 1923–1993*.
17. Anthony Polsky, "Premier Lee Kuan Yew and the Singapore Press Controversy" (speech given at the Hong Kong Foreign Correspondents Club, 20 July 1971).

18. Timothy P. Barnard and Jan van der Putten, "Malay Cosmopolitan Activism in Post-War Singapore", in *Paths Not Taken*, ed. Barr and Trocki.
19. Chen Ai Yen, "The Mass Media, 1819–1980", in *A History of Singapore*, ed. Ernest C.T. Chew and Edwin Lee (Singapore: Oxford University Press, 1991), pp. 288–311.
20. Barnard and van der Putten, "Malay Cosmopolitan Activism".
21. Ibid., p. 136.
22. Ibid., p. 137.
23. Quoted in Said Zahari, *Dark Clouds at Dawn: A Political Memoir* (Kuala Lumpur, Malaysia: Insan, 2001), p. 53.
24. Ibid.
25. Ibid.
26. Ainon Haji Kuntom, *Malay Newspapers, 1876–1973: A Historical Survey of the Literature* (1973), p. 44.
27. "Survey of All Newspapers in Singapore".
28. Zahari, *Dark Clouds at Dawn*, pp. 54–5.
29. Ibid., p. 63.
30. Salim, "A Pioneer in Malay Journalism", pp. 91, 105.
31. Zahari, *Dark Clouds at Dawn*, p. 61.
32. Ahmad Sebi, "Samad's Influence", in *A. Samad Ismail: Journalism and Politics*, ed. Cheah Boon Kheng (Kuala Lumpur, Malaysia: Utusan Publications & Distributors Sdn Bhd, 2000), p. 136.
33. Firdaus Haji Abdullah, *Radical Malay Politics: Its Origins and Development* (Selangor, Malaysia: Pelanduk Publications, 1985), p. 125.
34. Ibid.
35. Lee, *From Third World*, p. 218.
36. Ibid.
37. Ibid., p. 342.
38. See, for example, Ben H. Bagdikian, *The Media Monopoly*, 5th ed. (Boston: Beacon Press, 1997).
39. Chen Ai Yen, "The Mass Media, 1819–1980", pp. 297–8.
40. Francis Wong, "Nation Building and the Press" (speech at Seminar on Mass Media, University of Singapore Student Union, 18 July 1971).
41. Quoted in Francis T. Seow, *The Media Enthralled: Singapore Revisited* (Boulder, Colorado: Lynne Rienner Publishers, 1998), p. 44.
42. Turnbull, *Dateline Singapore*, p. 387.
43. Chen Ai Yen, "The Mass Media, 1819–1980".
44. Ibid., p. 130.
45. See, for example, Mitchell Stephens, *A History of News* (Fort Worth, Texas: Harcourt Brace, 1997).
46. Jeremy Iggers, *Good News, Bad News: Journalism Ethics and the Public Interest* (Boulder, Colorado: Westview Press, 1998).

47. Lee Boon Yang, "Towards a Global City" (speech given at the Singapore Press Club Lunch, Raffles Hotel, Singapore, 12 Nov. 2003), <http://stars.nhb.gov.sg> [accessed 17 Jan. 2011].
48. Barbie Zelizer, *Taking Journalism Seriously: News and the Academy* (Thousand Oaks, CA: Sage, 2008), p. 81.
49. Lee Kuan Yew, *From Third World to First*.
50. Eugene K.B. Tan. "Chinese-Singaporean Identity: Subtle Change Amidst Continuity", in *Impressions of the Goh Chok Tong Years in Singapore*, ed. Bridget Welsh, James Chin, Arun Mahizhnan and Tan Tarn How (Singapore: NUS Press, 2009), p. 331.
51. Ibid.
52. Hong Lysa and Huang Jianli. *The Scripting of a National History: Singapore and its Pasts* (Singapore: NUS Press, 2008), p. 96.
53. Ibid., p. 177.
54. Kwok Kian Woon, "Myth, memory, and modernity: Reflections on the situation of the Chinese-educated in post-independence Singapore". Paper for Hwa Chong alumni conference on "Identity: Crisis and Opportunity", 28 July 1996, p. 7.
55. Department of Statistics, "Key Indicators of the Resident Population", in *Census of Population 2010 Statistical Release 1: Demographic Characteristics, Education, Language and Religion* (Singapore: Department of Statistics, 2011), <http://www.singstat.gov.sg/pubn/popn/c2010sr1/indicators.pdf> [accessed 1 Aug. 2011].
56. Department of Statistics, *Yearbook of Statistics 2009>* (Singapore: Department of Statistics, 2009).
57. Department of Statistics, "Resident Households by Monthly Household Income from Work and Predominant Household Language", in *General Household Survey 2005* (Singapore: Department of Statistics, 2006), <http://www.singstat.gov.sg/pubn/popn/ghsr2/t82-89.pdf> [accessed 1 Aug. 2011].
58. Department of Statistics, "Statistical Tables: Language Most Frequently Spoken at Home", in *Census of Population 2010 Statistical Release 1: Demographic Characteristics, Education, Language and Religion* (Singapore: Department of Statistics, 2011), <http://www.singstat.gov.sg/pubn/popn/c2010sr1/t43-52.pdf> [accessed 1 Aug. 2011].
59. Hao Xiaoming and Cherian George, "Singapore Journalism: Buying into a Winning Formula", in *The Global Journalist in the 21st Century*, ed. D. Weaver and L. Willnat (Oxford, UK: Routledge, forthcoming).

Chapter 7

1. Francis T. Seow, *The Media Enthralled: Singapore Revisited* (Boulder, Colorado: Lynne Rienner Publishers, 1998).

2. S.R. Nathan, *An Unexpected Journey: Path to the Presidency* (Singapore: Editions Didier Millet, 2011).
3. Ian Stewart, "Papers Silent Over Government Raid on Business Times", *South China Morning Post*, 15 Aug. 1992, p. 9.
4. Leslie Fong, "S'poreans the Losers in Sterile Information Environment", *The Straits Times* 26 Sept. 1992, p. 33.
5. Chong Kai Xiong, et al., "World Press Freedom Day 2008", <http://www.scribd.com/doc/2873689/WORLD-PRESS-FREEDOM-DAY-2008> [accessed 19 Mar. 2011].
6. With nine daily newspaper titles in Singapore's four official languages, SPH enjoys a virtual monopoly of the local newspaper market. The national broadcaster, MediaCorp, runs one daily paper.
7. James Gomez, *Freedom of Expression and the Media in Singapore*, Article 19 <http://www.article19.org/pdfs/publications/singapore-baseline-study.pdf> [accessed 11 Mar. 2011].
8. Eric Ellis, "Court of the Lion Kings", *Sydney Morning Herald*, 30 Oct. 2010, <http://www.smh.com.au/business/court-of-the-lion-kings-20101029-177fu.html> [accessed 19 Mar. 2011].
9. "Report of the Seminar on Theatre in Singapore" (Singapore: Ministry of Community Development, 1987).
10. Clarissa Oon, "Theatre Life!: A History of English-Language Theatre", in *Singapore through The Straits Times (1958–2000)*, ed. Ong Sor Fern (Singapore: Singapore Press Holdings, 2001).
11. "Report of the Seminar on Theatre in Singapore" (Singapore: Ministry of Community Development, 1987).
12. Robert Iau, et al., *Report of Committee on Performing Arts*, Singapore, 1988.
13. Ong Teng Cheong, et al., *Report of the Advisory Council on Culture and the Arts*, Singapore, 1989, p. 5.
14. Robert Yeo, "Theatre and Censorship in Singapore", *Australasian Drama Studies* 25 (1994): 49–60; Ministry of Community Development, *Report of the Seminar on Theatre in Singapore*, Singapore, 1987; Oon, "Theatre Life".
15. Ong Keng Sen, "The Practice of English Language Theatre in Singapore", in *Prize Winning Plays Volume V*, ed. Thiru Kandiah (Singapore: UniPress, 1991), pp. 177–204.
16. Yeo, "Theatre and Censorship", pp. 49–60.
17. Anne Low, "Wooing Movie-Makers to Tinseltown, Singapore", *The Straits Times*, 3 June 1988, p. 48; Shaun Seow and Bee Ann Koh, "Tinseltown in Singapore", *The Straits Times*, 22 April 1989, p. 24.
18. Tan Hsueh Yun, "'Art' Acts at Parkway Parade Vulgar and Distasteful: NAC", *The Straits Times*, 5 Jan. 1994, p. 3; Koh Buck Song, "Liberalising the Arts Takes Time", *The Straits Times*, 8 Feb. 1994, p. 4; Ovidia Lim, "Is This Art?", *The New Paper*, 5 Jan. 1994, p. 12; Lois Ng, "Thumbs Down for 'Artists'", *The New Paper*, 7 Jan. 1994, p. 11.

19. T. Sasitharan, "Theatre Doyen Sells Himself to Raise Funds", *The Straits Times*, 11 May 1994, p. 2.
20. *Films Act* (Singapore, Cap 107, 2009 rev. ed.).
21. Leong Ching Ching, "Using Videotapes Will Debase Politics: Bg Yeo", *The Straits Times*, 28 July 1996, p. 3.
22. *Films Act*, above n 35, Sections 2(1), 2(2).
23. Tan Pin Pin, et al., "Film Act: Filmmakers Seek Clarification", *The Straits Times*, 11 May 2005, p. 8.
24. "Singapore Filmmakers Seek to Clarify Boundaries", *Reuters News*, 19:07, 11 May 2005; "Singapore Filmmakers Speak Up in Support of Director Under Police Probe", *Associated Press Newswires*, 15:26, 11 May 2005.
25. "MM Lee Speaks on Politics in Singapore, Faith", *The Straits Times*, 6 Dec. 2005.
26. Martyn See, "Speech at ASEM Seminar on Human Rights" (speech given at the 8th Informal ASEM Seminar on Human Rights, Siem Reap, Cambodia, Sept. 2007 <http://singaporerebel.blogspot.com/2007/09/police-probe-almost-farcical-martyn-see.html> [accessed 19 Mar. 2011]).
27. Clarissa Oon, "Films Act Amended", *The Straits Times*, 24 Mar. 2009; Clarissa Oon, "Reel Knots in Changes to Films Act", *The Straits Times*, 27 Mar. 2009; Clarissa Oon, "Independent, Non-Partisan Citizens to Advise Censors on Political Films", *The Straits Times*, 24 Mar. 2009.
28. Wong Kim Hoh, "New Film Makes Fun of Singapore Censors", *The Straits Times*, 7 Mar. 2004; Foong Woei Wan, "Censors Pass Cut Without Any Cuts", *The Straits Times*, 14 April 2004; "Royston Makes the Cut", *The Straits Times*, 26 May 2004.
29. "Basic Position", Arts Engage, <http://sites.google.com/site/artsengagesg/basic-position> [accessed 19 Mar. 2011].
30. "Position Paper on Censorship & Regulation", Arts Engage, <http://sites.google.com/site/artsengagesg/position-paper-on-censorship-regulation> [accessed 19 Mar. 2011].
31. "Benefits of Regulation", Arts Engage, <http://sites.google.com/site/artsengagesg/benefits> [accessed 19 Mar. 2011].
32. Ibid.
33. "Censorship Accounts", Arts Engage, <https://sites.google.com/site/artsengagesg/censorship-accounts> [accessed 19 Mar. 2011].
34. "Journalists Should Not Retail Government Disinformation", Yawning Bread, <http://yawningbread.wordpress.com/2010/06/22/journalists-should-not-retail-government-disinformation> [accessed 19 Mar. 2011].
35. "Recommendation", Arts Engage, <https://sites.google.com/site/artsengagesg/recommendation> [accessed 19 Mar. 2011].
36. "Artistic Community Responds to CRC Report", Arts Engage, <http://sites.google.com/site/artsengagesg/responsestocrc> [accessed 19 Mar. 2011].

37. Vincent Mosco, *The Political Economy of Communication*, 2nd ed. (London: Sage, 2009), p. 140.
38. Sue Curry Jansen and Brian Martin, "Making Censorship Backfire", *Counterpoise* 7, no. 3 (2003): 5–15.
39. Thomas Hanitzsch, *et al.*, "Modeling Perceived Influences on Journalism: Evidence from a Cross-National Survey of Journalists", *Journalism & Mass Communication Quarterly* 87, no. 1 (2010): 7–24.
40. Pierre Bourdieu, "The Field of Cultural Production, Or: The Economic World Reversed", in *The Field of Cultural Production: Essays on Art and Literature*, ed. Randall Johnson (New York: Columbia University Press, 1993), pp. 29–73.
41. "Proposals for Internet Freedom in Singapore", Citizen Journalism.sg, <http://citizen.journalism.sg/2008/04/21/proposals-for-internet-freedom-in-singapore> [accessed 10 Mar. 2011]. As editor of Journalism.sg, I was a member of Bloggers13 and a co-author of the report.
42. Joanna Hor, "Soft words over spiked story", *Nanyang Chronicle*, 6 Oct. 2008, 6, <http://www3.ntu.edu.sg/chronicle/archives/vol15no04.pdf> [accessed 19 Mar. 2011].
43. Lin Junjie, "It wasn't just Chee Soon Juan", *The Enquirer*, 14 Oct. 2009 <http://enquirer.sg/2009/10/14/it-wasnt-just-chee-soon-juan> [accessed 1 June 2011].
44. William Peterson, *Theater and the Politics of Culture in Contemporary Singapore* (Middletown, Connecticut: Wesleyan University Press, 2001), pp. 29–30.
45. Seow, *The Media Enthralled*.
46. Doug McAdam, Sidney Tarrow and Charles Tilly, *Dynamics of Contention* (Cambridge: Cambridge University Press, 2001).
47. Ong Teng Cheong, *et al.*, "Report of the Advisory Council on Culture and the Arts", Singapore, 1989, p. 12.
48. Ibid., p. 5.
49. S. Jayakumar, *et al.*, *Report of the Review Committee on Censorship* (Singapore: Ministry of Culture, 1981).
50. Meheroo Jussawalla, Toh Mun Heng and Linda Low, "Singapore: An Intelligent City-State", *Asian Journal of Communication* 2, no. 3 (1992).
51. Jason Tan, "Banning of 100 smut sites more a gesture of concern", *The Straits Times*, 2 Nov. 1997, p. 27.
52. Anil Samtani, "Re-Visiting the Singapore Internet Code of Practice", *Journal of Information, Law and Technology* 2 (2001).
53. Cherian George, *Contentious Journalism and the Internet: Toward Democratic Discourse in Malaysia and Singapore* (Singapore and Seattle: Singapore University Press and University of Washington Press, 2006).
54. Richard L. Florida, *The Rise of the Creative Class: And How It's Transforming Work, Leisure, Community and Everyday Life* (New York, N.Y.: Basic Books, 2002).

55. Bourdieu, "Field of Cultural Production".
56. Parvathi Nayar, "Art without Boundaries", *Business Times*, 13 May 2005.
57. Ong Sor Fen, "We Are Singapore", *The Straits Times*, 3 May 2005.
58. "Poll: World Divided on Press Freedom", BBC World Service, <http://news.bbc.co.uk/1/shared/bsp/hi/pdfs/10-12-07-worldservicepoll.pdf> [accessed 19 Mar. 2011].
59. Tan Pin Pin, *et al.*, "Film Act".

Chapter 8

1. Cherian George, "Internet Politics: Shouting Down the PAP", in *Voting in Change: Politics of Singapore's 2011 General Election*, ed. Kevin Y.L. Tan and Terence Lee (Singapore: Ethos Books, 2011), pp. 145–60.
2. Lawrence Lessig, *The Future of Ideas* (New York: Vintage, 2002). See also J.H. Saltzer, D.P. Reed and D.D. Clark, "End-to-End Arguments in System Design" (1981), <http://web.mit.edu/Saltzer/www/publications/endtoend/endtoend.pdf> [accessed 1 June 2011].
3. Jonathan Zittrain, *The Future of the Internet — And How to Stop It* (New Haven and London: Yale University Press, 2008).
4. Manuel Castells, *The Information Age: Economy, Society and Culture (Volume 1): The Rise of the Network Society*, 2nd ed. (Oxford: Blackwell, 2000), pp. 16–7.
5. "Singnet Will Allow Public to Access Data from July 1", *The Straits Times*, 25 June 1994.
6. George Yeo, "Speech at the Launch of Singapore Infomap", 8 Mar. 1995, <http://stars.nhb.gov.sg/stars/public> [accessed 1 June 2011].
7. Garry Rodan, "The Internet and Political Control in Singapore", *Political Science Quarterly* 113, no. 1 (1998): 63–89.
8. Media Development Authority, "Registration Form C for Class Licensable Broadcasting Services", <http://mda.gov.sg/Licences/OnlineServices/Pages/default.aspx> [accessed 1 June 2011].
9. Khairulanwar Zaini, "TOC Uncassetted: TOC's strenght lies in a collective heartbeat", The Online Citizen, 31 Jan. 2011, <http://theonlinecitizen.com/2011/01/toc-uncassetted-toc%E2%80%99s-strength-lies-in-a-collective-heartbeat/> [accessed 1 Sept. 2011].
10. "Singapore", OpenNet Initiative, <http://opennet.net/research/profiles/singapore> [accessed 26 June 2011].
11. Cherian George, *Contentious Journalism and the Internet: Toward Democratic Discourse in Malaysia and Singapore* (Singapore and Seattle: Singapore University Press and University of Washington Press, 2006).
12. Randolph Kluver, "Political Culture and Information Technology in the 2001 Singapore General Election", *Political Communication* 21, no. 4 (2004): 435–58.

13. Mark Deuze, Axel Bruns and Christoph Neuberger, "Preparing for an Age of Participatory News", *Journalism Practice* 1, no. 3 (2007): 322–38; J.D. Lasica, "What is Participatory Journalism?", *Online Journalism Review*, 7 Aug. 2003, <http://www.ojr.org/ojr/workplace/1060217106.php> [accessed 26 June 2011].
14. Lee S.C., "Should Wong Kan Seng resign?", life@anchorvale web log, 2 Mar. 2008, <http://anchorvale.wordpress.com/2008/03/02/should-wong-kan-seng-resign/> [accessed 20 Aug. 2008].
15. John D.H. Downing, *Radical Media: Rebellious Communication and Social Movements* (Thousand Oaks, CA: Sage, 2001).
16. Chris Atton, *Alternative Media* (London: Sage Publications, 2002).
17. Sidney Tarrow, *Power in Movement: Social Movements and Contentious Politics*, 2nd ed. (Cambridge: Cambridge University Press, 1998), p. 67.
18. Eugene Tan, "Singapore Shared Values", *Singapore Infopedia* (National Library Board, 21 Sept. 2001, <http://infopedia.nl.sg/articles/SIP-542-2004-12-18.html> [accessed 1 July 2011].
19. See, for example, Herbert J. Gans, *Deciding What's News: A Study of CBS Evening News, NBC Nightly News, Newsweek, and Time* (New York: Pantheon Books, 1979).
20. Doug McAdam, Sidney Tarrow and Charles Tilly, *Dynamics of Contention* (Cambridge: Cambridge University Press, 2001).
21. Singapore Rebel, <http://singaporerebel.blogspot.com> [accessed 26 June 2011].
22. Jay Rosen, *What Are Journalists For?* (New Haven, CT: Yale University Press, 1999), p. 69.
23. "HWZ Forums", HardwareZone.com, <http://forums.hardwarezone.com.sg> [accessed 26 June 2011].
24. "Forum", Sam's Alfresco Coffee, <http://sammyboy.com> [accessed 26 June 2011].
25. Joshua Chiang, personal communication, 29 Nov. 2010.
26. Alex Au, personal communication, 30 Mar. 2011.
27. "Lee Hsien Loong Scores a Nought for Political Nous", Yawning Bread, <http://yawningbread.wordpress.com/2011/05/15/lee-hsien-loong-scores-a-nought-for-political-nous> [accessed 26 June 2011].
28. John Perry Barlow, "A Declaration of the Independence of Cyberspace", <http://www.eff.org/~barlow/Declaration-Final.html> [accessed 26 June 2011].
29. Shanthi Kalathil and Taylor C. Boas, *Open Networks Closed Regimes: The Impact of the Internet on Authoritarian Rule* (Washington DC: Carnegie Endowment for International Peace, 2003), p. 136.
30. Hillary Rodham Clinton, "Remarks on Internet Freedom" (speech given at The Newseum, Washington, DC, 21 Jan. 2010), <http://www.state.gov/secretary/rm/2010/01/135519.htm> [accessed 26 June 2011].

31. Lawrence Lessig, *Code* (New York: Basic Books, 1999).
32. Ibid., p. 44.
33. Przeworski, *Democracy and the Market*, pp. 54–5.
34. Clay Shirky, "The Political Power of Social Media", *Foreign Affairs* 90, no. 1 (2011): 30.
35. Cherian George, "The Internet's Political Impact and the Penetration/Participation Paradox in Malaysia and Singapore", *Media, Culture & Society* 27, no. 6 (2005): 903–20.
36. "History Archive", People Like Us, <http://www.plu.sg/society/?cat=3> [accessed 26 June 2011]; "About Me", Yawning Bread, <http://yawningbread.wordpress.com/about-me> [accessed 26 June 2011].
37. "History", Transient Workers Count Too, <http://www.twc2.org.sg/site/who-we-are/history.html> [accessed 26 June 2011].
38. The Death Penalty in Singapore, <http://sgdeathpenalty.blogspot.com> [accessed 26 June 2011].
39. Arts Engage, <http://sites.google.com/site/artsengagesg> [accessed 26 June 2011].
40. Maruah Singapore, <http://maruah.org> [accessed 26 June 2011].
41. Singapore Democrats, <http://yoursdp.org> [accessed 26 June 2011].
42. Harakah Daily (English Edition), <http://en.harakah.net.my> [accessed 26 June 2011].
43. K. Bhavani, "Distorting the Truth, Mr Brown?", *Today*, 3 July 2006, <http://www.mrbrown.com/blog/2006/07/letter–from–mic.html> [accessed 26 June 2011].
44. Cherian George, "OB Markers and the Rules of Political Engagement", in *Singapore: The Air-Conditioned Nation — Essays on the Politics of Comfort and Control* (Singapore: Landmark Books), pp. 39–48.
45. "Excerpts from the Q&A", The Straits Times, 23 Mar. 2007.
46. "Malaysiakini Turns 10. So Where's Singaporekini?," Journalism.sg, <http://journalism.sg/2009/11/26/malaysiakini-turns-10> [accessed 26 June 2011].
47. Political Donations Act, Chapter 236, Section 2(1), "Interpretation".
48. Chris Anderson, *The Long Tail* (New York: Hyperion, 2006).
49. Nick Couldry, "Beyond the Hall of Mirrors? Some Theoretical Reflections on the Global Contestation of Media Power", in *Contesting Media Power*, ed. Nick Couldry and James Curran (Lanham, Maryland: Rowman and Littlefield, 2003).
50. Gerald Giam's Blog, <http://geraldgiam.sg> [accessed 26 June 2011].
51. "CNA, why different rules for PAP?", Singapore Democrats, <http://yoursdp.org/index.php/news/singapore/4694-cna-why-different-rules-for-pap> [accessed 26 June 2011].
52. "TNP refuses to apologize despite massive backlash from netizens", Temasek Review, <http://www.temasekreview.com/2011/05/05/tnp-refuses-

to-apologize-despite-massive-backlash-from-netizens> [accessed 26 June 2011].
53. Bill Kovach and Tom Rosenstiel, *Warp Speed: America in the Age of Mixed Media* (New York: Century Foundation, 1999).
54. Andrew Loh, "Looking Back on Five Years", The Online Citizen, 5 May 2011, <http://theonlinecitizen.com/2011/05/looking-back-on-five-years/> [accessed 1 June 2011].
55. Radha Basu, Personal communication, 17 July 2011.
56. James C. Scott, *The Art of Not Being Governed: An Anarchist History of Upland Southeast Asia* (New Haven: Yale University Press, 2009).
57. James C. Scott, *Domination and the Arts of Resistance: Hidden Transcripts* (New Haven: Yale University Press, 1990).
58. Ibid., p. 227.
59. Axel Bruns, "Gatewatching, Gatecrashing: Futures for Tactical News Media", in *Digital Media and Democracy: Tactics in Hard Times*, ed. Megan Boler (Cambridge, Mass.: MIT Press, 2008), p. 252.

Chapter 9

1. Gopalan Nair, "Singapore. Judge Belinda Ang's Kangaroo Court", *Singapore Dissident* (blog), 29 May 2008, <http://singaporedissident.blogspot.com/2008/05/singapore-judge-belinda-angs-kangaroo.html> [accessed 1 Feb. 2011].
2. Gopalan Nair, "Lee Kuan Yew: If bloggers who defame me identify themselves, I will sue them!," *Singapore Dissident* (blog), <http://singaporedissident.blogspot.com/2008/05/lee-kuan-yew-if-bloggers-who-defame-me.html> [accessed 1 Feb. 2011].
3. Ibid.
4. Nair was released after issuing an unreserved apology and withdrawing his allegations against the judiciary. He retracted his apology when he returned to the US, explaining that he had only apologised to shorten his jail term.
5. See, for example: H.M. Cleaver, Jr., "The Zapatista Effect: The Internet and the Rise of an Alternative Political Fabric", *Journal of International Affairs* 51, no. 2 (1998): 621–40; O. Froehling, "The Cyberspace 'War of Ink and Internet' in Chiapas, Mexico", *Geographical Review* 87, no. 2 (1997): 291–307; Jerry W. Knudson, "Rebellion in Chiapas: Insurrection by Internet and Public Relations", *Media, Culture & Society* 20, no. 3 (1998): 507–18.
6. Perry Anderson, "The Antinomies of Antonio Gramsci", *New Left Review* (1976): 5–80.
7. Hannah Arendt, *On Violence* (Orlando, Florida: Harcourt Brace Jovanovich, 1970), p. 106.

8. Sue Curry Jansen and Brian Martin, "Making Censorship Backfire", *Counterpoise* 7 (2003): 5–15.
9. Gene Sharp, *There Are Realistic Alternatives* (Boston, Mass: The Albert Einstein Institute, 2003), pp. 10–1.
10. Cherian George, "Consolidating Authoritarian Rule: Calibrated Coercion in Singapore", *The Pacific Review* 20 (2007): 127–45.
11. "Policies and Content Guidelines: Internet", Media Development Authority, <http://mda.gov.sg/Policies/PoliciesandContentGuidelines/Internet/Pages/default.aspx> [accessed 17 Jan. 2011].
12. Broadcasting Act (Chapter 28 Section 9), Broadcasting (Class Licence) Notification. Government Notification No. S 306/96, 15 July 1996. Amended by Government Notification Nos. S 496/2001 and S 555/2003.
13. OpenNet Initiative, "Country Profile: Singapore", 10 May 2007, <http://opennet.net/research/profiles/Singapore> [accessed 1 June 2011].
14. Ronald Deibert and Rafal Rohozinski, "Beyond Denial: Introducing Next-Generation Information Access Controls", in *Access Controlled: The Shaping of Power, Rights, and Rule in Cyberspace*, ed. Ronald J. Deibert, John G. Palfrey, Rafal Rohozinski and Jonathan Zittrain (Cambridge, MA: MIT Press, 2010), pp. 3–13.
15. "Man Allegedly 'Encouraged Law-Breaking on Web'", *The Straits Times*, 18 Nov. 2001.
16. Zulfikar Mohamad Shariff, "Fateha.com: Challenging Control Over Malay/Muslim Voices in Singapore", in *Asian Cyberactivism: Freedom of Expression and Media Censorship*, ed. S. Gan, J. Gomez and U. Johannen (Bangkok, Thailand: Friedrich Naumann Foundation, 2004), pp. 318–68.
17. Article 19, "Freedom of Expression and Defamation", in *International Seminar on Promoting Freedom of Expression* (Hilton Hotel London, United Kingdom, 2000).
18. Rachel Chang, "Govt will step in when efforts fail", *The Straits Times*, 6 Mar. 2010.
19. For a compilation of cases from 1996–2006, see Calibrated Coercion in Singapore, <http://calibratedcoercion.wordpress.com> [accessed 26 June 2011].
20. Cherian George, *Contentious Journalism and the Internet: Toward Democratic Discourse in Malaysia and Singapore* (Singapore and Seattle: Singapore University Press and University of Washington Press, 2006).
21. "Youths Let Off with 'Warning' for Organising Public Forum", Think Centre, <http://www.thinkcentre.org/article.cfm?ArticleID=5> [accessed 17 Jan. 2011].
22. James Gomez, *Internet Politics: Surveillance & Intimidation in Singapore* (Singapore: Think Centre, 2002), p. 77.
23. Ibid., pp. 76–9.
24. Ibid., p. 76.

25. Martyn See, "Martyn See Speaks out on Police Probe, Foreign 'Interference' and Burma", *Singapore Rebel* (blog), 30 Sept. 2007 <http://singaporerebel.blogspot.com/2007/09/police-probe-almost-farcical-martyn-see.html> [accessed 1 July 2011].
26. Martyn See, "Martyn See Speaks out on Police Probe, Foreign 'Interference' and Burma", *Singapore Rebel* (blog), <http://singaporerebel.blogspot.com/2007/09/police-probe-almost-farcical-martyn-see.html> [accessed 1 Mar. 2011].
27. Kenneth Paul Tan, *Cinema and Television in Singapore: Resistance in One Dimension* (Leiden: Brill, 2008), p. 268.
28. Martyn See, "'Singapore Rebel' Saga Ends after Police Issues 'Stern Warning'", *Singapore Rebel* (blog), <http://singaporerebel.blogspot.com/2006/08/singapore-rebel-saga-ends-after-police.html> [accessed 1 Mar. 2011].
29. George, *Contentious Journalism and the Internet*.
30. Martyn See, "'Zahari's 17 Years' Now Online", *Singapore Rebel* (blog), <http://singaporerebel.blogspot.com/2007/04/zaharis-17-years-now-online.html> [accessed 1 Mar. 2011].
31. Daniel Joseph Boorstin, *The image: A guide to pseudo-events in America* (New York: Vintage, 1961).
32. "Sign Letter of Protest Outside Burmese embassy", Singapore Democratic Party, <http://singaporedemocrat.org/articleburmaprotest2.html> [accessed 17 Jan. 2011].
33. "Singapore Police Warns Dr Chee at Burma Embassy", Singapore Democratic Party, <http://singaporedemocrat.org/articleburmaprotest5.html> [accessed 17 Jan. 2011].
34. "Steady Stream of Petitioners Despite Harassment by Singapore Police", Singapore Democratic Party, <http://singaporedemocrat.org/articleburmaprotest6.html> [accessed 17 Jan. 2011].
35. "Police Rejects SDP's Application for Protest March", Singapore Democratic Party, <http://singaporedemocrat.org/articleburmaprotest11.html> [accessed 17 Jan. 2011].
36. "Opposition Party Leaders Arrested During Burma Protest," Singapore Democratic Party, <http://singaporedemocrat.org/articleburmaprotest19.html> [accessed 17 Jan. 2011].
37. "The Propaganda Wing Swings Into Action", Singapore Democratic Party, <http://singaporedemocrat.org/articleburmaprotest22.html> [accessed 17 Jan. 2011].
38. Bamboozler68, comment on "Petition-Signing at Burmese Embassy in Singapore", singaporedemocrats, <http://www.youtube.com/watch?v=P7Yg05RDcZ4> [accessed 1 June 2008].
39. singaporedemocrats, "Petition-Signing at Burmese Embassy in Singapore", singaporedemocrats, <http://www.youtube.com/watch?v=P7Yg05RDcZ4> [accessed 1 June 2008].

40. "Steady Stream of Petitioners Despite Harassment by Singapore Police", Singapore Democratic Party, <http://singaporedemocrat.org/articleburmaprotest6.html> [accessed 17 Jan. 2011].
41. "SDP Members Arrested Outside the Istana, Singapore", YouTube video, 2:10, from theonlinecitizen showing SDP members arrested outside Singapore's Istana for protesting against the Singapore government's involvement with the Burmese Junta, posted by "theonlinecitizen", 8 Oct. 2007, <http://www.youtube.com/watch?v=PFlENeTb56E> [accessed ??].
42. Sharp, *There Are Realistic Alternatives*.
43. Tan Tarn How, *Fear of Writing*, staged by TheatreWorks, Sept. 2011.

Chapter 10

1. Larry Diamond, *The Spirit of Democracy: The Struggle to Build Free Societies Throughout the World* (New York: Henry Holt, 2009), p. 55.
2. Juan J. Linz and Alfred C. Stepan, *Problems of Democratic Transition and Consolidation* (Baltimore and London: The Johns Hopkins University Press, 1996), p. 5.
3. Larry Diamond, "Thinking About Hybrid Regimes", *Journal of Democracy* 13, no. 2 (2002): 21–35.
4. Raj K. Vasil, *A Citizen's Guide to Government and Politics in Singapore* (Singapore: Talisman, 2004), p. 118.
5. Kevin Tan, *An Introduction to Singapore's Constitution* (Singapore: Talisman, 2005), p. 80.
6. See, for example, U.S. Department of State (1986), "Singapore", *Country Reports on Human Rights Practices 1985*.
7. U.S. Department of State, *2009 Human Rights Report: Singapore*, <http://www.state.gov/g/drl/rls/hrrpt/2009/eap/136008.htm> [accessed 19 Feb. 2011].
8. United States Embassy in Singapore, "Singapore's Opposition", 18 Oct. 2004, released by Wikileaks, 30 Aug. 2011, <http:// wikileaks.org/cable/2004/10/04SINGAPORE3001.html> [accessed 1 Oct. 2011].
9. Robert A. Dahl, *On Democracy* (New Haven, London: Yale University Press, 1998). See also Charles Tilly's claim that "a regime is democratic to the degree that political relations between the state and its citizens feature broad, equal, protected and mutually binding consultation", in Charles Tilly, *Democracy* (Cambridge: Cambridge University Press, 2007), pp. 13–4.
10. Andreas Schedler, "The Menu of Manipulation", *Journal of Democracy* 13, no. 2 (2002): 37.
11. Carl A. Trocki, *Singapore: Wealth, Power, and the Culture of Control, Asia's Transformations* (New York: Routledge, 2005).
12. Vasil, *Citizen's guide*, pp. 153–4.

13. Han Fook Kwang, *et al.*, *Lee Kuan Yew: Hard Truths to Keep Singapore Going* (Singapore: Straits Times Press, 2011), pp. 109–10.
14. "Interview with Lee Kuan Yew", in *People's Action Party, For People Through Action By Party* (Singapore: People's Action Party Editorial Committee, 1999), pp. 132–3.
15. Chan Heng Chee, "The Structuring of the Political System", in *Management of Success: The Moulding of Modern Singapore*, ed. Kernial Singh Sandhu and Paul Wheatley (Singapore: Institute of Southeast Asian Studies, 1989), p. 73.
16. Raj Vasil, "Trade Unions", in *Management of Success*, ed. Sandhu and Wheatley, pp. 144–70.
17. Ho Khai Leong, "Political Consolidation in Singapore: Connecting the Party, the Government and the Expanding State", in *Management of Success: Singapore Revisited*, ed. Terence Chong (Singapore: Institute of Southeast Asian Studies, 2010), p. 75.
18. Justin Yeo and Calvin Liang, "*Shadrake Alan v Attorney-General* [2011] SGCA 26 — A look at the recent decision on the law of contempt of court for scandalising the judiciary", *Inter Se* (July 2011): 27–32.
19. Kevin Y.L. Tan, "State and institution building through the Singapore Constitution 1965–2005", in *Evolution of a revolution: forty years of the Singapore constitution*, ed. Li-ann Thio and Kevin Y.L. Tan (Abingdon, Oxon.: Routledge-Cavendish, 2009), p. 67.
20. Ibid.; Jaclyn Ling-Chien Neo and Yvonne C.L. Lee, "Constitutional supremacy: Still a little dicey?", in *Evolution of a revolution*, ed. Thio and Tan.
21. Anthony Lewis, *Freedom for the Thought that We Hate: A Biography of the First Amendment* (New York: Basic Books, 2007).
22. Kevin Tan, *Introduction to Singapore's Constitution* (Singapore: Talisman, 2005).
23. Chan Sek Keong, Keynote Address, New York State Bar Association Seasonal Meeting, 27 Oct. 2009, <http://app.supremecourt.gov.sg> [accessed 1 July 2011].
24. Han, *et al.*, *Lee Kuan Yew*, p. 54.
25. Ibid., p. 49.
26. Ibid., p. 62.
27. Miles Kahler, "Networked Politics: Agency, Power, and Governance", in *Networked Politics: Agency, Power, and Governance*, ed. Miles Kahler (Ithaca, New York: Cornell University Press, 2009), pp. 1–20.
28. Peter Ho, "Governance at the Leading Edge: Black Swans, Wild Cards, and Wicked Problems", *Ethos*, no. 4 (April 2008): 78–9.
29. Han, *et al.*, *Lee Kuan Yew*, p. 63.
30. "About REACH: Overview", REACH, <http://www.reach.gov.sg/AboutREACH/Overview.aspx> [accessed 19 Feb. 2011].

31. Constance Singam, Tan Chong Kee, Tisa Ng and Leon Perera, eds., *Building Social Space in Singapore: The Working Committee's Initiative in Civil Society Activism* (Singapore: Select Books, 2002).
32. Adam Przeworski, *Democracy and the Market: Political and Economic Reforms in Eastern Europe and Latin America* (Cambridge: Cambridge University Press, 1991).
33. Garry Rodan and Kanishka Jayasuriya, "The Technocratic Politics of Administrative Participation: Case Studies of Singapore and Vietnam", *Democratization* 14, no. 5 (Dec. 2007): 795–815.
34. "About Us", People Like Us, <http://www.plu.sg/society/?page-id=2> [accessed 26 June 2011].
35. "About IndigNation", IndigNation, <http://indignationsg.wordpress.com/about> [accessed 26 June 2011].
36. James Surowiecki, *The Wisdom of Crowds* (New York: Anchor Books, 2005); Charles Leadbeater, *We-Think: Mass Innovation, Not Mass Production* (London: Profile Books, 2009); Don Tapscott and Anthony D. Williams, *Wikinomics: How Mass Collaboration Changes Everything* (New York: Portfolio, 2008).
37. Jonathan Zittrain, *The Future of the Internet — And How to Stop It*, 1st ed. (Yale University Press, 2008).
38. Leadbeater, *We-Think*, p. 72.
39. Ibid., p. 68.
40. Tapscott and Williams, *Wikinomics*, p. 1.
41. Ann Florini, ed., "Introduction: The Battle Over Transparency", in *The Right to Know: Transparency for an Open World* (New York: Columbia University Press, 2007).
42. Ibid., p. 2.
43. Leadbeater, *We-Think*, pp. 71–2.
44. Open Government Partnership website, <http://www.opengovpartnership.org/> [accessed 2 Aug. 2011].
45. Cherian George, "Internet Politics: Shouting Down the PAP", in *Voting in Change: Politics of Singapore's 2011 General Election*, ed. Kevin Y.L. Tan and Terence Lee (Singapore: Ethos Books, 2011), pp. 145–60.
46. Chitra Rajaram, "GE: 'We hear all your voices', says PM Lee", Channel NewsAsia website, 8 May 2011, <http://www.channelnewsasia.com/stories/singaporelocalnews/view/1127451/1/.html> [accessed 1 Aug. 2011].
47. Donald Low, "What went wrong?", Facebook, 17 May 2011, <http://www.facebook.com/note.php?note-id=209993849034597> [accessed 1 July 2011].
48. Donald Low, "A reform agenda for a reformist government (part II)", Facebook, 28 May 2011, <http://www.facebook.com/note.php?note-id=212655728768409> [accessed 1 July 2011].

49. Donald Low, "PM Lee's Koizumi Moment?", Facebook, 13 May 2011, <http://www.facebook.com/#!/note.php?note-id=208989375801711> [accessed 1 July 2011].
50. "Newsmen with 'licence to kill'", *The Straits Times*, 18 June 1986.
51. Quoted in Cherian George.
52. Advisory Council on the Impact of New Media on Society, *Engaging new media: challenging old assumptions* (Singapore: Advisory Council on the Impact of New Media on Society, 2008), p. 38.
53. Lee Hsien Loong, Speech at the Swearing-In Ceremony, State Room, Istana, May 21, 2011, <http://stars.nhb.gov.sg/stars/public/> [accessed 2 Aug. 2011].
54. Han, *et al.*, *Lee Kuan Yew*, p. 359.
55. Thoughts of a Cynical Investor, "SPH: Another home for ex-ministers?" 7 Oct. 2011, <http://atans1.wordpress.com/2011/10/07/sph-another-home-for-ex-ministers/> [accessed 3 Nov. 2011].

Bibliography

Abdullah, Firdaus Haji. *Radical Malay Politics: Its Origins and Development.* Selangor, Malaysia: Pelanduk Publications, 1985.
Ahmad, Sebi. "Samad's Influence." In *A. Samad Ismail: Journalism and Politics*, ed. Cheah Boon Kheng. Kuala Lumpur, Malaysia: Utusan Publications & Distributors Sdn Bhd, 2000, p. 136.
Ainon, Haji Kuntom. *Malay Newspapers, 1876–1973: A Historical Survey of the Literature* (1973).
Anderson, Chris. *The Long Tail.* New York: Hyperion, 2006.
Anderson, Perry. "The Antinomies of Antonio Gramsci." *New Left Review* 100 (Nov.–Dec. 1976): 5–80.
Arendt, Hannah. *On Violence.* Orlando, Florida: Harcourt Brace Jovanovich, 1970.
Article 19, "Freedom of Expression and Defamation." In *International Seminar on Promoting Freedom of Expression.* Hilton Hotel London, United Kingdom, 2000.
Aspinall, Edward. *Opposing Suharto: Compromise, Resistance, and Regime Change in Indonesia.* Stanford, California: Stanford University Press, 2005.
Atton, Chris. *Alternative Media.* London: Sage Publications, 2002.
Bagdikian, Ben H. *The Media Monopoly*, 5th ed. Boston: Beacon Press, 1997.
Bandurski, David and Martin Hala. *Investigative Journalism in China: Eight Cases in Chinese Watchdog Journalism.* Hong Kong: Hong Kong University Press, 2010.
Barnard, Timothy P. and Jan van der Putten. "Malay Cosmopolitan Activism in Post-War Singapore." In *Paths Not Taken: Political Pluralism in Post-War Singapore*, ed. Michael D. Barr and Carl A. Trocki. Singapore: NUS Press, 2008.
Barr, Michael. "Singapore's Catholic Social Activists: Alleged Marxist Conspirators." In *Paths not Taken: Political Pluralism in Post-war Singapore*, ed. Michael Barr and Carl A. Trocki. Singapore: NUS Press, 2008.
Bertrand, Claude-Jean. "Media Accountability." *Pacific Journalism Review* 11, no. 2 (Sept. 2005): 5–16.
Boorstin, Daniel Joseph. *The image: A guide to pseudo-events in America.* New York: Vintage, 1961.

Bourdieu, Pierre. "The Field of Cultural Production, Or: The Economic World Reversed." In *The Field of Cultural Production: Essays on Art and Literature*, ed. Randall Johnson. New York: Columbia University Press, 1993, pp. 29–73.

Bruns, Axel. "Gatewatching, Gatecrashing: Futures for Tactical News Media." In *Digital Media and Democracy: Tactics in Hard Times*, ed. Megan Boler. Cambridge, Mass.: MIT Press, 2008, p. 252.

Carey, James W. "The Press and Public Discourse." *The Center Magazine*, March 1987.

Case, William. *Politics in Southeast Asia: Democracy or Less*. Richmond, Surrey: Curzon, 2002.

Castells, Manuel. *The Information Age: Economy, Society and Culture (Volume 1): The Rise of the Network Society*, 2nd ed. Oxford: Blackwell, 2000.

Cenite, Mark, et al. "Perpetual development journalism? Balance and framing in the 2006 Singapore election coverage." *Asian Journal of Communication* 18, no. 3 (2008): 280–95.

Chalaby, Jean K. "New Media, New Freedoms, New Threats." *Gazette* 62, no. 1 (2000): 19–29.

Chambers, Simone and Anne Costaine, eds. *Deliberation, Democracy and the Media*. Maryland: Rowman & Littlefield Publishers, 2000.

Chan Heng Chee. "Political Developments, 1965–1979." In *A History of Singapore*, ed. Ernest C.T. Chew and Edwin Lee. Singapore: Oxford University Press, 1991.

———. *Singapore: The Politics of Survival, 1965–1967*. Singapore: Oxford University Press, 1971.

———. "The Structuring of the Political System." In *Management of Success: The Moulding of Modern Singapore*, ed. Kernial Singh Sandhu and Paul Wheatley. Singapore: Institute of Southeast Asian Studies, 1989.

Chan Sek Keong. Keynote Address, New York State Bar Association Seasonal Meeting, 27 Oct. 2009, <http://app.supremecourt.gov.sg> [accessed 1 July 2011].

Chen Ai Yen. "The Mass Media, 1819–1980." In *A History of Singapore*, ed. Ernest C.T. Chew and Edwin Lee. Singapore: Oxford University Press, 1991, pp. 288–311.

Chen Mong Hock. *The Early Chinese Newspapers of Singapore 1881–1912*. Singapore: University of Malaya Press, 1967.

Cheong Yip Seng. "The Singapore Press: How Free, How Credible?." *The Asean Journalist* 1, no. 1 (1981): 28–9.

Christians, Clifford G., Theodore L. Glasser, Denis McQuail, Kaarle Nordenstreng, and Robert A. White. *Normative Theories of the Media: Journalism in Democratic Societies*. Urbana and Chicago, Ill.: University of Illinois Press, 2009.

Cleaver, H.M., Jr. "The Zapatista Effect: The Internet and the Rise of an Alternative Political Fabric." *Journal of International Affairs* 51, no. 2 (1998): 621–40.

Clinton, Hillary Rodham. "Remarks on Internet Freedom." Speech given at The Newseum, Washington, DC, 21 Jan. 2010 <http://www.state.gov/secretary/rm/2010/01/135519.htm> [accessed 26 June 2011].

"Commission on Freedom of the Press." In *A Free and Responsible Press. A General Report on Mass Communication: Newspapers, Radio, Motion Pictures, Magazines, and Books*, ed. Robert D. Leigh. Chicago: University of Chicago Press, 1947, pp. xii. 138.

Coronel, Sheila S. "Investigative Reporting and the Struggle for the Public Sphere." In *Free Markets Free Media? Reflections on the Political Economy of the Press in Asia*, ed. Cherian George. Singapore: Asian Media Information and Communication Centre and Wee Kim Wee School of Communication and Information, Nanyang Technological University, 2008, pp. 87–108.

Couldry, Nick. "Beyond the Hall of Mirrors? Some Theoretical Reflections on the Global Contestation of Media Power." In *Contesting Media Power*, ed. Nick Couldry and James Curran. Lanham, Maryland: Rowman and Littlefield, 2003.

Dahl, Robert A. *On Democracy*. New Haven, London: Yale University Press, 1998.

Davenport, Christian. "Multi-Dimensional Threat Perception and State Repression: An Inquiry into Why States Apply Negative Sanctions." *American Journal of Political Science* 39, no. 3 (1995): 683–713.

Davies, Nick. *Flat Earth News*. London: Vintage Book, 2009.

Deibert, Ronald and Rafal Rohozinski. "Beyond Denial: Introducing Next-Generation Information Access Controls." In *Access Controlled: The Shaping of Power, Rights, and Rule in Cyberspace*, ed. Ronald J. Deibert, John G. Palfrey, Rafal Rohozinski, and Jonathan Zittrain. Cambridge, MA: MIT Press, 2010, pp. 3–13.

Deuze, Mark, Azel Bruns, and Christoph Neuberger. "Preparing for an Age of Participatory News." *Journalism Practice* 1, no. 3 (2007): 322–38.

Diamond, Larry. "Thinking About Hybrid Regimes." *Journal of Democracy* 13, no. 2 (2002): 21–35.

Donsbach, Wolfgang. "Factors Behind Journalists' Professional Behavior: A Psychological Approach to Journalism Research." In *Global Journalism Research: Theories, Methods, Findings, Future*, ed. Martin Loffelholz and David Weaver. Malden, Maine: Blackwell, 2008, pp. 65–78.

Dorman, William A. "Press Theory and Journalistic Practice: The Case of the Gulf War." In *Do the Media Govern?: Politicians, Voters, and Reporters in America*, ed. Shanto Iyengar and Richard Reeves. Thousand Oaks, CA: Sage Publications, 1997, pp. 118–25.

Downing, John D.H. *Radical Media: Rebellious Communication and Social Movements*. Thousand Oaks, CA: Sage, 2001.
Ettema, James S. and Theodore L. Glasser. *Custodians of Conscience: Investigative Journalism and Public Virtue*. New York: Columbia University Press, 1998.
Evans, Harold. *Good Times, Bad Times*. London: Weidenfeld & Nicolson, 1983.
Fernandez, Michael and Kah Seng Loh. "The Left-Wing Trade Unions in Singapore, 1945–1970." In *Paths Not Taken: Political Pluralism in Postwar Singapore*, ed. Michael Barr and Carl A. Trocki. Singapore: NUS Press, 2008, pp. 206–26.
Florida, Richard L. *The Rise of the Creative Class: And How It's Transforming Work, Leisure, Community and Everyday Life*. New York, N.Y.: Basic Books, 2002.
Florini, Ann, ed. "Introduction: The Battle Over Transparency." In *The Right to Know: Transparency for an Open World*. New York: Columbia University Press, 2007.
Froehling, O. "The Cyberspace 'War of Ink and Internet' in Chiapas, Mexico." *Geographical Review* 87, no. 2 (1997): 291–307.
Fukuyama, Francis. *The End of History and the Last Man*. New York: Avon Books, 1993.
Gans, Herbert J. *Deciding What's News: A Study of CBS Evening News, NBC Nightly News, Newsweek, and Time*. New York: Pantheon Books, 1979.
Gartner, Scott Sigmund and Patrick M. Regan. "Threat and Repression: The Non-Linear Relationship between Government and Opposition Violence." *Journal of Peace Research* 33, no. 3 (1996): 273–87.
Geertz, Clifford. "Thick Description: Toward an Interpretive Theory of Culture." In *The Interpretation of Cultures* (New York: Basic Books, 1973).
George, Cherian. "'Asian' Journalism: More Preached than Prized?." Paper presented at the Association for Education in Journalism and Mass Communication Western Conference, Stanford, California, 2002.
———. "Consolidating Authoritarian Rule: Calibrated Coercion in Singapore." *The Pacific Review* 20 (2007): 127–45.
———. *Contentious Journalism and the Internet: Toward Democratic Discourse in Malaysia and Singapore*. Singapore and Seattle: Singapore University Press and University of Washington Press, 2006.
———. "The Internet's Political Impact and the Penetration/Participation Paradox in Malaysia and Singapore." *Media, Culture & Society* 27, no. 6 (2005): 903–20.
Glasser, Theodore L. "The Idea of Public Journalism." In *The Idea of Public Journalism*, ed. Theodore L. Glasser (New York: Guilford Press, 1999).
Goh Chok Tong. Speech given at the 5th Anniversary Dinner of Today Newspaper, Shangri-La Hotel, Singapore, 31 Oct. 2005 <http://www.stars.nhb.gov.sg> [accessed 16 Jan. 2011].

―――. "The Singapore Press." Speech given at the Straits Times 150th Anniversary Gala Dinner, Singapore International Convention and Exhibition Centre, Singapore, July 15, 1995 <http://stars.nhb.gov.sg> [accessed 16 Jan. 2011].

Gomez, Edmund Terence and Jomo K.S. *Malaysia's Political Economy: Politics, Patronage and Profits*, 2nd ed. Cambridge: Cambridge University Press, 1999.

Gomez, James. *Internet Politics: Surveillance & Intimidation in Singapore*. Singapore: Think Centre, 2002.

GPI. "Methodology, Results & Findings." <http://www.visionofhumanity.org/wp-content/uploads/PDF/2007/2007%20%20%20%20Results%20Report.pdf> [accessed 14 Jan. 2011].

Green, Philip, ed. "Part IV: The Theory of Democratic Elitism." In *Democracy*. New Jersey: Humanities Press, 1993, pp. 67–118.

Gupta, Dipak K., Harinder Singh, and Tom Sprague. "Government Coercion of Dissidents: Deterrence or Provocation." *The Journal of Conflict Resolution* 37, no. 2 (1993): 301–39.

Habermas, Jurgen. *The Structural Transformation of the Public Sphere*. Cambridge, Mass.: MIT Press, 1991.

Hallin, Daniel C. and Paolo Mancini. *Comparing Media Systems: Three Models of Media and Politics*. Cambridge, UK: Cambridge University Press, 2004.

Han Fook Kwang, Warren Fernandez, and Sumiko Tan. "What People Want is Good Government." In *Lee Kuan Yew: The Man and his Ideas*. Singapore: Times Edition, 1998, p. 381.

Han Fook Kwang, et al. *Lee Kuan Yew: Hard Truths to Keep Singapore Going*. Singapore: Straits Times Press, 2011.

Hanitzsch, Thomas, et al. "Modeling Perceived Influences on Journalism: Evidence from a Cross-National Survey of Journalists." *Journalism & Mass Communication Quarterly* 87, no. 1 (2010): 7–24.

Hao Xiaoming and Cherian George. "Singapore Journalism: Buying into a Winning Formula." In *The Global Journalist in the 21st Century*, ed. D. Weaver and L. Willnat. Oxford, UK: Routledge, forthcoming.

Hartley, John. "Journalism as a Human Right: The Cultural Approach to Journalism." In *Global Journalism Research: Theories, Methods, Findings, Future*, ed. Martin Loffelholz and David Weaker. Malden, Mass.: Blackwell, 2008, pp. 39–51.

Harvey, David. *A Brief History of Neoliberalism*. Oxford: Oxford University Press, 2005.

Held, David. *Political Theory and the Modern State*. Stanford, California: Stanford University Press, 1989.

Henderson, Conway W. "Conditions Affecting the Use of Political Repression." *The Journal of Conflict Resolution* 35, no. 1 (1991): 120–42.

Herman, Edward S. and Noam Chomsky. *Manufacturing Consent: The Political Economy of the Mass Media*. New York: Pantheon, 1988.

Himelboim, Itai and Yehiel Limor. "Media Institutions, News Organizations, and the Journalistic Social Role Worldwide: A Cross-National and Cross-Organizational Study of Codes of Ethics." *Mass Communication and Society* 14, no. 1 (2011): 71–92.

Ho Khai Leong. "Political Consolidation in Singapore: Connecting the Party, the Government and the Expanding State." In *Management of Success: Singapore Revisited*, ed. Terence Chong. Singapore: Institute of Southeast Asian Studies, 2010.

Ho, Peter. "Governance at the Leading Edge: Black Swans, Wild Cards, and Wicked Problems." *Ethos*, no. 4 (April 2008): 78–9.

Hong Lysa and Huang Jianli. *The Scripting of a National History: Singapore and its Pasts*. Singapore: NUS Press, 2008.

Huang Jianli. "Positioning the Student Political Activism of Singapore: Articulation, Contestation and Omission." *Inter-Asia Cultural Studies* 7, no. 3 (2006): 403–30.

Huntington, Samuel P. *Political Order in Changing Societies*. New Haven: Yale University Press, 1996.

Huntington, Samuel P., Joji Watanuki, and Michael Crozier. "Chapter III — The United States." In *The Crisis of Democracy: Report on the Governability of Democracies to the Trilateral Commission*. New York: New York University Press, 1975, pp. 53–119.

Iau, Robert, et al. *Report of Committee on Performing Arts*. Singapore, 1988.

Iggers, Jeremy. *Good News, Bad News: Journalism Ethics and the Public Interest*. Boulder, Colorado: Westview Press, 1998.

IMD. "IMD 2010 World Competitiveness Yearbook rankings." <http://www.imd.org/news/IMD-World-Competitiveness-Yearbook-2010-Rankings.cfm> [accessed 14 Jan. 2011].

Jacques, Martin. *When China Rules the World: The Rise of the Middle Kingdom and the End of the Western World*. New York: Penguin Press, 2009.

Jansen, Sue Curry and Brian Martin. "Making Censorship Backfire." *Counterpoise* 7, no. 3 (2003): 5–15.

Jayakumar, S., et al. *Report of the Review Committee on Censorship*. Singapore: Ministry of Culture, 1981.

Josephi, Beate. "On the Cusp Between Global and Local: Young Journalists at the Straits Times." *Asia Pacific Media Educator*, no. 12/13 (2002): 123–38.

Jussawalla, Meheroo, Toh Mun Heng, and Linda Low. "Singapore: An Intelligent City-State." *Asian Journal of Communication* 2, no. 3 (1992).

Kahler, Miles. "Networked Politics: Agency, Power, and Governance." In *Networked Politics: Agency, Power, and Governance*, ed. Miles Kahler. Ithaca, New York: Cornell University Press, 2009.

Kalathil, Shanthi and Taylor C. Boas. *Open Networks Closed Regimes: The Impact of the Internet on Authoritarian Rule*. Washington DC: Carnegie Endowment for International Peace, 2003.

Kausikan, Bilahari. "The 'Asian Values' Debate: A View from Singapore." In *Democracy in East Asia*, ed. Larry Diamond and Marc F. Plattner. Baltimore, Maryland: John Hopkins University Press, 1998, pp. 17–27.

Kluver, Randolph. "Political Culture and Information Technology in the 2001 Singapore General Election." *Political Communication* 21, no. 4 (2004): 435–58.

Knudson, Jerry W. "Rebellion in Chiapas: Insurrection by Internet and Public Relations." *Media, Culture & Society* 20, no. 3 (1998).

Kovach, Bill and Tom Rosenstiel. *Warp Speed: America in the Age of Mixed Media*. New York: Century Foundation, 1999.

Kwok Kian Woon. "Myth, memory, and modernity: Reflections on the situation of the Chinese-educated in post-independence Singapore." Paper for Hwa Chong alumni conference on "Identity: Crisis and Opportunity," 28 July 1996, p. 7.

Leadbeater, Charles. *We-Think: Mass Innovation, Not Mass Production*. London: Profile Books, 2009.

Lee Boon Yang. "Towards a Global City." Speech given at the Singapore Press Club Lunch, Raffles Hotel, Singapore, 12 Nov. 2003 <http://stars.nhb.gov.sg> [accessed 17 Jan. 2011].

Lee, Edwin. *Singapore: The Unexpected Nation*. Singapore: Institute of Southeast Asian Studies, 2008.

Lee Khoon Choy. *On the Beat to the Hustings: An Autobiography*. Singapore: Times Books International, 1988.

Lee Kuan Yew. "Exciting Times Ahead." Speech given at the Tanjong Pagar GRC National Day Dinner, World Trade Centre, Hall 1, Singapore, 12 Aug. 1995 <http://stars.nhb.gov.sg> [accessed 19 Feb. 2011].

―――. *From Third World to First: The Singapore Story: 1965–2000: Memoirs of Lee Kuan Yew*. Singapore: Times Editions and Singapore Press Holdings, 2000.

―――. Speech given to the American Society of Newspaper Editors, Washington DC, 14 April 1988 <http://stars.nhb.gov.sg> [accessed 16 Jan. 2011].

―――. Speech given at the Asian Media Conference, Los Angeles, 29 Oct. 1998 <http://stars.nhb.gov.sg> [accessed 23 Jan. 2011].

―――. Speech given at the PAP Paya Lebar Branch 15th Anniversary Dinner, Singapore, 13 May 1971. <http://stars.nhb.gov.sg> [accessed 23 Jan. 2011].

―――. "The Mass Media and New Countries." Speech given at the General Assembly of the International Press Institute, Helsinki, 9 June 1971 <http://journalism.sg/lee-kuan- yews-1971-speech-on-the-press> [accessed 23 Jan. 2011].

_____. *The Singapore Story: Memoirs of Lee Kuan Yew*. Singapore: Times Editions, 1998.

Lessig, Lawrence. *Code*. New York: Basic Books, 1999.

_____. *The Future of Ideas*. New York: Vintage, 2002.

Lewis, Anthony, ed. *Freedom for the Thought that We Hate: A Biography of the First Amendment*. New York: Basic Books, 2007.

Lim Jim Koon, ed. *Our 70 Years 1923–1993: History of Leading Chinese Newspapers in Singapore*. Singapore: Chinese Newspapers Division, Singapore Press Holdings, 1993.

Lim, Peter. "No monopoly on wisdom." In *150 Years of The Straits Times*, ed. Cherian George. Singapore: Singapore Press Holdings, 1995.

Linz, Juan J. "Opposition in and under an authoritarian regime: The case of Spain." In *Regimes and Oppositions*, ed. Robert A. Dahl. New Haven, CT, and London: Yale University Press, 1973.

Linz, Juan J., and Alfred C. Stepan. *Problems of Democratic Transition and Consolidation*. Baltimore and London: The Johns Hopkins University Press, 1996.

Lippmann, Walter. *The Phantom Public*. New York: Harcourt, Brace and Company, 1925.

Lule, Jack. *Daily News, Eternal Stories: The Mythological Role of Journalism*. New York: The Guilford Press, 2001.

McAdam, Doug, Sidney Tarrow, and Charles Tilly. *Dynamics of Contention*. Cambridge: Cambridge University Press, 2001.

_____. *Dynamics of Contention*. Cambridge: Cambridge University Press, 2001.

McChesney, Robert W. *The Political Economy of Media: Enduring Issues, Emerging Dilemmas*. New York: Monthly Review Press, 2008.

Mindich, David. *Just the Facts: How "Objectivity" Came to Define American Journalism*. New York: NYU Press, 2000.

Ministry of Community Development. "Report of the Seminar on Theatre in Singapore." Singapore, 1987.

Moore, Will H. "The Repression of Dissent: A Substitution Model of Government Coercion." *The Journal of Conflict Resolution* 44, no. 1 (2000): 107–27.

Mosco, Vincent. *The Political Economy of Communication*, 2nd ed. London: Sage, 2009.

Muhlmann, Géraldine. *Journalism for Democracy*. Cambridge: Polity, 2010.

Nathan, S.R. *An Unexpected Journey: Path to the Presidency*. Singapore: Editions Didier Millet, 2011.

Nerone, John C., ed. *Last Rights: Revisiting Four Theories of the Press*. Urbana: University of Illinois Press, 1995.

OHCHR. "International Covenant on Civil and Political Rights, Article 20." <http://www2.ohchr.org/english/law/ccpr.htm> [accessed 14 Jan. 2011].

Olson, Mancur. *Power and Prosperity: Outgrowing Communist and Capitalist Dictatorships*. New York: Basic Books, 2000.
Ong, Keng Sen. "The Practice of English Language Theatre in Singapore." In *Prize Winning Plays Volume V*, ed. Thiru Kandiah. Singapore: UniPress, 1991, pp. 177–204.
Ong Teng Cheong, et al. *Report of the Advisory Council on Culture and the Arts*. Singapore, 1989.
Oon, Clarissa. "Theatre Life!: A History of English-Language Theatre." In *Singapore through The Straits Times (1958–2000)*, ed. Ong Sor Fern. Singapore: Singapore Press Holdings, 2001.
Peterson, William. *Theater and the Politics of Culture in Contemporary Singapore*. Middletown, Connecticut: Wesleyan University Press, 2001.
Plott, David and Michael Vatikiotis. "The Life and Times of the Far Eastern Economic Review." In *Free Markets Free Media? Reflections on the Political Economy of the Press in Asia*, ed. Cherian George. Singapore: Asian Media Information and Communication Centre, 2008, pp. 137–58.
Polsky, Anthony. "Premier Lee Kuan Yew and the Singapore Press Controversy." Speech given at the Hong Kong Foreign Correspondents Club, 20 July 1971.
Przeworski, Adam. *Democracy and the Market: Political and Economic Reforms in Eastern Europe and Latin America*. Cambridge: Cambridge University Press, 1991.
Rajah, Jothie. *Authoritarian Rule of Law: Legislation, Discourse and Legitimacy in Singapore*. New York: Cambridge University Press, 2012.
Rajah, K.S. "Negotiating Boundaries: Ob Markers and the Law." In *Impressions of the Goh Chok Tong Years in Singapore*, ed. Bridget Welsh, James Chin, Arun Mahizhnan, and Tan Tarn. Singapore: NUS Press, 2010, p. 77.
Rodan, Garry. "The Internet and Political Control in Singapore." *Political Science Quarterly* 113, no. 1 (1998): 63–89.
———. *Transparency and Authoritarian Rule in Southeast Asia: Singapore and Malaysia*. London: RoutledgeCurzon, 2004.
Rodan, Garry and Kanishka Jayasuriya. "The Technocratic Politics of Administrative Participation: Case Studies of Singapore and Vietnam." *Democratization* 14, no. 5 (Dec. 2007): 795–815.
Ron, James. "Varying Methods of State Violence." *International Organization* 51, no. 2 (1997): 275–300.
Rosen, Jay. *What Are Journalists For?* New Haven, CT: Yale University Press, 1999.
Said, Zahari. *Dark Clouds at Dawn: A Political Memoir*. Kuala Lumpur, Malaysia: Insan, 2001.
———. *The Long Nightmare: My 17 Years as a Political Prisoner*. Cheras, Kuala Lumpur: Utusan Publications & Distributors, 2007.

Samtani, Anil. "Re-Visiting the Singapore Internet Code of Practice." *Journal of Information, Law and Technology* 2 (2001): 23–46.
Schedler, Andreas. "The Menu of Manipulation." *Journal of Democracy* 13, no. 2 (2002): 37.
Schudson, Michael. *Discovering the News: A Social History of American Newspapers*. New York: Basic Books, 1978.
Schumpeter, Joseph A. *Capitalism, Socialism and Democracy*. New York: Harper & Row, 1950.
Scott, James C. *Domination and the Arts of Resistance: Hidden Transcripts*. New Haven: Yale University Press, 1990.
———. *The Art of Not Being Governed: An Anarchist History of Upland Southeast Asia*. New Haven: Yale University Press, 2009.
See, Martyn. "Speech at ASEM Seminar on Human Rights." Speech given at the 8th Informal ASEM Seminar on Human Rights, Siem Reap, Cambodia, Sept. 2007 <http://singaporerebel.blogspot.com/2007/09/police-probe-almost-farcical-martyn-see.html> [accessed 19 Mar. 2011].
Sen, Amartya Kumar. "Democracy as a Universal Value." *Journal of Democracy* 10, no. 3 (1999): 3–17.
Seow, Francis T. *The Media Enthralled: Singapore Revisited*. Boulder, Colorado: Lynne Rienner Publishers, 1998.
———. *To Catch a Tartar: A Dissident in Lee Kuan Yew's Prison*. New Haven, Connecticut: Yale Center for International and Area Studies, 1994.
Sesser, Stan. *Lands of Charm and Cruelty: Travels in Southeast Asia*. New York, N.Y.: Vintage, 1994.
Shanmugam, K. Speech given at the "A Free Press for a Global Society" Forum, Columbia University, New York, 4 Nov.2010 <http://app2.mlaw.gov.sg/News/tabid/204/Default.aspx? ItemId=515> [accessed 23 Jan. 2011].
Shariff, Zulfikar Mohamad. "Fateha.com: Challenging Control Over Malay/Muslim Voices in Singapore." In *Asian Cyberactivism: Freedom of Expression and Media Censorship*, ed. S. Gan, J. Gomez, and U. Johannen. Bangkok, Thailand: Friedrich Naumann Foundation, 2004, pp. 318–68.
Sharp, Gene. *There Are Realistic Alternatives*. Boston, Mass: The Albert Einstein Institute, 2003.
Shirky, Clay. "The Political Power of Social Media." *Foreign Affairs* 90, no. 1 (2011): 30.
Siebert, Fred S., Theodore Peterson and Wilbur Schramm. *Four Theories of the Press: The Authoritarian, Libertarian, Social Responsibility and Soviet Communist Concepts of what the Press should be and do*. Urbana: University of Illinois Press, 1956.
Singam, Constance, Tan Chong Kee, Tisa Ng, and Leon Perera, eds. *Building Social Space in Singapore: The Working Committee's Initiative in Civil Society Activism*. Singapore: Select Books, 2002.

Singh, Manmohan. *A critical analysis of the Straits Times' reporting on the Singapore Armed Forces: the RSS courageous and dunking incidents in 2003*. Singapore: Nanyang Technological University Master of Mass Communication Thesis, 2008.

Shoemaker, Pamela J. and Stephen D. Reese. *Mediating the Message: Theories of Influences on Mass Media Content*, 2nd ed. New York: Longman, 1996.

Sigal, Leon V. "Who? Sources Make the News." In *Reading the News: A Pantheon Guide to Popular Culture*, ed. Robert K. Manoff and Michael Schudson. New York: Pantheon Books, 1986, pp. 9–37.

Soh Lung Teo. *Beyond the Blue Gate: Recollections of a Political Prisoner*. Kuala Lumpur, Malaysia: Strategic Information and Research Development Centre, 2010.

Soros, George. *The Soros Lectures: At the Central European University*. New York, N.Y.: Public Affairs, 2010.

Stephens, Mitchell. *A History of News*. New York: Viking, 1988.

———. *A History of News*. Fort Worth, Texas: Harcourt Brace, 1997.

Surowiecki, James. *The Wisdom of Crowds*. New York: Anchor Books, 2005.

Tan, Eugene K.B. "Chinese-Singaporean Identity: Subtle Change Amidst Continuity." In *Impressions of the Goh Chok Tong Years in Singapore*, ed. Bridget Welsh, James Chin, Arun Mahizhnan and Tan Tarn How. Singapore: NUS Press, 2009.

Tan, Kenneth Paul. *Cinema and Television in Singapore: Resistance in One Dimension*. Leiden: Brill, 2008.

Tan, Kevin. *An Introduction to Singapore's Constitution*. Singapore: Talisman, 2005.

Tan, Kevin Y.L. "State and institution building through the Singapore Constitution 1965–2005." In *Evolution of a revolution: forty years of the Singapore constitution*, ed. Li-ann Thio and Kevin Y.L. Tan. Abingdon, Oxon.: Routledge-Cavendish, 2009.

Tapscott, Don and Anthony D. Williams. *Wikinomics: How Mass Collaboration Changes Everything*. New York: Portfolio, 2008.

Tarrow, Sidney. *Power in Movement: Social Movements and Contentious Politics*, 2nd ed. Cambridge: Cambridge University Press, 1998.

Tey Tsun Hang. "Confining the Freedom of the Press in Singapore: A 'Pragmatic' Press For 'Nation-Building'?" *Human Rights Quarterly* 30, no. 4 (2008): 876–905.

The Right to be Heard: Singapore's Dispute with TIME magazine & the Asian Wall Street Journal: The Facts. Singapore: Ministry of Communications & Information, May 1987.

Tilly, Charles. *Democracy*. Cambridge: Cambridge University Press, 2007.

———. "War Making and State Making as Organized Crime." In *Bringing the State Back In*, ed. Peter Evans, Dietrich Rueschemeyer and Theda Skocpol. Cambridge, UK: Cambridge University Press, 1985.

Tong, Jingrong. *Investigative Journalism in China: Journalism, Power, and Society*. London and New York: Continuum International Publishing Group, 2011.

Trocki, Carl A. *Singapore: Wealth, Power, and the Culture of Control, Asia's Transformations*. New York: Routledge, 2005.

Tuchman, Gaye. "Objectivity as Strategic Ritual: An Examination of Newsmen's Notions of Objectivity." *The American Journal of Sociology* 77, no. 4 (1972): 660–79.

Turnbull, Mary C. *Dateline Singapore: 150 years of The Straits Times*. Singapore: Singapore Press Holdings, 1995.

Vasil, Raj. "Trade Unions." In *Management of Success: The Moulding of Modern Singapore*, ed. Kernial Singh Sandhu and Paul Wheatley. Singapore: Institute of Southeast Asian Studies, 1989.

Vasil, Raj K. *A Citizen's Guide to Government and Politics in Singapore*. Singapore: Talisman, 2004.

Wang, Georgette and Eddie C.Y. Kuo. "The Asian communication debate: culture-specificity, culture-generality, and beyond." *Asian Journal of Communication* 20, no. 2 (2010): 152–65.

Whimster, Sam, ed. *The Essential Weber: A Reader*. London: Routledge, 2004.

Wong, Francis. "Nation Building and the Press." Speech given at Seminar on Mass Media, University of Singapore Student Union, 18 July 1971.

Wong Kan Seng. "The Real World of Human Rights." Speech given at the World Conference on Human Rights, Vienna, 14 June 1993.

World Economic Forum. "The Global Competitiveness Economic Report." <http://www.weforum.org/reports/global-competitiveness-report-2010-2011-0> [accessed 14 Jan 2011].

Yap, Sonny, Richard Lim, and Weng Kam Leong. "Puppets in a Dangerous Game." In *Men in White: The Untold Story of Singapore's Ruling Political Party*. Singapore: Marshall Cavendish, 2010.

Yeo, Justin and Calvin Liang. "Shadrake Alan v Attorney-General [2011] SGCA 26 — A look at the recent decision on the law of contempt of court for scandalising the judiciary." *Inter Se* (July 2011): 27–32.

Yeo, Robert. "Theatre and Censorship in Singapore." *Australasian Drama Studies* 25 (1994): 49–60.

Zakaria, Fareed. *The Future of Freedom: Illiberal Democracy at Home and Abroad*. London and New York: W.W. Norton & Company, 2003.

Zelizer, Barbie. *Taking Journalism Seriously: News and the Academy*. Thousand Oaks, CA: Sage, 2008.

Zittrain, Jonathan. *The Future of the Internet — And How to Stop It*. New Haven and London: Yale University Press, 2008.

Zulfikar Mohamad Shariff. "Fateha.com: Challenging Control Over Malay/Muslim Voices in Singapore." In *Asian Cyberactivism: Freedom of Expression and Media Censorship*, ed. S. Gan, J. Gomez and U. Johannen. Bangkok, Thailand: Friedrich Naumann Foundation, 2004.

Index

Asian values, 5, 17, 53–4, 56–7, 118–9, 121, 127, 132
journalism, 51, 53
Asian Wall Street Journal, 38–9, 42
Asiaweek, 38, 43
authoritarian regime, 2, 5–6, 19, 25, 30–1, 42, 44, 63, 69, 95, 116, 147, 202, 214
authoritarianism, 8, 92, 95–6, 201–2, 225
Aw family, 28

Barisan Sosialis, 103, 206
BBC, xi, 45, 155, 166, 197, 207
World Service, 89
Berita Harian, x, 103, 117, 119, 124, 126, 170
Bloomberg, 41–2
Bourdieu, Pierre, 15, 147, 153
British colonial
government/rule, 120, 123
period, 27
broadcasting, 3, 31–2, 113, 161, 163, 170, 207
act, xi
Bush, George W., 9, 62
Business Times, x, 35, 40, 45, 137–8, 154, 170

capitalism, 7–8, 14, 27, 30, 43–4
censorship, 4, 6, 8–9, 25, 44, 84, 106, 108, 116, 137, 139–41, 143–51, 153–7, 163–4, 170–1, 176, 178, 184–6, 191–2, 197
Censorship 1.0, 27, 40
Censorship 2.0, 29, *see also* Newspaper and Printing Presses Act (NPPA) of 1974
Review Committee, 213
self-censorship, 4, 37, 40, 44, 89, 139, 147, 149–50, 174, 177, 186, 188, 192, 197, 223
Channel NewsAsia, x, 177
Chee Soon Juan, 143, 148–9, 177, 183–4, 191–2, 198, 213
China, 7–8, 13, 16–7, 26, 44, 61, 63–4, 67, 74, 76, 82, 88, 93–4, 114, 116, 120–1, 132–3, 135, 147, 171, 184, 217
Citibank, 30
civil society, 6, 105, 168, 170, 172–3, 210, 213
organisations, 25, 53, 68, 212
CNBC Asia, xi
CNN, xi, 197
Cold War, 12, 73–4
Communist Party (China), 44, 96, 121
contempt of court, xi, 6, 41–2, 63, 104, 170, 208
contempt of parliament, 40
Corrupt Practices Investigation Bureau, 17, 207

Index

DBS Bank, 30–1
defamation, 6, 9–10, 40–3, 63, 78, 104, 170, 184, 187, 205, 208
democratisation, 6–7, 171
detention without trial, *see* Internal Security Act
Dow Jones, 43

Eastern Sun, 28, 98
economic growth, 7, 40, 66, 116, 152, 203
Economist, The, 38

Far Eastern Economic Review (FEER), 37–9, 41, 43, 66, 104, 154
Fernandez, Warren, 35
Fridae, 166–7, 215
Foreign Correspondents' Association, 42, 220
Fox News, 8, 62
freedom of expression, vii, 1, 9, 78–81, 84–5, 91–2, 139–40, 148, 155–6, 171–3, 187, 190, 197–8, *see also* freedom of speech *and* freedom of the press
freedom of information, 39, 79, 217
freedom of speech, 189, *see also* freedom of expression
freedom of the press, xi, 74, 155, *see also* freedom of expression

Geertz, Clifford, 15
Germany, 14
Goh Chok Tong, ix, 2, 35, 38, 75, 77, 84, 105, 117, 160, 218, 222
Gramsci, Antonio, 9, 45, 96, 185
Great Eastern Life Assurance, 31

Hammer, 28, 104
Han Fook Kwang, 25, 35, 45

Ho Ching, 41
Hong Kong, 13, 25, 37, 66, 76, 82, 98, 138, 154
HSBC, 30

India, 14, 25, 82, 208
Indian Ocean, ix, 74
Indonesia, ix, 14, 43, 64, 95, 122, 170, 172, 221
Internal Security
  Act (ISA), 29, 94, 98, 119, 137, 140
  Department (ISD), 24, 33, 56, 115, 137, 189
International Herald Tribune, 41–2, 154
Iraq, 9, 62–3
ISA, *see* Internal Security Act (ISA)
ISD, *see* Internal Security Department (ISD)

Japan, ix, 1
Japanese Occupation, 51
Jeyaretnam, J.B., 38, 88, 109, 111, 142, 177, 188, 211, 220
journalism
  citizen, 4, 6, 33, 165–6
  watchdog, 17, 44, 63–4, 92, 133, 158

Kuala Lumpur, 16, 32, 80, 124–5

language
  English, x, 28, 35, 52, 76, 80, 117–9, 121–2, 126–8, 131, 133–5
  Malay, x, 16, 35, 52, 103, 117–9, 122, 126
  Mandarin, x, 122, 132, 134
  Tamil, x, 32, 117, 135

Lee Boon Yang, 33, 224
Lee Hsien Loong, ix, 41, 75, 115,
    143, 169, 183, 209, 220, 222
Lee Kuan Yew, ix, xi, 2, 18, 26, 28,
    30, 32–5, 37, 41, 43, 71, 75,
    81, 90, 93, 97–8, 102–3,
    106–7, 111, 113, 116, 118,
    120–1, 124, 126, 130, 132,
    143, 160, 181, 183, 207,
    209–10, 212, 217–8, 224
    Helsinki speech, 88–9
Lianhe Wanbao, x, 127
Lianhe Zaobao, x, 117, 127, 133
liberal democracy, 9, 88, 201
licensing, *see* Newspaper and
    Printing Presses Act
Lim Kim San, 33
Lim, Peter, 34–5, 50, 68, 109–11
London, 45, 89

mainstream
    journalism, 48–9, 65, 103,
        119, 124, 130, 156, 167,
        179–80
    media, 9–10, 65–6, 68, 84,
        113, 139, 148–9, 158–9,
        166–7, 169, 173, 176–81,
        186, 191, 194, 197, 219,
        223–4
    press, 4, 23, 26, 167, 223
Malaya, Federation of, ix, 32, 75,
    91, 123, 125
Malaysia, ix, 3, 13, 16, 31–2, 41,
    63, 67, 89–90, 94, 97, 102–3,
    113, 116, 121, 125, 159,
    172–3, 186, 197, 221
Malaysiakini, 173–4, 181
Maria Hertogh Riots, 82, 125
media
    controls, 3–6, 29, 83, 201
    freedom, 1, 9, 17, 23, 37, 76,
        125, 140, 154, 197, 208

    system, 3–5, 12, 14–5, 18–9,
        21–2, 25–6, 41, 45, 50,
        75–6, 78, 89, 92, 95, 108,
        119, 139, 166, 222–3, 225
Media Development Authority, xii,
    185, 213
MediaCorp, x–xi, 3, 32–3, 35, 64,
    104, 146, 149, 177, 197
mioTV, xi
Mr Brown, 173–4, 186
Murdoch, Rupert, 8
Myanmar, 15, 26, 184, 193–6

Nair, Gopalan, 183–4, 197
Nanyang Siang Pau, x, 16, 28, 76–7,
    98, 103, 119, 121–2, 126–8,
    130–1, 137
Nathan, S.R., 33, 109–11, 137
nation-building, 16, 26, 75, 83, 85,
    99, 128, 153
neoliberalism, 7, 45
New Paper, The, x, 40, 53, 55, 60,
    112, 177, 194
New Straits Times, 32, 104
New York, 43, 81, 89
New York Times, 31, 42, 92
New Yorker, 105
Newspaper and Printing Presses Act
    (NPPA) of 1974, xi, 30, 38,
    99, 126, 138, 147
newspaper licensing, *see* Newspaper
    and Printing Presses Act
newspaper permits, *see* Newspaper
    and Printing Presses Act
Newseum, 1, 8
Nixon, Richard, 8, 58, 73
NPPA, *see* Newspaper and Printing
    Presses Act (NPPA)
North America, 1, *see also* United
    States (US)
Norway, 13
NTUC Income, 31, 169

OCBC Bank, 31
Official Secrets Act (OSA), 40, 63, 137–8
OSA, *see* Official Secrets Act (OSA)
"out of bounds" (OB) markers, 4, 48, 65, 186

PAP, *see* People's Action Party (PAP)
People's Action Party (PAP), ix, xi, 2–7, 10–1, 14, 16–8, 21–37, 41–5, 48, 57, 69–73, 75–92, 94, 103, 105, 107–9, 113–6, 118–9, 121, 124–6, 128–9, 131–4, 136, 139–40, 145, 155–60, 169, 172–8, 180–2, 185–6, 193, 196, 198, 201–12, 214–5, 218–25
Philippines, 13, 77, 97
Potential Net Migration Index, 22
Pravda, 3
press freedom, 1–2, 4, 16, 25, 39, 42, 44, 65, 71, 74, 78–80, 84–5, 98, 123, 138, 140, 147, 155, 172, 208, 225, *see also* RSF Press Freedom Index
Prime Minister's Office, xii, 38, 206
Public Service Commission, 34

race, 66, 84, 128, 189, 215
Rajaratnam, S., 110, 220–1
Reagan, Ronald, 7
religion, 66, 74, 84, 101, 123, 150, 163, 189
Reporters Sans Frontieres (RSF), 1–3
  Press Freedom Index, 1, 3
riots, 74, *see also* Maria Hertogh Riots
RSF, *see* Reporters Sans Frontieres (RSF)
Reporters Without Borders, *see* Reporters Sans Frontieres (RSF)

Sedition Act, 66, 188–9
self-determination, 12–3, 85
Shanmugam, K., 10, 75, 78, 84, 90
Shin Min Daily News, x, 60, 135
Singapore Constitution, 81
Singapore Democratic Party, 142, 159, 168, 173, 177, 184, 188, 193
Singapore Herald, 28, 66, 72, 98, 137
"Singapore Paradox", 7
Singapore Press Holdings (SPH), x, 2–3, 30, 32–3, 52, 127, 137–8, 224
Singapore Technologies, xi
Singapore Telecom, xi, 31, 163
Singh, Pritam, 10
Sintercom, 164, 168, 177
Soros, George, 7, 174
South Korea, 1, 181
Star, 41
Starhub, xi
status quo, 3, 5, 17, 26, 48, 64, 91, 119, 136, 148, 170, 192, 220, 225
Straits Times, x, 2–3, 16, 20, 23–5, 29, 35, 40, 45–7, 49, 51, 53, 60, 67, 69, 80, 83, 94, 103, 106, 109–10, 113, 117, 127, 135, 137–8, 141–3, 149, 154, 161, 165, 177–9, 188
Straits Times group, 32–4, 50, 111, 126–7, 134, 137
Suharto, 43, 95, 97, 172

Taiwan, 1, 67, 77
Talking Cock, 186
Tamil Murasu, x, 32, 117, 170
Tan, Tony, 33, 112, 222
Temasek Holdings, 41, 212
Temasek Review, xi, 168–9
Thatcher, Margaret, 7

The Online Citizen, xi, 148, 164–5, 168–9, 173–6, 179–80, 198
Thomson Reuters, xi, 51, 61, 137, 154
Think Centre, 164, 168, 177, 190–2, 198
Tiger Balm, 28
Time magazine, 37–8, 43, 93, 143
Today, x, 32, 60, 112, 173–4

UMNO, 32
United Nations, 84, 93
    Human Development Index, 21
United Overseas Bank, 30–1
United States (US), 11, 25, 34, 41, 44, 50, 52, 62–4, 73, 80, 83–4, 113, 147, 159, 169–70, 196–7, 208
Utusan Melayu, 16, 28, 103, 119, 122–5

Wall Street Journal, 31, 43, 54
Washington D.C., 1, 8, 197
Washington Post, 92
Watergate, 8, 58, 109
Workers' Party, 28, 104, 109, 176, 178, 198, 211

Yawning Bread, 148, 168–9, 172, 176, 178, 186